Politicking and Emergent Media

The publisher gratefully acknowledges the generous support of the Valerie Barth and Peter Booth Wiley Endowment Fund in History of the University of California Press Foundation.

Politicking and Emergent Media

US Presidential Elections of the 1890s

Charles Musser

UNIVERSITY OF CALIFORNIA PRESS

University of California Press, one of the most
distinguished university presses in the United States,
enriches lives around the world by advancing scholarship
in the humanities, social sciences, and natural sciences. Its
activities are supported by the UC Press Foundation and
by philanthropic contributions from individuals and
institutions. For more information, visit www.ucpress.edu.

University of California Press
Oakland, California

Library of Congress Cataloging-in-Publication Data

Names: Musser, Charles, author.
Title: Politicking and emergent media : US presidential
    elections of the 1890s / Charles Musser.
Description: Oakland, California : University of
    California Press, [2016] | "2016 | Includes
    bibliographical references and index.
Identifiers: LCCN 2016011311 (print) | LCCN
    2016012957 (ebook) | ISBN 9780520292727 (cloth :
    alk. paper) | ISBN 9780520292734 (pbk. : alk. paper) |
    ISBN 9780520966123 (ebook)
Subjects: LCSH: Presidents—United States—Elections—
    History—19th century. | Mass media—Political
    aspects—United States. | Press and politics—United
    States—History—19th century. | Political campaigns—
    United States—History—19th century. | United
    States—Politics and government—1885–1899.
Classification: LCC JK524 .M87 2016 (print) | LCC
    JK524 (ebook) | DDC 324.973/087—dc23
LC record available at http://lccn.loc.gov/2016011311

Manufactured in the United States of America

25 24 23 22 21 20 19 18 17 16
10 9 8 7 6 5 4 3 2 1

For my daughter Hannah
In memory of Danny Schechter

"The moving picture machine is to figure in the campaign. The moving picture machine learned how to cheat some time ago."

—*Washington Post*, August 16, 1900

"No matter what the story, there is always another story— the media story."

—Danny Schechter

Contents

Acknowledgments

This book came into being through a circuitous route. In 1990 and 1991 I published an informal trilogy of books on the early years of American cinema. The culmination of more than a decade of research and writing, much of it examined the moving picture world of the 1890s. My subsequent dilemma in terms of future scholarship was intense and undoubtedly familiar to many of my academic colleagues. On one hand I was extremely eager to move on to new areas of scholarship—to return to my interest in contemporary documentary, to develop a still-preliminary engagement with issues of race and representation, to explore the dynamic relations of the stage and screen, and to extend my historical knowledge of motion picture practices into the later years of silent cinema—all while assuming a more international outlook. I was not at all eager to have the inscription on my gravestone read "Charles John Musser (1-16-1951/XX-XX-2XXX), Here Lies the Dean of Early Cinema." On the other hand, I found it hard to entirely escape the pull of my established area of expertise. Certainly I had a stake in the various debates surrounding early cinema, but more importantly there were significant areas of research and new analytic paradigms that I was eager to pursue. One result of my continued investment in the 1890s was the publication of *Edison Motion Pictures, 1890–1900: An Annotated Filmography* (1997). My investigations outside early cinema included *Oscar Micheaux and His Circle: African American Filmmaking and Race Cinema of the Silent Era* (2001), a volume of essays

I coedited with Pearl Bowser and Jane Gaines. Nevertheless, much of my work in the last two decades has appeared in article form. Since my list of publications can readily be found online, I will not enumerate them here. Most were connected to various book projects. One examined changing conceptions of truth in documentary film practice from the 1850s to the present day. When that undertaking proved too broad, I narrowed it to the often-promised *Truth and Documentary in the Age of George W. Bush.* Inevitably I became fascinated by the use of documentary and other nonfiction forms as they were mobilized in the electoral campaigns of 2004 and 2008. Then at the March 2009 Udine conference on the Histories of Film Theories, I examined the use of new and established media in these two elections and compared them to the elections of 1892 and 1896. I was humbled but also enchanted as my modest research on the 1890s led to so many unexpected discoveries. This new turn then morphed into an ambitious book entitled *Media Shifts and US Presidential Elections: Stereopticon/Cinema/Television/ Internet,* which looked at six US presidential campaigns—the two others being 1948 and 1952. Then, in an ironic twist, I expanded the first section of that undertaking for this book and found myself having come full circle.

My scholarly path that produced *Politicking and Emergent Media* is deeply indebted to essential support from the Academy of Motion Picture Arts and Sciences, which made me an Academy Film Scholar in 2005, and the Clark Art Institute, which awarded me a Residential Fellowship in 2006. Not only did these enable me to focus my energies on research and writing, but they had a profound impact on my personal life. On my way to receive my Academy award in December 2004, I took a detour to the Philippines to consult on a forthcoming conference on early cinema in Southeast Asia, then being organized by the film scholar and filmmaker Nick Deocampo. There I met my wife, Maria Threese Serana, who was working as a journalist and had been teaching political science at University of the Philippines-Cebu. The first stages of our son's journey through life began during my residency at the Clark Art Institute in Williamstown, Massachusetts.

This book is dedicated to my daughter, Hannah Grace Zeavin Musser—generally known as Hannah Zeavin. Hannah's birth in July 1990 briefly interrupted the indexing of my three books on early cinema and contributed immeasurably to the productivity of that year; nevertheless, she has been deeply frustrated by the meandering nature of my subsequent scholarship, waiting impatiently for a finished book that would be dedicated to her. Her wait has, I hope, produced some deeper satisfactions. Certainly it has for me. Whether speaking as the youth representative for a Not in Our Name rally at Union Square during the 2004 Republican National Convention or publishing a book of poetry, *Circa* (2009), with Hanging Loose Press, Hannah has always charted an independent path. Thinking she had chosen the life of a poet, I was delighted when she entered the PhD program in the Department of Media, Culture, and Communication at NYU in 2012. I was also grateful when she interrupted work on her dissertation to become the first person to read this book's introduction and provide me with much-appreciated feedback.

I first met News Dissector Danny Schechter at Film Fest New Haven in September 2004 as he was screening his newly completed documentary *WMD: Weapons of Mass Deception,* about the George W. Bush administration's ability to control the media in ways that enabled Bush to launch the Iraq War. His compelling documentary and his interest in media, war, and politics resonated with my own interests in documentary. Over the next ten years I brought him to my Yale classes and met him for meals in New York. We often traded stories about our daughters' various accomplishments, and I was delighted that Hannah could join us for dinner on more than one occasion. He also provided Threese with her first job in the United States. I benefited intellectually and emotionally from our friendship, which lasted almost ten years and sadly came to a premature end with his death.

A book such as this has many starting points. One moment was certainly a visit to the office of Lisa Gitelman, who was teaching at NYU's Department of Media, Culture, and Communication. We had known each other since our days at the Thomas A. Edison Papers but had been out of touch. I explained to her my interest in widening my scholarly investigations to take in the broader media studies field and asked for counsel. Maria Tortajada at l'Université de Lausanne encouraged me to think through the problems of the stereopticon as a platform or media form, which renewed my investigations of audiovisual media in the second half of the nineteenth century. My colleague Francesco Casetti has not only done much to propel this book into being but also contributed wording for its title. The most immediate motivation for the book perhaps involves academic politics. When I arrived at Yale more than two decades ago, I was a filmmaker-scholar who had essentially left filmmaking behind even though I was expected to teach documentary filmmaking. Through the good graces and modest funding of the provost's office, notably Deputy Provost Lloyd Suttle, I was eventually able to turn Documentary Film Workshop over to D. A. Pennebaker, Chris Hegedus, and most recently Laura Poitras. After the university unexpectedly defunded this line, I resumed teaching the course, which also necessitated a return to filmmaking: my seventy-two-minute documentary *Errol Morris: A Lightning Sketch* (2014) was one immediate result. But then a funny thing happened. In separate conversations, several of my humanities-based colleagues assumed that I had given up on traditional scholarship for filmmaking—as if I had gone through some belated midlife crisis. In fact I have always seen my filmmaking and my scholarship as deeply interconnected. Their well-intentioned if disconcerting comments propelled me to channel my somewhat diffused exploration of audiovisual practices and focus on a book-length manuscript: what follows is the result.

Many individuals and institutions deserve my heartfelt thanks. I have been blessed to have a group of supportive colleagues in Yale's Film and Media Studies Program, including Brigitte Peucker, Dudley Andrew, Katerina Clark, John MacKay, Aaron Gerow, Katie Trumpener, Thomas Elsaesser, J. D. Connor, Laura Wexler, Katherine Germano, Jon Andrews, and Marc Lapadula. Past members of this group who continue to be part of my world include Terri Francis, Noa Steimatsky, Angela Dalle Vacche, and Josh Glick. Our graduate program has been blessed with an engaging group of students, all of whom have taken my course Historical Methods in Film Study, which is focused on pre-1920 cinema (particularly in the United States). I am deeply grateful for their hard work and our lively discussions. Indeed, I presented elements of this book to the graduate-run Rough Cut seminar. My fall 2012 course on Media and US Presidential Elections, which I had taught the previous summer at Stockholm University (thanks to Tytti Soila and Jan Olsson), was also an important opportunity to think through these ideas. The scholarly community at Yale, which includes my many colleagues in American Studies and others—notably for this undertaking, Jeffrey Alexander—has been an essential support.

I am also grateful for a large community of film and media scholars who have made my scholarly and professional life so fulfilling, including Dan Streible, Walter Forsberg, and the many friends associated with Orphan Film Movement; Jane Gaines, Michael Renov, Faye Ginsburg, Ruby Rich, Brian Winston, and the Visible Evidence convocators; Tom Gunning, Andre Gaudreault, Yuri Tsivian, Greg Waller, Tami Williams, Scott Curtis, Vanessa Toulmin, and other Domitor participants; Patrice

Petro, Anna Lopez, officers, staff, and members of the Society for Cinema and Media Studies, which has supplied me with an essential base of support since the late 1970s; Shelley Stamp, Richard Abel, Monica Dall'Asta, and the members of Women and Film History International (aka Women and the Silent Screen); David Robinson, Livio Jacob, Paolo Cherchi Usai, Piera Patat, Jay Weissberg, and the wonderful colleagues at Le Giornate del Cinema Muto in Pordenone, Italy; David Francis and Josh Marsh of the Kent Museum of the Moving Image; Jack Judson of the Magic Lantern Castle Museum; Terry and Debbie Borton, Richard Balzer, Artemis Willis, and Kentwood D. Wells of the Magic Lantern Society; film archivists Jan-Christopher Horak, Michael Mashon, Eileen Bowser, Paul Spehr, Robert Rosen, and Patrick Loughney; as well as many other friends and colleagues with whom I share a history from my NYU days, including William Uricchio, Roberta Pearson, Richard Koszarski, Antonia Lant, Richard Allen, Jonathan Buchsbaum, William Boddy, and Alison Griffiths. All have contributed directly or indirectly to these pages, but I owe special thanks to manuscript readings from Lisa Gitelman, Greg Waller, Thomas Elsaesser, and John MacKay.

For more than two decades my university has provided essential funds for research and for leaves which, though generally compromised by the pressing needs of Film and Media Studies, have been invaluable. I have also been blessed with the support of my friend and the long-standing Yale Film Study Center Director Michael Kerbel, along with his associates Archer Nielson (manager) and Brian Meacham (archivist); the amazing Lee Faulkner and his several assistants in the Digital Media Center for the Arts; Molly Wheeler and the Yale University Library; as well as Anthony Sudol, Pete Monroy, Jim Blau, Robert Chang, and Steve Ongley in Information Technology Services.

Threese Serana, our son John Carlos, and my nephew Binhi Serana have provided patience and the joys of family life as I worked on this and other projects. My college roommate, Warren Bierwirth, his partner, Anne Priol, the filmmaker Lorna Johnson, and her spouse, Richard Frizell, have been the most supportive of friends. I have been particularly fortunate to forge a relationship with Raina Nadine Polivka, the film and humanities editor at University of California Press. Our association and her editorial advice have been invaluable. Thanks also to Zuha Khan and Lindsey Westbrook for patiently guiding me through this editorial process.

Further research and analysis has deepened and transformed elements of this manuscript, which have appeared in published anthologies.

Portions of chapters 1 and 3 appeared in "The Media Reconfigured: The US Presidential Elections of 1892 and 1896," in Jeff Menne and Christian Long, eds., *Film and the American Presidency* (New York: Routledge, 2015), 19–38. Portions of chapter 2 appeared in "The Stereopticon and Cinema: Media Form or Platform?" in François Albera and Maria Tortajada, eds., *Cine-Dispositives: Essays in Epistemology Across Media* (Amsterdam: University of Amsterdam Press, 2104), 129–60. Sections of chapter 4 were presented at the conference "The Impact of Technological Innovations on the Historiography and Theory of Cinema" in November 2011 as "When Did Cinema Become Cinema? Problems in Historiography and Theory." This book supersedes them all in important respects.

Charles Musser
February 2016

Introduction

In 2008 Barack Obama utilized the new possibilities of the Internet far more effectively than did his rivals Hillary Clinton and John McCain, giving the young senator a crucial edge in the Democratic nominating process and general election. For example: after suffering unexpected defeat in the New Hampshire primary, Obama delivered an inspirational speech on live television in the late evening: "Yes We Can." Although this address to his disheartened supporters went largely unseen due to the late hour and the many competing campaign narratives of the day, his campaign organization immediately reposted the broadcast to the candidate's YouTube channel, where it became an Internet phenomenon.[1] Its impact was further augmented by will.i.am's immensely popular "Yes We Can" music video, which echoed Obama's New Hampshire oratory as an array of performers voiced what may be the most potent campaign song in US political history.[2] This speech is often said to have propelled Obama to the nomination and ultimately the presidency, but it was the Internet that made that possible. Likewise, Obama supporters from around the world expressed their heartfelt enthusiasm for his candidacy on the Internet, usually in song. This ran the gamut from a popular video showing members of Obama for Obama—a group from Obama, Fukui, in Japan—joyously singing "O-B-A-M-A OBAMA!" to a YouTube posting by a young Swedish woman of Finnish ethnicity who was working in England as a nanny. Alone in her small, under-furnished room in the early hours of the morning, she sang a song to celebrate his nomination. It would barely receive one hundred views.[3]

The rapidly changing, dynamic interplay between media and the politics of presidential elections has been one of the always fascinating, often exhilarating, and sometimes distressing aspects of the last dozen years. If television and to a lesser extent print journalism were the keystones of electoral politics in the second half of the twentieth century, they were rapidly replaced by the Internet and digital media in the twenty-first. Early in the 2004 presidential campaign season Robert Greenwald used the Internet and the newly popular DVD (digital versatile disc) technology to launch a series of documentaries, including *Uncovered: The Whole Truth About the Iraq War* (2003) and *Outfoxed* (2004), creating a network of nontraditional screening venues (in particular house parties) that became potent sites for progressive activism and grassroots political organizing. Nevertheless, the old-fashioned feature-length political documentary made an unexpected comeback as Michael Moore's *Fahrenheit 9/11* (2004) moved into more than two thousand theaters and became the highest-grossing documentary of all time.[4] It seemed destined to prevent George W. Bush from being reelected for a second term as president—until the Right was able to demonize and largely neutralize Moore and his message. Meanwhile, a group of Vietnam War veterans, Swift Boat Veterans for Truth, managed to damage his Democratic rival with a series of excoriating television advertisements, which accused former navy lieutenant and medal recipient John Kerry of being a liar and a traitor. They were never effectively rebutted and proved to be crucial to Bush's victory, particularly in the swing state of Ohio. Clearly the emergence of this new yet ever-changing media reality has not had a simple, straightforward trajectory.

As News Dissector Danny Schechter has remarked, "No matter what the story, there is always another story—the media story."[5] To understand the media story does not usually involve focusing on just one specific mode of communication—film or television, newspapers or the Internet—but on the media in all of its diversity. To understand how individual texts (or series of texts) functioned, we need to grapple with the ways they functioned within a larger media system. And so, while trying to make sense of the broader media formation that emerged over the course of the last three presidential elections—often with the benefit of Danny's wisdom—I also deepened my investigations into the ways that media were used for political purposes in the 1890s.[6] This has been fruitful, for political campaigns began to deploy modern forms of audiovisual media in the long 1890s: the illustrated lecture, the cinema, the phonograph, the telephone, and more. The media formation of the 1890s was certainly multifaceted, but because the nation was smaller and technology less developed, it was presumably somewhat less complex and potentially easier to fully grasp. In any case, historical perspective—the gap between our present-day awareness of what this world of new media would become and the immediate experiences of political operatives, amusement entrepreneurs, journalists, and voters in the 1890s—provides a productive vantage point. Likewise, a better understanding of this formative period can provide a perspective on the present.

Presidential elections hold a unique place in American politics. In the entire process of electing governmental officials, they are the only time when citizens go to the polls as a nation and vote for candidates to fill national offices. In fact there are only two such positions, one being that of president of the United States, the role of leader of "the greatest nation on Earth."[7] It is a high-stakes political struggle for power that reaches a fevered pitch in the months, weeks, and days before the actual votes are cast. Unlike the democratic process in some other countries, US presidential elections are regularly occurring events, creating a ritualistic pattern to the whole process. As James W. Carey might point out, they involve a coordinated series of communication acts that give "life an overall form, order and tone."[8] Whether the wearing of campaign buttons, the posting of candidates' portraits, the act of notifying candidates that they have been nominated by their party, or the culminating parades on behalf of their chosen candidate, campaigns and citizens alike embraced a set of reassuring rituals over the course of the long 1890s. John B. Thompson has likewise emphasized the mundane, everyday character of such activities.[9] For this reason, although issues, candidates, and the kinds of available media may have changed between the 1890s and the 2000s, the overall pattern of politicking has remained remarkably stable and recognizable. The pages that follow offer a limited window onto a politicized media economy that is often quite strange and unexpected but also very familiar.

Jeffrey Alexander, looking at Barack Obama's two presidential campaigns, has observed that the candidates were symbolically constructed, with the discourse of civil society divided into either/or binaries. Political candidates have been typically constructed as rational or impulsive, honest or deceitful, concerned for the interests of all the citizenry or just a few special interests. This binary language "constitutes a symbolic reality that those who struggle for democratic power must align themselves with or go down trying."[10] As Alexander and his collaborator Bernadette Jaworsky summarize:

> Political campaigning tells a story about purity and pollution, about who is qualified to protect and extend solidarity and who would narrow and endanger it. To be associated with "anti-civil" qualities is to be symbolically constructed as immoral. Electing such a polluted figure would threaten the solidarity upon which democracy depends. Successful political performers plant their feet squarely inside the civil sphere. Demonstrating their moral trustworthiness, they work furiously to push their opponents outside the world of civility into the immoral world outside.[11]

This characterization, which Alexander has explored in relationship to the presidential campaigns of 2008 and 2012, holds true for the campaigns of the 1890s as well. How new and established media were used to symbolically construct these candidates is an important dimension of *Politicking and Emergent Media*.

Although insurgent third parties have been a recurrent and complicating feature in American politics—with the People's Party, or Populists, remarkably successful in 1892—two parties, the Republicans and the Democrats, have been the preeminent contestants in this high-stakes quadrennial struggle that culminates at the polls. Unfolding around an array of issues and personalities, these contests display first and foremost a fierce rivalry that the participants—as well as more dispassionate observers—understand as similar to a game, a blood sport, or, to offer an analogy that was still quite explicit in the 1890s: war. In the aftermath of the Civil War, it is perhaps understandable that politics—particularly presidential politics—were seen as analogous to war, perhaps even as war by peaceful means. At election time, loyal party members were mobilized and new recruits sought. These citizens were then often organized into military-style units, particularly when they displayed their political loyalties through parades and other forms of public pageantry.

Although presidential candidates play the starring roles in these quadrennial rituals, in the early 1890s they were often careful to appear above the fray. At a time when technologies of reproducibility and communication were rudimentary by comparison to our own time, political surrogates played more prominent roles than they do now—as inter*media*ries or relays between the presidential candidate and the nation's citizenry. They were stand-ins who represented the presidential candidates. (As technologies of reproducibility became more accomplished, the need for such human substitutes—one might even think of them as embodying pre-technological forms of reproducibility—faded, though it did not disappear.) As Geoffrey Craig has noted, the new media of the 1890s began to reestablish "linkages between public and visibility that had diminished with the rise of the print media."[12] Given the prominence of the phonograph and telephone, which as Lisa Gitelman has pointed out worked *against* the traditional visuality of audio production in which one saw as well as heard a musician or orator, we might better think of this as an increase in a particular kind of perceptibility.[13] The virtual presence of presidential candidates rather than their actual presence was becoming more and more noticeable. This has often been characterized in film studies as the absence of presence. Although this moved away from the traditional publicness of co-presence between candidates and voters, spectators still frequently experienced an unsettling illusion of continued presence—particularly in the initial introduction of these new media.

Politicking and Emergent Media examines the four presidential elections of the long 1890s (1888 through 1900), in which new but now-familiar media forms first emerged on the political stage. It looks at just two sets of leading candidates. Democrat and US President Grover Cleveland faced the Republican challenger, former Senator Benjamin Harrison, in 1888. Harrison won that election, which produced an 1892 rematch in which ex-President Cleveland defeated sitting President Harrison. International commerce and the tariff proved the central issue of both campaigns, with Republicans wanting a "protective tariff" that would favor domestic industry while the Democrats wanted a less onerous tariff that would enable imports and encourage competition, thus lowering the cost of goods for ordinary citizens. Cleveland and the Democrats counted on the popular press, particularly in large cities such as New York, where they enjoyed an advantage. Democratic-leaning newspapers were responsible for Cleveland's victory in 1884, and the well-funded Republicans were desperate to find new and innovative campaign methods that could reverse that humiliating defeat. They were able to introduce at least one significant innovation in the 1888 campaign: an illustrated lecture entitled *The Tariff Illustrated*, which we can now recognize as the progenitor of the modern-day political documentary made for campaign purposes. Many considered it to have been an important contribution to Harrison's victory. Four years later Republicans made greater use of stereopticon lectures that favored the protective tariff, but the 1892 presidential election was generally notable for its comparative lack of innovations, as the two campaigns chose to work within a familiar mediascape.[14]

Both Republicans and Democrats offered a fresh slate of candidates in 1896. Former Republican Governor of Ohio William McKinley confronted former Democratic Congressman William Jennings Bryan of Nebraska as the principal issue of the campaign, after a sustained period of deflation and depression, shifted from the tariff to the money supply. Bryan wanted "Free Silver," in which the government would back its currency with silver as well as gold, at a ratio of sixteen to one. This would increase the money supply, stimulate the economy, and help farmers, who could expect the prices paid for their crops to rise. Considering this idea to be positively communistic, Republicans favored "Sound Money" and retaining the Gold Standard.

The 1896 election not only offered voters a fresh slate of candidates. Republicans, and to a lesser extent Democrats, mobilized an array of media novelties in their efforts to achieve victory. This included the first uses of motion pictures, the telephone, the phonograph, and the bicycle for campaign purposes. Nevertheless, the most decisive development of the campaign with respect to media was the shifting allegiance of traditionally Democratic newspapers, most of which rejected Bryan's radicalism and embraced Sound Money and the Republican candidate. McKinley's victory led to another electoral rematch in 1900. Given the booming economy and the McKinley administration's efforts to establish an overseas empire in the wake of the 1898 Spanish-American War, the key campaign issue had shifted. As the US military battled Filipino patriots in an ultimately successful effort to colonize the Philippines, Bryan made anti-imperialism the "paramount issue" of his campaign. The press continued to favor McKinley, while lantern lectures on the Spanish-American War and armed struggle in the Philippines bolstered his cause. In respect to new media forms, the radical innovations of 1896 were normalized. Once again McKinley, assisted by his vice presidential candidate Theodore Roosevelt, proved victorious.

The 1890s mediascape was shaped by a variety of advances in communication and transportation that had emerged over the previous sixty years. The introduction of the railroad and the telegraph in the 1830s and 1840s created the first modern industrial networks and decisively separated communication from transportation.[15] By the 1880s these networks had so penetrated American life that they required a new way of managing time: no longer local time tied to the sun but railroad time or industrial time, which was tied to the clock. This shift was formalized in the United States and Canada when railroads introduced four time zones in November 1883, less than a year before Grover Cleveland's first successful presidential campaign. New high-speed presses made possible the cheap and rapid printing of newspapers and the penny press: the *Philadelphia Inquirer* (established 1829), the *New York Sun* (1833), and the *New York Herald* (1835) were followed by the *Philadelphia Public Ledger* (1836), the *Baltimore Sun* (1837), the *New York Tribune* (1841), the *Brooklyn Eagle* (1841), the *Boston Herald* (1846), the *Chicago Tribune* (1847), the *New York Times* (1851), the *Washington Star* (1852), and the *Chicago Times* (1854). The Associated Press, formed in 1846 (the same year that a limited telegraphic network was established with New York as the hub), reached an exclusive agreement with Western Union to transmit and share news reports in 1856.[16] With the telegraph making it possible to report news from around the country and across the globe simultaneously and with unprecedented rapidity, newspapers were crucial agents of modernity and active players in the political realm. Mass-circulation dailies proliferated in the post–Civil War era as E. W. Scripps launched the *Cleveland Press* (1878) and the *Cincinnati Post* (1881), then formed the modern newspaper chain in the 1890s.[17] Joseph Pulitzer owned the *St. Louis Post-Dispatch* (1879), followed by the *New York World* (1883), while William Randolph Hearst had the *San Francisco Examiner* (1887) and the *New York Journal* (1895), then launched the *Chicago American* (1900). They served as crucial agents of persuasion and communication for presidential campaigns.

Photography was also in an early experimental stage in the 1830s, culminating with the successful daguerreotype system in 1839. Photography subsequently underwent a rapid series of technological innovations and improvements as it was integrated into many different aspects of daily life. One of these has particular importance in this study—the ability from 1850 onward to transfer a positive image to a glass or transparent surface—as it enabled photographers to create slides that could be projected onto a screen using the magic lantern or, as its modernized variant was often called in the United States, the stereopticon. Photography could boast two noticeable innovations in the 1890s. First, George Eastman introduced the Kodak camera in 1888 and offered a series of refinements over the following decade. With the slogan "You press the button, we do the rest," he made photography available to ordinary people. Kodak snapshots would play a modest but noteworthy role in the 1900 presidential campaign as they were incorporated into illustrated lectures by returning military personnel. Second, Thomas Edison began pursuing his ideas for a modern motion picture system in 1888, which achieved commercial reality with the peep-hole kinetoscope in 1894, followed two years later by cinema itself. Photography altered people's sense of space and time, as lifelike images depicting family, friends, the nation, and the world could circulate. Within a few short months of cinema's debut, film screenings featured iconic images of presidential candidates McKinley and Bryan.

Edison's phonograph had been widely shown as a technological marvel and novelty to assembled audiences in the late 1870s but soon faded from view. In 1888 major refinements turned it into a viable instrument for audio recording and playback, launching the phonograph industry in the subsequent decade. Likewise Alexander Graham Bell, who invented the telephone in 1876, began to establish a series of increasingly ambitious long-distance lines in this same period: Boston–New York (1884), Philadelphia–New York (1885), New York–Chicago (1892), Chicago–Nashville (1895), and New York–Omaha (1897).[18] Parallel achievements occurred in the realm of transportation. The safety bicycle was developed in the mid- to late 1880s and launched the bicycle craze of the 1890s. The automobile entered American life slightly later: the Duryea Motor Wagon Company became the first US manufacturer of gasoline automobiles in 1895, while Henry Ford tested his first self-propelling vehicle in 1896. These would provide opportunities for campaign novelties as the century came to a close.

The rapidly evolving mediascape was only one aspect of what is often called the Second Industrial Revolution (1870–1914). As Warren Susman and John Higham have observed, the 1890s was its epicenter: a turning point in American society and culture.[19] It was the end of the Gilded Age, a term coined by Mark Twain to refer to the period from 1870 to 1900, in which ostentatious wealth concealed underlying poverty and industrial turbulence. Historians have had other names for much of this period: the Great Depression of 1873 to 1896, or the Great Deflation that lasted from 1870 to 1896.[20] This period of rapid industrialization, financial speculation, and monetary deflation was accompanied by labor unrest. The American Federation of Labor, formed in 1886 (the same year as the bloody Haymarket Affair), was actively fighting for the eight-hour workday by the time of the 1888 election. The brutal Homestead Steel Strike occurred a few months before the presidential election of 1892 and was soon followed by the Financial Panic of 1893, the worst economic depression of the nineteenth century. Unemployment, below 4 percent in 1892, rose steeply. Estimates vary, but the unemployment rate fluctuated between 8.1 percent and 18.4 percent between 1893 and 1899 and was consistently more than 10 percent between 1894 and 1898.[21] Only in 1900 did it fall to 5 percent. Through all this, working-class Americans were not generally drawn to a radical political party specifically focused on their interests and concerns. Only 1.31 percent of voters supported the Union Labor Party in 1888, while Eugene Debs and the Socialist Democratic Party received a mere 0.69 percent of the vote in 1900. Rather, Republican and Democratic candidates sought to appeal to working-class voters as well as the middle class and elites.

The United States had a population of 62,947,714 according to the 1890 census—an increase of more than 12 million in ten years. By 1900 it would be 76,212,168. Improved steamship travel facilitated a boom in US immigration, with 5,246,613 people arriving between 1881 and 1890, and another 3,687,564 between 1891 and 1900. Since recently arrived immigrants were not yet citizens and did not have the right to vote, political parties tended to direct their appeals to more established ethnic groups, particularly Germans and the Irish rather than those from eastern and southern Europe. Likewise, mass-circulation dailies were less concerned with these groups because they tended to be illiterate or read the ethnic press. Recent immigrant groups might encounter hostility and exploitation, but political organizations—in New York City it was Tammany Hall—provided a variety of services that helped to integrate them into American life, including acquiring citizenship and the vote.

African Americans, in contrast, were being stripped of their legal rights and protections. The Civil Rights Act of 1875 provided that "all persons within the jurisdiction of the United States shall be entitled to the full and equal enjoyment of the accommodations, advantages, facilities, and privileges of inns, public conveyances on land or water, theaters, and other places of public amusement; subject only to the conditions and limitations established by law, and applicable alike to citizens of every race and color." The Supreme Court ruled it unconstitutional in 1883 by an eight-to-one margin.[22] This setback was followed by Plessy v. Ferguson, which affirmed the right of states to require segregation in public facilities. The Supreme Court decided the case in May 1896 by a seven-to-one margin. A Republican, Henry Billings Brown, wrote the majority opinion. The desperate state of race relations in the United States is evident in the fact that African Americans still voted overwhelmingly for Republican candidates—when and where they could vote.

White women, on the other hand, achieved increased rights during the 1890s. In the 1888 election, not a single state gave women the opportunity to vote for president. Twelve years later, women could vote for president in four of them: Wyoming (1890), Colorado (1893), Utah (1896), and Idaho (1896).[23] The National American Woman Suffrage Association, formed at a Washington, DC, convention in 1890, had established local organizations in every state by 1899, although the next state to add women's suffrage would only do so in 1910. By the 1890s, women represented more than a third of those attending college.[24] The Woman's Art Club of New York, which eventually became the National Association of Women Artists, was founded in 1890 with annual exhibitions, reflecting women's significant progress in the arts. Actresses such as Sarah Bernhardt, Minnie Maddern Fiske, Olga Nethersole, and May Irwin headed important theatrical companies. They provided powerful models of independence for young women, while the bicycle gave greater mobility and independence to those from the middle class. Although the rituals of politicking frequently remained exclusively male affairs, women began to participate in campaign rituals in many parts of the nation.

The 1890s witnessed the robust rise of consumer culture as electricity, telephones, and phonograph players entered an increasing number of homes. Consumerism extended beyond the domestic sphere and included a boom in commercial amusements. Burlesque, variety, and vaudeville were on the rise. Touring theatrical companies took advantage of the improved transportation network to bring drama to cities and towns across the country. In the 1880s and early 1890s, lectures, musical recitals, phonograph concerts, and other forms of proper and refined culture rapidly lost ground to more sensational performances, such as Olga Nethersole's *Carmen* (1895). Over the course of the play the actress kissed three men with unprecedented realism: Was it great art or pornography? People filled the theater to find out for themselves. Illustrated lectures, which were part of the discourse of sobriety and propriety, were presented in auditoriums, church halls, and other nontheatrical venues. Cinema, which appeared in the second half of the 1890s, was typically shown in commercial theaters, particularly vaudeville houses, and was part of the world of amusement that Baptists, Methodists, and other evangelical groups strongly opposed.

Tom Gunning has characterized the films of this period as "inciting visual curiosity, and supplying pleasure through an exciting spectacle—a unique event, whether fictional or documentary, that is of interest in itself. The attraction to be displayed may also be of a cinematic nature, such as the early close-ups . . . or trick films in which a cinematic manipulation (slow motion, reverse motion, substitution, multiple exposure) provides the film's novelty."[25] Scantily clothed dancers, boxing matches, semi-naked strongmen, kissing couples, and scenes of Coney Island were among the most popular subjects. So, too, were scenes of distant lands. As Robert Grau remarked, when the Lumière cinématographe appeared in Keith's Union Square Theater in July 1896, weekly receipts jumped from $3,000 to $7,000.[26] Polite, proper entertainment was giving way to more risqué and lively fare. These shifting dynamics were also evident in the political realm. The theatrical world and the world of political theater had long been at odds: presidential elections negatively impacted the box office as potential patrons abandoned the amusement world to participate in the rituals of political campaigning. Beginning with the 1896 election, political operatives and amusement entrepreneurs began to find ways to reconcile the two as politics entered entertainment venues.

Although scholars always face the danger of recycling ideas and information when returning to familiar subject matter, this book departs from my previous work on screen practice and early cinema of the 1890s in three respects. First, as has already been made clear, this book resituates cinema within a much broader media formation. This reorientation parallels changes in the scholarly discipline in which I participate, as film studies has become film and media studies. Thus the study of cinema's first two decades, which has operated under the "early cinema" rubric, has gone through a succession of changes such that the emerging intellectual formation, at least as encountered in the course of this study, operates under the banner of "media archaeology."[27] Certainly scholars of early cinema have examined the role of audiovisual media in the 1896 election, including *McKinley at Home* (1896), made by the American Mutoscope Company.[28] Yet, from a more inclusive media perspective, we discover that the Republicans simultaneously employed the telephone in ways that throws new light on their use of cinema and the way we understand its operation as a novelty. Of course we can and should also reverse the order of this insight by observing that the Republicans' use of cinema throws new light on their use of the telephone. I will return to the role and relevance of media archaeology for this present project in the concluding coda.

What is the "media" of media studies? Many have traditionally conceived of the media as involving newspapers, radio, and television—what might be called the mass media.[29] The Internet is now usually included as part of this configuration. In contrast, Thomas Elsaesser, Wanda Strauven, and Michael Wedel are representative of many in film and media studies who take a quite different stance. "'Media' in our case," writes Elsaesser, "refers in principle to all imaging techniques and sound technologies, but cinema has provided the conceptual starting point and primary historical focus."[30] In this context, newspapers and magazines are essentially excluded—even as radio, television, the Internet, cellphones, and social media are embraced.

In her influential book *When Old Technologies Were New*, Carolyn Marvin has defined media more broadly as "devices that mediate experience by re-presenting messages originally in a different mode."[31] Seeking a more elaborated and theoretical definition, Lisa Gitelman sees "media as socially realized structures of communication, where structures include both technological forms and their associated protocols, and where communication is a cultural practice, a ritualized collocation of different people on the same mental map, sharing or engaged with popular ontologies of representation."[32] Gitelman's definition resonates closely with Walter Benjamin's oft-mentioned interest in an era of technological reproducibility.[33] It is also similar to the term *dispositif* being used by many current European cinema and media scholars, such as François Albera and Maria Tortajada.[34]

Although this study is largely focused on media that involve technological reproducibility, it cannot be limited to these concerns. Rather, in order to adequately describe the cultural system of communications at work during these (and other) presidential campaigns, it considers the role of public oratory and public pageantry.[35] Since these practices do not have clear technological components, a workable conception of media requires a somewhat different definition than these scholars have offered. By shortening Gitelman's definition somewhat, we can include these vital areas of interest. Media might then be described as "socially realized structures of communication, where communication is a cultural practice, a ritualized collocation of different people on the same mental map, sharing or engaged with popular ontologies of representation." This then would include all kinds of public performances that are unmediated by film, photography, the phonograph, or other technologies of transmission and reproducibility. Public protests, heckling, and other forms of disruptions, even by solitary individuals, also fall within this media configuration. One might argue that this verges on a cultural studies approach, as evidenced in Asa Briggs and Peter Burke's *A Social History of the Media* (2002), but perhaps scholars of communications have paid relatively little attention to nineteenth-century political campaigns because their technological biases are at a tangent to this reality.[36]

My investigation's expanded reach is not meant to minimize those structures that "include both technological forms and their associated protocols." Quite the contrary: emergent media remains the focus of this book, and like Elsaesser and his colleagues I am particularly interested in the audiovisual. In this respect, this book returns to a theoretical framework that I have pursued in the past: that of screen practice. Although I have certainly looked at cinema within quite different intermedial contexts since I wrote *The Emergence of Cinema: The American Screen to 1907* (1990)—for instance by treating cinema and live stage performances as a single, unified field of theatrical entertainment—the projected image and its sound accompaniment return full force in this book both as a reality and a theoretical conundrum.[37] This has been made necessary by one of the early and unexpected discoveries of this current undertaking: the importance of the stereopticon to political campaigning in the late nineteenth century.

What was the stereopticon, and where does it fit in the history of modern media? "Stereopticon" was an American term: in Britain the equivalent was "optical lantern." Indeed, the stereopticon was often considered as something like a "new media," as it combined photography with state-of-the-art projection in a way that anticipated cinema as a combination of motion pictures with the lantern. The reality is that media scholars have given it relatively little notice. Historical surveys of the media by Anthony Fellow, Paul Starr, and John B. Thompson as well as more scholarly and specialized accounts by Carolyn Marvin and Lisa Gitelman have ignored it.[38] Although Jay Bolter and Richard Grusin make some brief gestures toward the past in *Remediation: Understanding New Media* (2000), they overlook both the magic lantern and the stereopticon.[39] But why? The reasons are inevitably complicated. At first glance, the lantern might not appear to involve technological reproducibility, its relation to cinema perhaps not unlike that of the eighteenth-century semaphore to the telegraph—though this can certainly be disputed.[40] Perhaps the once-new technologies spawned by the late sixteenth- and seventeenth-century revolution in optics and other science-based achievements, which include the microscope and the telescope as well as the magic lantern, remain too remote for most people interested in the archaeology of modern media.

Although Siegfried Zielinski certainly deals with the lantern and other optical devices in his investigations around Athanasius Kircher, he does not pursue it as he examines later time periods.[41] Perhaps its old newness is felt to be not just old but ancient. And yet, between the phantasmagoria of the 1790s and cinema of the 1890s, screen practices actively participated in the many technological innovations of the nineteenth century. Various historians have examined this history but typically as a self-contained phenomenon.[42] It has been viewed at best as minor media. By examining lantern practices in a broad media context, this book can help to end that isolation.

This book's main topic—that of the application of media to political campaigns—is interrupted at two points in order to grapple with the question: What constitutes a "media form"? Although the term was certainly not in use in the nineteenth century, the concept of a media form can be useful for interrogating the status and contours of specific practices. The first section of chapter 2 pauses to ask: Are the magic lantern and the stereopticon the same media form? That is, do they constitute a single cultural practice but at different stages of development, like silent and sound motion pictures, or were they seen as two separate media, like painting and photography? Or, whether taken separately or together, perhaps they do not constitute "media" as such, in the strong sense of the term? Perhaps they are merely a single platform that has become technologically more sophisticated over time. Platforms provide a means of transmission, exhibition, and/or presentation. Besides the projector (or lantern), other platforms for turn-of-the-century motion pictures would include the mutoscope and the kinetoscope. The relationships among platforms, mediums, and media forms is complex and fluid. That is, one might claim that the lantern or projector, which goes back to the mid-seventeenth century, is merely a means to present a wide variety of distinctive media over time, including paintings, lithographs, photographs, and motion pictures. On the other hand, one might argue that the lantern or projector is an essential component of a series of different media forms. For instance, photography was understood as a new media form, and its various means of display—whether fixed on the silver surface of the daguerreotype or the cheaper metal-surfaced tintype, printed on photographic paper, reproduced in books and newspapers, or transferred onto the glass lantern slide that needed to be projected to be seen (and much later digitized so that it comes into being on a computerized screen)—were perceived simply as variants under photography's rubric. Camera clubs in the nineteenth century often used the lantern as a suitable platform to show their work. Grappling with this conundrum surrounding the stereopticon has been one of this book's most interesting challenges.

The stereopticon—photography plus a powerful (modern) light source plus sharp lenses—was hailed as a new media form in part because it was felt to be a scientific reaction to what had become the nonobjective and fantastic qualities of the magic lantern. Yet the stereopticon as a name and as a new cultural practice emerged in the early 1860s, some ten years after William and Frederick Langenheim began showing photographic glass slides with the magic lantern. In this respect, I was fascinated to discover that the "illustrated lecture" as a term and coherent cultural practice emerged at roughly the same time as the term "stereopticon," and that the two were profoundly interrelated. Most platform orators who delivered illustrated lectures did so using the stereopticon. Operators certainly used the stereopticon for other purposes, and not all individuals giving illustrated lectures used photographic slides or even the lantern, but there was a powerful conjunction between the two. The term "stereopticon lecture" became relatively common and was pivotal to the ways in which its practitioners came to think of the stereopticon as a media form. Although many Americans saw the stereopticon as a media form in the 1880s and the 1890s, its constructed identity was never fully institutionalized. Some persisted in seeing the stereopticon as an extension of the magic lantern, while others probably saw it as one possible component of the public lecture, which could easily be imagined as a distinctive media form with its own protocols. From yet another perspective, early advocates of projected motion pictures often saw the cinema as a special kind of stereopticon. The only way to confront these contradictions and conundrums is through historical investigation and some theoretical speculation. In the end, this study treats the stereopticon as a key instance of emergent media despite the fact that it may have been a largely national formation that went through various hesitations and repetitions in its development.

The first part of chapter 4 likewise looks at the term "cinema," inspired in part by André Gaudreault, who has recently posed the question: When did cinema become cinema? When we talk about the invention of cinema by the Lumières and their contemporaries, "cinema" would seem to be defined as projected motion pictures shown in a theatrical setting. Yet as Gaudreault's question makes clear, the term does not possess a single, constant meaning. He seems to be asking: When does the cinema become "a socially realized structure of communication"?[43] This can be slightly rephrased as: When did cinema become its own distinct or autonomous media form? That is, technological innovations and changing cultural formations pose the problem of media specificity as well as cultural and social constructedness. In crucial respects projected motion pictures operated within the overarching context of the stereopticon until about 1903. At that moment a wholesale reorganization of the *dispositif* occurred, giving cinema a new and more recognizable identity. During the US presidential elections from 1888 to 1900, the stereopticon possessed a hegemonic preeminence in the audiovisual realm that it would not possess before or after. When the modern era of technological reproducibility is considered, the stereopticon provided politicking with an essential audiovisual foundation.

The mediascape of the 1896 election was surprisingly different from its immediate predecessor. Although the stereopticon continued to be used, political operatives generally directed their energies elsewhere. Newly emergent media was central to this presidential contest—and cinema was only one of these forms. Both nickel-in-the-slot phonographs using individual earphones and phonograph concerts had become popular as early as 1890. While campaign managers could have used them in the 1892 election, this did not transpire. The phonograph was first used for politicking four years later, motivated in part by the heightened attention given to the political oratory of the two main candidates. More surprisingly, the GOP used the long-distance telephone for high-profile campaign events—not merely to communicate between their New York and Chicago headquarters. In a rather unexpected development, technologically savvy Republicans responded to McKinley's front porch campaign by connecting his home in Canton, Ohio, with a large-scale demonstration in Chicago, enabling columns of marchers to relay their chants to the distant candidate in real time. And yet this also had a context of sorts, for long-distance "telephone concerts" had become something of a technological novelty by 1890. Grover Cleveland and Benjamin Harrison could have adapted these practices for political purposes in 1892, but did not do so. Four years later the Republicans embraced new media forms, making technological innovation and novelty the powerful subtexts of their appeal to voters, and as it turned out, they were highly successful. In many ways the adoption of newly emergent media came to have symbolic value that far exceeded the media's actual reach and direct impact. To a significant degree, the media truly was the message.

Newspapers were the only mass media of the 1890s, and as the sole form of mass communication, they were central to the political process. Benedict Anderson has written eloquently about the ways in which newspapers have been central to the construction of national communities.[44] While most US newspapers of the 1890s offered a clear conception of the nation, they also did much to construct distinct political communities. Mainstream newspapers tended to have strong ties to one of the two major political parties—allegiances that were reflected in their news reporting as well as their editorial policies. They were central to the political process, and when a core group of Democratic newspapers shifted allegiance to the Republicans, as they did in the second half of the decade, it had a profound impact on the conduct and outcome of subsequent presidential campaigns.

Finally, in looking at American politics within a larger media system, we must take seriously the role of public oratory and public pageantry—two forms of communication, and two media forms that had preceded the printing press by millennia. In large cities, parades of supporters in the days and weeks leading up to an election tested the relative strength of each party's candidate—both synchronically in relation to the rival party's demonstrations and diachronically in comparison to similar parades organized by the same party in previous years. Novel forms of oratory and pageantry were also pursued, particularly in the 1896 contest. These speeches and parades were reported on extensively in the press, creating an important feedback loop that was central to the campaigns. Daniel Boorstin might have characterized them in an uncomplimentary fashion as pseudo–news events, but they were pervasive, potent symbols of participatory democracy.[45]

· ·

Besides a shift of focus from cinema to a more inclusive media system, this book offers a second distinctive approach that has to do with its investigation of historical change. This was made possible by the political calendar's regularity, which held significant advantages for those invested in the art of presidential campaigning. Party operatives could reflect on the triumphs and mistakes of the previous electoral cycle and recalibrate their campaigns accordingly. This was particularly true with respect to audio, pictorial, and audiovisual media, all of which experienced rapid if uneven change and expansion throughout the long twentieth century. Not surprisingly, this regularity provides somewhat similar advantages for today's media scholars. Presidential elections, in their regularity, offer a set of useful delimitations. Individual media are constantly changing in big ways and small, but the few months prior to Election Day provide a snapshot of maximal media mobilization: thirty-two such snapshots between 1888 and 2012. Each of these presidential contests produced its own unique media formation—a distinct set of relationships and interplay among the full range of utilized media forms. Technology and technological innovation was only one factor in defining the characteristics of each quadrennial media formation. The candidates, their managers and political allies, the issues, and finances all significantly impacted the ways that different media were mobilized and prioritized. Yet Republicans and Democrats always mobilized the media for the same purpose—to bring victory to their respective presidential candidate. There was a consistent purity of intent over time.

By giving equal weight to the media formations of the 1892 and 1896 elections, we can investigate the nature of the shift from one to the other and speculate on how and why it took place as well as what that shift meant. By exploring the ways that media was deployed in 1892 and how it was likely seen as successful or unsuccessful, we gain a new perspective on, and so a new understanding of, the media formation (as well as the emergent media) of 1896. What were the significant continuities across the two campaigns? What changed and what emerged? Democrats could rely on a robust press during the 1892 election, and it proved sufficient for Grover Cleveland's electoral victory. Republicans, knowing that the press working on their behalf was weak by comparison, were heavy users of the stereopticon in 1892, with at least six operatives giving evening-length illustrated lectures on the election's key issue: the tariff. When they lost that election, Republicans largely lost interest in the stereopticon—but not in the screen. With no reason to expect that much of the traditionally Democrat-leaning press would back McKinley in 1896, they reconceptualized their approach and sought a more robust audio-visual campaign presence, which emphasized novelty. The American Mutoscope Company was essentially a Republican-controlled media company. Not surprisingly, the Republican National Committee hosted the film program that debuted Biograph's short film *McKinley at Home*. This was not by chance and should not escape our notice. The Republicans' film activities become far more explicable and significant when their past involvement with the stereopticon is considered.

This book privileges the stereopticon, the cinema, and emergent media. Chapter 1 begins by laying out the broad media formation of the 1892 election, then looks back at the 1888 election, when Judge John L.

Wheeler first introduced *The Tariff Illustrated*, and finally concentrates on that lecture's expanded mobilization four years later. The first part of chapter 2 considers the technological and cultural innovations that produced the stereopticon as a media form, while the second half examines the early uses of the stereopticon for political purposes from 1872 to 1884. Chapter 3 then focuses on the 1896 campaign, as Republicans continued to be interested in the screen as a source of effective politicking even as they created a wide range of new media moments. Correspondingly, the first half of chapter 4 lays out a succession of changes in early motion picture practice as a way to understand the different ways it was deployed for political purposes. The second section of chapter 4 looks at the ways party operatives used cinema, the phonograph, and the telephone in the 1900 election and investigates the large number of illustrated lectures using lantern slides and occasionally films that fostered the imperialist, expansionist agenda of the Republicans, as opposed to the anti-imperialist stance of the 1900 Bryan Democrats. In this respect the stereopticon lecture as a political force regained its prominence as the nineteenth century came to an end.

I have chosen to tell this story of presidential politicking and the media in a manner that is not strictly linear. The four core chapters go back and forth in time. Superficially they might even seem out of order, but they mime the way I as a historian found myself moving back and forth in time as I tried to better understand my subject. I hope that they have a similar utility for the reader. I started out by focusing on the transformation in media politicking between the 1892 to 1896 elections but gradually, almost reluctantly, found myself going back in time—to find out what had happened in the 1888 presidential campaign. A firmer understanding of that election enabled me to return to the 1892 election with new insight—and pushed me back to the beginnings of the stereopticon itself. Much later, almost out of a sense of duty, I looked into the last US presidential election of the nineteenth century—only to become intrigued and then amazed as random word searches revealed dozens of lantern programs that heralded American expansionism. History unfolds chronologically, and while there are moments of crisis, breaks, regressions, and transformations, it moves forward along a linear pathway. This is not, however, how we necessarily encounter it as researchers and historians. Nor as ordinary people making sense of our past. As readers we often peruse one section of a book and then another rather than start at its beginning and follow the author's intended path to its conclusion. Encountering the history of politicking and media in a nonlinear fashion can produce insights and enjoyment. Perhaps the reader will read this book—or portions of this book—in this way as well. In any case, the following chapters reveal a fascinating story of political parties, particularly Republicans, mobilizing a variety of new and unfamiliar media forms to outwit their rivals and regain (or retain) political power.

. . .

Third, this book's insights and subject matter both build on and depart from previous scholarship. Past scholarship on early cinema has generally focused on general overviews, individual companies, or a variety of other topics such as exhibition histories, questions of representation, and so forth. By focusing on cinema and other screen practices that were mobilized during these presidential elections, I found myself uncovering new information and new connections. For instance, the Democrats managed to respond to Biograph's filming of presidential candidate William McKinley by arranging for the Edison-Vitascope entrepreneurs to film his rival, William Jennings Bryan, a mere five days later. This coincidence was lost to me and no doubt others as we dealt with a massive number of films: *Bryan Train Scene* seemed obscure relative to many other motion picture subjects of that period. (Terry Ramsaye went so far as to suggest that such a film never actually existed, while today it remains a lost film.)[46] The alacrity of the Democrats' response cannot but strike us as astounding. Did they have someone in Canton, Ohio, who reported on unusual events such as the filming of McKinley? Were these events mentioned in the press? Or, more likely, did the Democrats have a mole inside the Biograph company itself so that their plans to film McKinley were known well in advance? All of which is not to completely dismiss the possibility of fortuitous coincidence. Perhaps there is no mystery: perhaps the idea of filming the candidates seemed self-evident, mere common sense. Somewhat ironically, by investigating a small group of films within a framework other than cinema as its own self-generating cultural practice, this book can enable us to better understand cinema's disruptive force and significance.[47]

This return to familiar territory but within a fresh framework is also facilitated by the radically new potential of digital research. The accessibility of primary-source documents has been changing over the years. Newspapers were still being microfilmed when I started doing my research on early cinema in the late 1970s, providing a relatively new basis for research. The digitization of old newspapers—or the digitizing of microfilm of old newspapers—began on an experimental basis in the 1980s and became more viable in the mid- to late 1990s. ProQuest Historical Newspapers, the Media History Digital Library, the American Memory Project at the Library of Congress, Newspaperarchive.com (started in 1999), and similar undertakings have made new kinds of information—including the proverbial needle in the haystack—accessible in ways that change how we can do history in general and certainly film and media history.[48] This should, I hope, be evident on almost every page of this book, but I can offer one example. Abner McKinley worked so effectively behind the scenes on behalf of his older brother William that his contributions to McKinley's 1896 presidential campaign have gone completely unmentioned in various reputable histories.[49] Although his activities were rarely reported in the press, random word searches of digitized newspapers reveal enticing details of his influence. A book about emergent media in the 1890s depends on emergent digital technologies for research some one hundred years later. Digitization has produced a new kind of archive that provides a new kind of access—and with it new opportunities and challenges. "The authorization that the archive gives can be understood as a gift as well as a responsibility . . . in terms of a very close, scrupulous and critical attention to the traces of the past," notes Patrick Joyce.[50] Certainly these newspapers cannot be read naively as simple sources of information, particularly when dealing with a subject of this kind. They are more or less always political documents.

Digitization projects provide us with increased access to major newspapers of the day but also many obscure ones from small cities and towns. While these can contribute to a picture of the nation as a whole, *Politicking and Emergent Media* generally takes a more limited geographic focus. William McKinley may have served as governor of Ohio and lived in Canton, but Abner McKinley worked in finance on Wall Street, and Wall Street was a powerful force in politics even in the 1890s. New York was also the nation's media center, particularly when it came to the newspaper business. It also served as an incubator for many new media forms such as motion pictures, the phonograph, and the telephone. Correspondingly, New York was the center of Republican and Democratic politics: both had national headquarters in Manhattan. Finally, New York State was the key to electoral victory. The candidate who won New York in the 1880, 1884, and 1888 elections won the presidency—and it would happen again in 1892, 1896, and beyond.[51] For the 1892 election, Democratic presidential candidate

Grover Cleveland had been governor of New York State while Harrison's vice presidential running mate, Whitelaw Reid, was also from New York. Since the Democratic margin of victory in New York City was crucial to the outcome, campaign activities in the city and its surroundings possessed a disproportionate importance that make them an appropriate focus for this study. When Illinois became a critical state in 1896 and 1900 as William Jennings Bryan ran for president, this book likewise pays greater attention to Chicago.

What follows then is a thick description, which the reader will hopefully find as lively and engaging as it is informative. I have chosen to present a selection of newspaper items as illustrative documents. Stereopticon lectures such as Wheeler's *The Tariff Illustrated* and Mason Mitchell's *How We Placed "Old Glory" on San Juan Hill* do not survive, and the best way for the reader to gain a clear sense of their substance and trajectory is through detailed and representative newspaper accounts of actual presentations. These and similar kinds of news items have been placed in the appendix even as they have been referenced in the main body of the book. The reader is urged to consult them, for they often remind us that in the highly competitive newspaper business of the 1890s, lively prose was a necessary means for capturing the reader's attention.

CHAPTER I

The Stereopticon, *The Tariff Illustrated*, and the 1892 Election

The 1892 US presidential election was a rematch that pitted former President Grover Cleveland against President Benjamin Harrison. Cleveland was a conservative or "Bourbon Democrat" who had been elected governor of New York State in 1882 by a landslide. In 1884 he became the first Democratic president since the Civil War, defeating former Senator James Blaine, a Maine Republican, by the thinnest of margins. His victory depended on winning his home state, which he did by 1,047 votes out of the 1,171,312 that were cast. His strongest supporter—the one most responsible for his success—was the publisher of the *New York World*, Joseph Pulitzer. Pulitzer, a longtime Democrat and owner of the *St. Louis Post-Dispatch*, had purchased the *World* in 1883. Barely a year later he was working hard on behalf of Cleveland's nomination for president. During the actual campaign the *World* savagely attacked his Republican opponent for corruption and for his sweetheart deals with the railroads. Pulitzer's *World* was particularly effective during the final days of the campaign. For the first time, and with some justice, Republicans could blame the liberal media for their loss of the White House, where they had enjoyed a twenty-eight-year occupancy. Mass-circulation daily newspapers had proved themselves to be a dominant political force, and Pulitzer had become a kingmaker.[1]

Four years later, Cleveland's Republican challenger was former Indiana Senator Benjamin Harrison, the grandson of the ninth US president, William Henry Harrison. His running mate was former New York

Congressman and Minister to France, Levi Morton. Although Cleveland won the popular vote, Harrison took New York State by 15,000 votes and so won the election. Republicans had seemingly found the means to counter the Democrats' newspaper advantage (more on this later). In the resulting 1892 redo, Harrison chose a new vice presidential running mate—another New Yorker, Whitelaw Reid. Not only did Reid provide geographic balance, but he was the publisher of the nation's preeminent Republican newspaper, the *New York Tribune*. The Democratic Party chose Adlai Stevenson, a former two-term congressman from Illinois, to be Cleveland's running mate. Stevenson's positions were more Populist than Cleveland's, and it was seen as a purposeful slap at the nominee.[2]

Republicans and Democrats faced a serious third-party insurgency. Various farm alliances combined with labor and reform groups to organize the People's Party in 1892. Under the banner "Equal Rights to All, Special Privileges to None," these Populists became a potent force in the West, where they would win the states of Nevada, Colorado, Idaho, and Kansas as well as a delegate in North Dakota. In fact, Cleveland did not appear on the ballot in these states—nor in Wyoming, which the Republicans won by a narrow margin. In the South the Populists would take votes away from the Republicans: in Alabama, the People's Party received more than 36 percent of the vote while Republicans were reduced to less than 4 percent. The Populists favored women's suffrage, and for the first time some women could cast ballots for the nation's highest office: they resided in Wyoming, the least populous state, which had been admitted into the union on July 10, 1890.[3] The Populists, however, were much less of a factor in the East and the Midwest, receiving less than 1 percent of the vote in New England, New Jersey, Pennsylvania, and Maryland; less than 2 percent of the vote in Ohio and New York; less than 3 percent in Illinois and Wisconsin; and less than 5 percent in Indiana, South Carolina, Virginia, and Iowa. For the Northeast and Midwest, where the election would be largely won or lost, the familiar two-party system remained very much intact. In this regard the political steadfastness of the prominent daily newspapers was undoubtedly important.

Many assumed that this 1892 contest would be a vicious grudge match, but such was not the case. As the *New York Herald* observed, it "had been marked by an obvious calmness"—a comment echoed by Cleveland in the closing days of the campaign.[4] Harrison and Cleveland had each faced major, even treacherous rivalries from within their own party in order to secure their nominations.[5] Now, for the first time in

FIGURE 1. This 1888 Cleveland-Thurman campaign poster features slogans that addressed the primary issue of the election: the tariff. Courtesy the Library of Congress.

history, two American presidents (one former, one current) faced each other. Perhaps they were just being "presidential," but Harrison stayed by the side of his seriously ill wife, while Cleveland refused to take advantage of his opponent's misfortune. In any case, it was an election in which the candidates and their campaign methods were equally familiar to voters. In a nation that had seen a brutal Civil War, economic panics, and civil unrest, candidates and their politicking offered a degree of ritual comfort and reassurance.

The principal issue dividing Republicans and Democrats was the tariff—a tax on goods imported into the United States. During his first term in office President Cleveland had been a strong advocate for reducing the tariff as a way to make goods more affordable. In contrast, the Republicans demanded a strong tariff to foster and protect American businesses. Joanne Reitano argues, "The year 1888 was unique in American history because it was so singularly dedicated to the discussion of ideas. A decade of ferment over economic theory among academics and reformers culminated in the adoption of the tariff issue by the president, Congress, the two major parties, and the press as a cause célèbre."[6] Following Harrison's 1888 victory the Republicans passed the Tariff Act of 1890. The higher tariff proved unpopular: along with an economic setback, it helped the Democrats win the 1890 midterm elections by a robust margin. The stage was thus set for an electoral contest in which the tariff would once again be the paramount issue. As in the past, the key to electoral victory was New York State, with Illinois, Indiana, New Jersey, and Connecticut seen as other potential swing states.

POLITICAL ORATORY, PARTISAN PAGEANTRY, AND THE PUBLIC SPHERE

The public sphere remained a vital force in New York City, as numerous political gatherings and public demonstrations remained a central feature of the 1892 presidential election. Although political oratory was crucial to this era's media formation, the actual candidates were remarkably parsimonious in making public appearances and speechifying. Perhaps the most notable exception was an "unprecedented" moment in July when Cleveland, joined by vice presidential candidate Stevenson, departed from his home in Buzzard's Bay, Massachusetts, and arrived by steamer to accept his party's nomination at New York's Madison Square Garden before a crowd of 20,000 people.[7] Traditionally the nominating committee left the party's convention and visited the candidate at his home and offered a modest if formal notification. Cleveland's appearance was an effort to unify and energize the badly fractured Democratic Party in New York State (the entire New York delegation at the Democratic convention had declared that he could not carry the state and so would lose the election).[8] With this goal in mind, ex-President Cleveland expressed tried-and-true Democratic sentiments: "No plan of tariff legislation shall be tolerated which has for its object and purpose a forced contribution from the earnings and incomes of the mass of our citizens to swell directly the accumulation of a favored few."[9] Cleveland declared himself to be the people's candidate who would defend the interests of ordinary Americans against the high-tariff Republicans who were seeking to line the pockets of a few Wall Street capitalists. Indeed, in informing Cleveland of his nomination as the Democrats' standard bearer, Colonel William L. Wilson noted that the Democratic Party was engaged in "a never-ending warfare with the strongest and most enduring force of human nature—the lust of power and the lust of greed" as represented (of course) by the Republicans. Democratic newspapers wrote enthusiastically of the event, and following this grand gesture, Cleveland returned to Buzzard's Bay where he remained, except for two additional brief visits to New York City for political consultations, until the second week of October.[10]

Even after Cleveland moved to his Manhattan home for the last four weeks of the campaign, he gave only a handful of speeches in New York. Most were brief, with two notable exceptions: he addressed a large assembly of German Americans at Cooper Union on October 27 and a crowd of 4,000 people gathered under the auspices of the Businessmen's Democratic Association at the Lenox Lyceum on November 1.[11] Since Democratic vice presidential candidate Stevenson had been born in Kentucky, he actively campaigned throughout the South in a successful effort to make sure those states did not leave the Democratic Party for the Populists. As a sitting president, Benjamin Harrison did not campaign at all (he might have broken with this custom except for his ill wife).[12] A New Yorker, Republican vice presidential candidate Whitelaw Reid campaigned actively in his home state. He, too, spoke to an overflowing crowd of German Americans at Cooper Union on November 3, complimenting this ethnic group for its commitment to honesty and integrity.[13] On the Saturday before the election he spoke to a huge crowd in Mamaroneck, New York, and then was whisked by train to nearby Port Chester for another event.[14] Both candidates were represented by numerous surrogates, who gave speeches throughout the city: Governor William McKinley of Ohio played a particularly prominent role in support of Harrison.[15] Political clubs, composed of members who shared work-related interests such as the Wholesale Dry Goods Republican Club or the Democratic New York Stock Exchange Club, organized many of these events.

There was an interactive feedback loop between the two political parties and the media—that is, the daily press—when it came to carefully orchestrated political demonstrations. As Paul Starr has noted, American newspapers both "helped their readers to act as competent citizens and enabled them to organize for political purposes. The channel that the press provided for communication between parties and the electorate raised levels of voting participation."[16] New York City's major newspapers were closely aligned with either the Democrats or the Republicans: they covered both sides—though hardly evenhandedly. They also played an organizational role by communicating information to the public for their respective parties. The *New York Press* used prime space on its editorial page to promote "another great Republican demonstration" at the Cooper Union in which ex-Governor Foraker of Ohio would speak: "No Republican who can go to Cooper Union on

Tuesday night can afford to stay away," it added.[17] The Republican *Brooklyn Standard Union* kept a full "Republican Calendar" on its editorial page. For Monday, October 17, it listed seven gatherings in the Brooklyn area, including a "rally and mass meeting" of the Harrison and Reid Campaign Club of College Point, a Third Assembly District Republican Convention at the Town Hall in Jamaica, and regular weekly meetings of the Harrison and Reid Tippecanoe Club of the Seventh Ward and similar clubs.[18]

New York newspapers would then report on activities they had been promoting, using an appropriately enthusiastic tone and giving front-page coverage to the most important events. When nearly a dozen local Republican clubs organized an evening parade in Harlem, which culminated in a reception for vice presidential candidate Whitelaw Reid, the *New York Tribune* devoted a column and a half to describing the event: "All along the line hundreds of Republicans cheered the parade. The sidewalks were crowded and all Harlem seemed alive with political activity. Many loyal Republicans who lived along the line of march had decorated their houses, and fireworks were discharged in great profusion as the clubs went by."[19] The several thousand club members ambled through Harlem's streets for almost an hour and a half before reaching Reid at the reviewing stand, where the persistence of the marchers forced him to make a brief speech in which he "hoped that he would be able to rejoice with them a few weeks hence in a common victory."[20]

Through editorials and investigative articles, these newspapers made arguments for or against the high tariffs advocated by the Republicans. The pro-Democratic *New York Herald*, for instance, asserted that Republican tariffs would suck in cheap labor from abroad, undercutting wages. The Republican *New York Tribune*, in contrast, claimed that tariffs made possible the high standard of living enjoyed by working people in comparison to the conditions they endured in Europe. On the same page as its "Republican Calendar," the *Brooklyn Standard Union* ran a lengthy column reporting the speech of President John Rooney of the Kings County Protective League, which he had delivered to the Second Ward Republicans. He asserted that more than $450,000,000 in goods were imported duty free, more than twice the amount in 1884: "The goods imported free of duty were goods that are not produced in this country, so that the people obtain the kinds of goods they do not produce themselves at the lowest possible price."[21] The Republicans, he argued, were looking out for the average American.

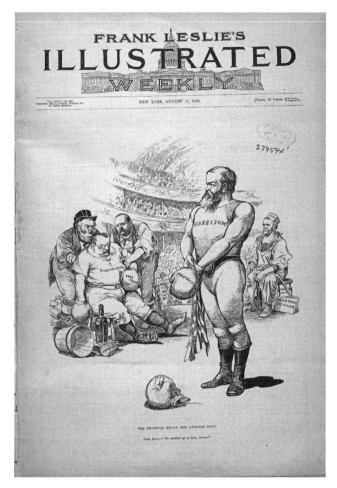

FIGURE 2. A trim Benjamin Harrison waits for a presidential rematch with Grover Cleveland, whom he previously defeated. A battered Cleveland is being sent into the ring by Adlai Stevenson (his running mate) and John Bull (a personification of Britain, which favored free trade). *Frank Leslie's Illustrated Weekly*, August 11, 1892. Courtesy the Library of Congress.

The preeminence of the press at this moment is evident through two men. Before becoming the Republican candidate for vice president, Whitelaw Reid was (and continued to be) the owner of the *New York Tribune*—the foremost Republican newspaper in New York City and so in the nation. On the Democratic side, Pulitzer was no longer Cleveland's champion. Rather there was Henry Villard, the owner of the

Democratic *New York Evening Post* and *The Nation*. Villard claimed chief responsibility for engineering Cleveland's presidential nomination in 1892. He soon became a constant presence at the Democratic national headquarters in New York City, raised money for Cleveland, and supported his campaign in other ways as well.[22]

Given New York State's pivotal position, it is worth noting the loyalties of its various newspapers. The Republicans had notable advantages outside the large cities; but in Manhattan and Brooklyn, the balance of forces favored the Democrats. The *New York Tribune*, the *New York Press*, the *New York Mail and Express*, and the *Brooklyn Standard Union*—as well as *Harper's Weekly* and *Judge* magazine—were solidly Republican. As it had been in 1884 and 1888, the *New York Times* was pro-Cleveland. So too was Villard's *New York Evening Post*, Joseph Pulitzer's *New York World*, St. Clair McKelway's *Brooklyn Daily Eagle*, James Gordon Bennett Jr.'s *New York Herald* (along with its afternoon counterpart, the *New York Evening Telegram*), and Joseph Keppler's *Puck* magazine.[23] Charles Dana's *New York Sun* had traditionally been a Democratic newspaper but refused to back Cleveland in 1884 and 1888 for largely personal reasons. In 1892 Dana's *Sun* supported the Democratic ticket even though his endorsement of Cleveland was at best lukewarm.[24] These newspapers not only detailed the success of their party's choreographed events, they tried to stoke factionalism and despair among their political rivals. Typically the *New York Tribune* compared the meetings of German Republicans and German Democrats at the Cooper Union, finding the Republicans to be filled with mirth and joy while the Democrats suffered in a state of despondency under the shadow of the nation's great prosperity, largely credited to Republican governance.[25]

The political parties looked for spectacle and arresting visuals to balance speeches and the written word. Many newspapers complemented their accounts with elaborate illustrations of the most notable events. Ephemera such as campaign buttons were common on both sides. The Cleveland and Stevenson campaign had the Red Bandana. Harrison and Reid had blue bandanas and white campaign top hats. (The switch in colors associated with each party occurred relatively recently.) Both sets of candidates had colorful broadsides with portraits of their respective candidates. Cleveland Democrats had silver-colored tokens with portraits of Cleveland and maxims such as "Democracy. The Party of the People 1892." The Harrison camp favored gold-colored tokens featuring portraits of the Republican candidates. Banners and other decorations were displayed wherever possible.

Tammany Hall Orators Arousing Wild Enthusiasm by Their Ringing Speeches in Behalf of Their Standard Bearers, Cleveland and Stevenson.

FIGURE 3. Outside their headquarters, 20,000 Tammany Hall Democrats gather for a nighttime rally in support of Grover Cleveland, November 3, 1892. *New York Herald*, November 4, 1892, 1. "The Great Wigwam was in a blaze of light and enthusiasm. There was victory in the air, it was in the voices of those who spoke, it was in the very music of the band, and it lurked in the rub-a-dub-dub of the big brass drum. Everybody was enthusiastic," wrote a *New York Times* reporter. November 4, 1896, 1.

Most importantly there was public pageantry. The Republicans were busy organizing the Business Men's Republican parade for Saturday, October 29, which was to follow the standard path up Broadway, jogging over to Fifth Avenue at Waverley Place. President Harrison, his then–vice president, New Yorker Levi Morton, and Reid were all invited to review some 30,000 marchers from the Tobacco Trade Republican Club, the University of Dentistry Republican Club, the Boot and Shoe Trade Republican Association, and many others. To pump up enthusiasm, speakers flooded the business districts and regaled lunchtime crowds; banners were unfurled and club members marched through the streets to their respective headquarters.[26] Then Caroline Scott Harrison, the president's wife, died on October 25, and these plans for the Business Men's Republican parade had to be cancelled.[27]

The Democrats culminated their campaign with several large-scale events. Five days before the election, they held a huge evening rally centered around Fourteenth Street opposite Tammany Hall but with a dozen speakers' stands scattered about the area.[28] This rally had special symbolic importance since the tensions between candidate Cleveland and the Tammany Hall machine remained considerable. Dana's *New York Sun*, which had its own issues with Cleveland, boosted the event: "From up town, from down town, from east and from west, the organizations were marching in, each headed by a band or drum corps to add its music to the crash of the bands already there. There seemed to be half a dozen great armies coming toward the one centre. Far beyond the brightness of the colored fires one could see long arrays of people, filling the sidewalks, spanning the streets from curb to curb, streaming forward from every direction."[29] Cleveland did not attend the rally lest he alienate the reform wing of his party by paying direct homage to Tammany Hall. Rather it was "Tammany's Rally for Cleveland. With Mass Meetings Inside and Outside the Wigwam the Unterrified Braves Attest Their Loyalty to the Ticket."[30] This was followed by a Saturday parade in which at least 35,000 members of the businessmen's Cleveland and Stevenson clubs marched past Cleveland, who was in a reviewing stand at Madison Square.[31]

The relationship between political campaigning and other cultural modes varied considerably during the 1892 election. Although these campaign speeches were obviously performances and the rallies involved a great deal of political theater, presidential politics were rarely present inside actual theaters. On November 6, the Sunday before Election Day, theatrical impresario Henry C. Miner, a district leader for the Tammany Hall Democrats, turned the People's Theater over to party loyalists for an evening of rousing speeches. The evening was not leavened, however, with any specialties from the resident performers.[32] Surely vaudevillians joked about aspects of the presidential contest, but mixing politics with theatrical amusements was downplayed. Political theater and theatrical entertainments were rivals in that presidential elections had a negative impact on theatergoing as potential ticket buyers attended campaign events instead. Likewise, betting focused on the election rather than sporting events: with voting only a few days away, the *New York Sun* claimed that the betting line favored Cleveland ten to nine.[33]

Audiovisual media, in particular the stereopticon, were employed for campaign purposes, though in limited and unequal ways. If the 1892 election witnessed a relative absence of noisy demonstrations, torchlight processions, and campaign songs, the illustrated lecture, which was part of what Bill Nichols has called "the discourse of sobriety," played a noteworthy role.[34] With the tariff the central issue in 1892 as it had been in 1888, politicians spoke and newspapers published endlessly on the subject. Arguments for and against the tariff must have become extremely familiar, challenging speakers to find ways to keep their audiences attentive and entertained. The illustrated lecture provided one solution. It functioned as a form of political oratory while adding a visual dimension that could bolster a speaker's rhetorical effectiveness. In this arena, the Republicans had a monopoly as they developed a template that had been introduced by Judge John L. Wheeler in the 1888 presidential campaign.

JUDGE WHEELER, *THE TARIFF ILLUSTRATED*, AND THE 1888 PRESIDENTIAL ELECTION

Judge Wheeler should be recognized as the progenitor and pioneering advocate of what we now recognize as the political campaign documentary. Born in Buffalo on March 13, 1847, Wheeler was in his teens when he served in the Eighth New York Cavalry during the Civil War. He later settled in Red Bank, New Jersey, where he became active in Democratic politics and eventually developed a billiard and pool ball business.[35] A lay judge, Odd Fellows grand master, and assistant adjunct general of the New Jersey GAR (Grand Army of the Republic), Wheeler began to give illustrated lectures on the Civil War.[36] After delivering a sequence of three presentations at the Brooklyn YMCA in February and March of 1886, he offered a course of four stereopticon lectures on *The Great Battles of the Civil War* at Manhattan's Chickering Hall in April.[37] He then toured smaller towns in upstate New York such as Ogdensburg, Gouverneur, and the village of Hermon.[38] Given the effectiveness of his illustrated presentations, Wheeler continued to give lantern lectures in a variety of New York venues.[39]

The Honorable John L. Wheeler had also become a well-regarded speaker at Democratic campaign rallies. Then, in March 1888, he met a reporter for the *New York Tribune* and declared that he had switched sides: "I am a strong protectionist; I have for some time called myself a Randall Democrat, but the way things look at present I can no longer sail under false colors, and am a good Republican, for that party has proclaimed its policy to protect American industry."[40] He then added, "I shall take the platform, as I always do in Presidential campaigns, for the National ticket which has the strongest protective tariff plank in its platform." Wheeler declared himself a man of conscience who was so concerned for the nation and his fellow Americans that he was ready to suffer the ridicule of past associates as he changed parties.

A few months later, Wheeler unveiled the vehicle he would use in the upcoming campaign: an illustrated lecture entitled *The Tariff Illustrated*. Perhaps not too surprisingly, the Republican *New York Tribune* gave enthusiastic attention to his lantern lecture, describing the ways he situated the tariff as a positive force in the broad expanse of American history and stymied efforts of rebuttal by the Democrats. (See document 1 in the appendix.) Wheeler gave several subsequent presentations in the metropolitan area: for the Sixth Ward Harrison and Morton Campaign Club at Grand Union Hall in Brooklyn (August 6), for the East River Park Harrison and Morton Club at Bruning's Hall, 206 East 86th Street in Manhattan (August 10), and for the American Protective Tariff Association at Phoenix Park (August 14).[41]

Wheeler's *The Tariff Illustrated* was not an independent effort, but rather depended for its prominence and effectiveness on the sponsorship of the foremost political action committee of the day, the American Protective Tariff League. The league was started in May 1885, shortly after Cleveland's first inaugural, and became active on a number of fronts to aid protective-tariff candidates (initially for the 1886 midterm elections). As Cleveland became more vocal about reforming the tariff, the league began to publish pro-tariff pamphlets and the *Tariff League Bulletin*, which started as a monthly in the second half of 1887 and then became a weekly from January 1888 onward. "*The Tariff League Bulletin* came into existence under the pressure of a special emergency, war having been declared upon our industrial institutions and through them—indirectly and, to some extent unconsciously—upon our political institutions as well," according to its editors. "It at once entered the fight to sustain the American economic policy of making the home market (or consumption of wealth by the laboring classes) the basis of our industrial and commercial prosperity, against the attempt to supplant it by the English economic doctrine of foreign markets, the chief features of which are Free-Trade and cheap labor (or small consumption of wealth by the masses)."[42]

By the end of the 1888 campaign, league president Edward Ammidown claimed that the organization had distributed 150 million pages of documents; its *Bulletin* was sent "to the press, and to influential men in all parts of the country, as well as to regular subscribers and to all our members."[43] The league also employed speakers in New York and its adjacent states to advocate for the protective tariff. Ammidown then added:

The most serious and effective work of this kind was done under our direction by Judge John L. Wheeler, of New Jersey, in his lectures on the Tariff, illustrated by stereopticon views. During the months of August, September and October last Judge Wheeler delivered more than 80 lectures, always to crowded and enthusiastic audiences, in the most important cities and towns of New York, New Jersey and Connecticut. So well satisfied are we of the effectiveness of this kind of work in attracting and convincing average audiences that it is now proposed to continue it, as one of the best means of popular Tariff education.[44]

Early in the campaign Wheeler traveled through his home state of New Jersey, including Trenton, New Brunswick, Patterson, Woodbridge, Perth Amboy, and South Amboy. The *New York Tribune* noted, "He covered the same territory four years ago for Cleveland, but this year came out for protection rather than English free trade."[45] Wheeler proved himself effective at the podium. "As a speaker the Judge is earnest and at times eloquent, his use of language is simple and plain, so that the 'plain people' fully and clearly understand him," the *Newark Union* (New York) remarked.[46] During the first part of September, Wheeler toured Connecticut, where his presentation at Bridgeport's Hawes Opera House was hailed as a Republican success. All 1,300 seats were taken, and standing room was also fully occupied. The theater had never held a larger audience. "An immense screen was displayed on the stage, and upon this were reflected pictures thrown from a stereopticon located in the gallery," explained the *Bridgeport News*. It added: "Judge Wheeler is a good speaker, and possesses a pair of stentorian lungs. He handled his subject—Protection—in a novel way, and one that made it decidedly entertaining."[47] The pro-Cleveland *New York Times* offered a different account of the evening: When Democrat Patrick Cassidy passed out anti-tariff literature to those entering the opera house, he was promptly arrested on complaints, placed by telephone from the Republicans. The police chief who arrested Cassidy was a Republican, and soon released him in the resulting brouhaha. The Democratic newspaper dismissed the Republicans' behavior as overly sensitive, calling their civic values into question.[48]

As the presidential contest intensified, Wheeler focused most of his time and energy on the crucial swing state of New York, visiting small cities and towns such as Mount Kisco, Cortland, Troy, and Newark as well as larger cities such as Syracuse and Buffalo. The *Buffalo Sunday Morning News* also lauded Wheeler's rhetorical effectiveness in a front-page account of his presentation. (See document 2 in the appendix.)

According to this unusually detailed description, he spoke with impressive moral authority as a former Democrat who had crossed party lines because he found the stakes around the tariff issue to be of overriding importance. His title of "judge" (rarely "ex-judge") suggested dispassionate impartiality, and his strong, self-confident voice further added to that sense of authority. The heroic sweep of US history and the images of past presidents clearly elicited a strong emotional response from his audiences. Wheeler began by quoting George Washington's support for protection of native industries, then declaimed: "Then was passed the first tariff law. The country began with the protective policy. Now here is Alexander Hamilton, the first Secretary of the Treasury, the man who brought into life the great American system of protection. (Cheers.) This system has lasted until the present day. It has fought back all the assaults of free trade."[49]

The savvy orator then evoked a series of national heroes who supported the tariff (Thomas Jefferson, James Madison, Abraham Lincoln, and so forth) and pariahs who did not (Martin Van Buren, Henry Clay, Jefferson Davis). He placed Harrison in the former category and Cleveland in the latter. A closing set of images of the American flag was contrasted with the Democrats' Red Bandana, which was refigured as a symbol warning of danger. At other moments Wheeler's arguments depended upon tables and statistics that had the appearance of objective facts as well as evidence that relied on photographic truth, including reproductions of newspaper advertisements for clothing. The carefully selected and organized images enabled him to present an overarching historical narrative, with free trade undermining the US economy and tariffs fostering prosperity: such a totalizing account proposed a compelling logic. For those who came with an open mind, as an undecided or wavering voter, these elements reverberated through the enthusiasm of the more partisan crowd. Only the *Syracuse Daily Journal* described a Wheeler presentation where "a good many Democrats" were in attendance and made "manifestations of disapproval at the facts demonstrated."[50]

In 1888 Wheeler's illustrated lecture was an unprecedented novelty. Never before had such a documentary-like program been used in conjunction with a political campaign for an elected office. Yet it certainly had a context beyond Wheeler's illustrated lectures on the Civil War and other historical subjects. One notable antecedent was the illustrated lecture *The Other Half—How It Lives and Dies in New York*, which Jacob Riis presented at the regular monthly meeting of the Society of

Amateur Photographers on January 25, 1888, and at many subsequent venues.[51] It became the basis for his groundbreaking book *How the Other Half Lives: Studies Among the Tenements of New York*, in which the photographer-investigator "aimed to tell the truth as I saw it."[52] Poverty and its causes were a topic Riis and Wheeler shared even though their underlying concerns differed substantially—not surprising, given that Riis was employed by Charles Dana's *New York Sun*, which had a strong Democratic affiliation.

A TALE OF TWO SCREENS: THE DEMOCRATIC PARTY'S USE OF THE STEREOPTICON IN 1888

The Tariff Illustrated was a significant departure from prior uses of the lantern for political purposes, for the stereopticon itself had had—and continued to have—a modest if familiar role in the political campaigns of both parties. The Democrats in particular preferred to project miscellaneous collections of words and images onto large outdoor canvases. Thus in Boston's Scollay Square, enterprising young "patriots" of the Young Men's Democratic Club projected "flashes of wit and nuggets of wisdom" on a twenty-five-foot-square canvas. Most of these were directed against Republican James Blaine, who four years before had run for president against Cleveland and lost, though he remained a potent force in the party. The club's slides featured such political poetry as

> Some things are dark
> But this is plain—
> Blaine owns the party
> And the trusts own Blaine[53]

Later in the campaign season, it offered an array of "campaign paragraphs" such as "Protectionism is the art of taxing the many for the benefit of the few."[54]

Much the same was happening in New York City. The *Sun* chortled as it reported on the activities of "the wicked stereopticon man of Madison square, who has been guying the Republicans for a week past on the roof of the Flat Iron, at Broadway and twenty-third street." At nightfall it fired off a series of tariff maxims. The crowd cheered:

> The perfection of the people's government is the lightness of its burden on the people.
> Up to 1850 we exported cotton cloths largely to China and the East Indies. When the tariff was raised the trade dwindled and finally ceased.[55]

In Watertown, New York, the Democratic Party used the stereopticon to project contradictory statements on the tariff made by the town's Republican *Watertown Daily Times*—to the delight of its Democratic rival, the *Watertown Re-Union.*[56] Finally, John Boyd Thacher, former mayor of Albany and president of the League of Democratic Clubs, outfitted a large boat, the *Thomas Jefferson*, to travel the Erie Canal. It was refurbished with a heavy platform on which "speakers stand to address the crowds on the bank" as well as a stereopticon. Traveling though Republican territory, the boat and its crew were often objects of abuse. Near Syracuse, "Admiral Thacher's stereopticon man was having a fine time standing in the crowd on shore and flinging his pictures of eminent Republicans with their tariff reform declarations to go with each picture, when suddenly the Republicans began to blot out the views by throwing the glare of a calcium light on his screen on the boat." The lanternist's defeat turned to victory when he "discovered a blank wall and flung his pictures there, instead of on his screen. The Republicans could not get at that wall, and so the canallers scored a victory."[57] Public spaces often became sites for symbolic struggle and confrontation. In this case, Republican interference was depicted as uncivil—and ineffective.

The Democrats were using techniques developed by early advertisers. They were appealing primarily to random, distracted viewers who would be attracted by the bright, colorful images at night. Perhaps it is worth pausing for a moment to reflect on urban life, particularly nightlife, during these quadrennial exercises in democracy. Political campaigns were above all masculinist and homosocial. As citizens who would cast their vote, men were expected to participate in the democratic process, which meant participating in the public sphere. This also meant being active—out and about—at night as the days became shorter and nights became colder. Moving about the city, these mobile spectators possessed the qualities of Charles Baudelaire's flaneur, whose "passion and his profession are to become one flesh with the crowd." It was a time to enjoy the pleasures of personal freedom from enforced domesticity when it became "an immense joy to set up house in the heart of the multitude, amid the ebb and flow of movement, in the midst of the fugitive and the infinite. To be away from home and yet to feel oneself everywhere at home; to see the world, to be at the centre of the world, and yet to remain hidden from the world." Baudelaire declared the spectator to be "a prince who everywhere rejoices in his incognito."[58] Clerks, bricklayers, and manual laborers during the day became democratic princes at night, thanks to presidential campaigns. At the ballot box, financial titans and their humblest employees became equals. Election season provided a fleeting but potent sense of democracy's utopian aspiration.

At this moment two kinds of screens were matched by two kinds of spectatorship: the casual, ephemeral, and unrestrained spectator who was free to roam the streets—for whom electioneering was a kind of holiday and a moment in which the citizen could feel his own importance—and the more genteel and attentive spectator, for whom citizenship meant participating in a solemn exercise that relied on, or at least claimed to rely on, discourses of sobriety. Looking for analogies, we might say the Democratic stereopticon was more like the newspaper, particularly those popular newspapers such as the *New York Herald* and the *New York World* that used illustrations, while Wheeler's illustrated lectures offered an epic account of national formation not entirely different from historical accounts of the Civil War. The Democrats were appealing to those moving through the city who might stop for and enjoy the witticisms and cartoons projected onto the wall of a building—and then move on. Of course, one should not forget that Democrats also took pleasure in annoying those Republicans who passed through these same urban spaces.[59]

Although Cleveland won the popular vote on the national level by a margin of 90,000, Benjamin Harrison carried New York State by 15,000 votes and so won the 1888 US presidential election. What were the factors that contributed to Cleveland's defeat? Internecine warfare inside the Democratic Party, with Tammany Hall refusing to enthusiastically support Cleveland, was one consideration. Many citizens may have also voted their pocketbooks: a brief recession and increase in unemployment in 1888 must have hurt the incumbent.[60] How much credit was due to Judge Wheeler's *The Tariff Illustrated*? This kind of question recurs again and again when dissecting the results of a presidential election: impossible to avoid, it is also impossible to answer. Ammidown's enthusiasm for Wheeler's contribution can be placed against the historian H. Wayne Morgan's assessment: "Republicans used funds to advertise tariff protection and the party's nationalism, and although industrialists provided most of the money, the GOP did not speak merely for business. It could never have won an election with a monolithic constituency. All observers agreed that millions of people read closely the pamphlets that filled the mails, and listened attentively to speakers who discussed protection. The tariff was one of the most

FIGURE 4. When the Democratic *New York Herald* announced that Harrison had won New York State, Republican victory was certain. Madison Square, election night, November 6, 1888. *Harper's Weekly*, November 17, 1888. Courtesy Jack Judson and the Magic Lantern Castle Museum.

vital and meaningful issues in American political history, reflecting the material self-interest of workers, farmers, and businessmen. It also appealed to all the emotions and security around political national-ism."[61] In this context, Wheeler's efforts were taken seriously and seen as a significant factor in Harrison's victory. To Republican eyes, *The Tariff Illustrated* had proved a new and valuable weapon in their cam-paign repertoire. It was a media form that could counter Democratic dominance of the press. They would try to use it more systematically in 1892.

Democrats, in contrast, saw the stereopticon with its miscellaneous combination of title slides and pictorial attractions as a visual flourish—at best a sideshow. One commentator on the campaign felt that the Democratic National Committee was avoiding any serious exertion. His evidence? "A stereopticon man in New York is nightly employed to blazon on his canvas in monumental letters, gibes and flings at the republicans. This is an agreeable kind of oratory for hot weather, but indicates lack of usual spirit in the committee."[62] The Democrats' use of the stereopticon, it seemed, revealed a certain intellectual laziness, a lack of seriousness that put them on the wrong side of the ethical binary.

If the stereopticon had been a strong positive for the Republicans, it was arguably a mild negative for the Democrats.

THE STEREOPTICON AND THE 1892 ELECTION

Following Harrison's election the Protective Tariff League declared victory and sought to institutionalize its organization and broaden its scope, rebranding its journal the *American Economist*. An expanded protective tariff bill was obviously going to be one of the hallmarks of the new administration, and the result was the Tariff Act of 1890, generally known as the McKinley Tariff after Representative William McKinley (R-Ohio) who managed the bill to passage.[63] The new bill raised tariffs on many goods to a rate approaching 50 percent.[64] This plus a faltering economy enabled the Democrats to win the midterm elections of 1890 by a landslide margin—even unseating Representative McKinley himself.[65] The stage was set for a presidential rematch in which the tariff would once again be the central issue. This time the Republicans rather than the Democrats were on the defensive. For both sides, the new tariff on tin plate had become the locus of dispute. As the *American Economist* explained, "No other provision of the new law has been so bitterly assailed as that framed to establish tin-plate making in the United States. Even the Democrats who do not go the full length of the Chicago platform in denouncing Protection, but believe that it may sometimes be beneficial, profess to see in the tin-plate Tariff only pure abomination."[66]

Americans needed to be convinced anew of the tariff's value to their political economy, and the Protective Tariff League once again enlisted Wheeler and his stereopticon. In early January 1889 its staff began working with Wheeler on a new edition of *The Tariff Illustrated*—about the same time that the *American Economist* published at least one article by Wheeler, on protection in the South, where free-trade sentiments had had long-standing support.[67] After publicizing this arrangement in mid-June 1892, the league began lining up venues. This time, *The Tariff Illustrated* would be offered as two separate lectures, each with one hundred or more lantern slides: "A History of the American System" and "Protection, Reciprocity and Business." Since the first of these bore a strong resemblance to the 1888 edition, Wheeler would deliver the second of these in places where only one presentation would be given.[68] In practice, however, it seems that Wheeler generally delivered a single lecture that combined the two. Even for those who attended his spiel four years before, hearing some portions again could be seen as a useful refresher.

Wheeler debuted his 1892 version of *The Tariff Illustrated* in Harlem on July 25, after which the *American Economist* offered weekly updates of his itinerary during the 1892 campaign. In late July he gave a week's worth of lectures in different New York City venues. He toured Brooklyn halls for another week in early August. On September 21 he participated in a "monster meeting" at Cooper Union under the auspices of the Tariff League itself.[69] "The telling effect of the use of stereopticon views presenting the conditions of people in countries which would compete with us under the Free-Trade system cannot be overestimated," opined the *American Economist*.[70] By the time Wheeler had reach Middletown, Connecticut, in mid-October, he and his lanternist, a Mr. Brower, had given "his famous lecture" for eleven weeks and had "nightly spoken to an audience which filled the houses to overflowing."[71]

Most newspaper accounts of his presentation are brief, but the *Middletown Daily Press* offered a detailed, full-column, front-page account of his well-attended lecture. The journalist found, "The illustrations were captivating of themselves, but when accompanied by strong, convincing arguments in favor of protection, became doubly attractive."[72] Its first section was quite similar to what Wheeler had delivered in 1888, beginning with George Washington and wending his way to Lincoln and the post–Civil War Republican presidents (see "Pictured Politics" in the *Buffalo Sunday Morning News*, document 2 in appendix). Wheeler then focused the second half of his lecture on the ups and downs of the last decade, giving more emphasis to the contemporary moment than in his earlier iteration—including a defense of the McKinley tariff that had been instituted in the interim. "He showed pictures of cotton mills, fields, etc., stating that there were 500 cotton mills in this country which would be closed were the Democrats to have their way."[73] Wheeler claimed to be offering the truth of photographic evidence to sustain his cause. The Middletown reporter readily concurred: "The effect of this presentation of true facts in this happy manner can not but be felt in the coming election."[74]

Wheeler's *The Tariff Illustrated* had been unique in 1888 and contributed to victory in the pivotal state of New York. The Protective Tariff League confessed, "It is a source of regret that we cannot duplicate the now famous presentation of the cause of Protection by Hon. John L. Wheeler."[75] More illustrated lectures on the protective tariff would presumably multiply its impact. Yet the league's expression of regret proved misplaced, for that is precisely what happened. As often occurred to creators of successful lantern programs, Wheeler's presentation was soon being imitated, in this instance by least five men: Elijah R. Kennedy, T. De Quincy Tully, Judge Lucius P. Deming, S. W. (Samuel Widdows) Reese, and Daniel. G. Harriman.

D. G. Harriman was based in Brooklyn, where he had been active in the Republican Party for many years.[76] Even before the campaign season, the American Protective Tariff League sometimes assigned him to debate people advocating tariff reform.[77] During the 1892 campaign he wrote a short article entitled "Protection a Necessity" for the mid-September issue of the *American Economist*.[78] Harriman also began to give illustrated lectures on the protective tariff, perhaps as Wheeler's substitute when the latter was otherwise engaged. Or else some other speaker's bureau provided him with these opportunities. In September he presented at Brooklyn's Grand Union Hall under the auspices of the joint Campaign Committees of the Sixth and Tenth wards.[79] In early October Harriman went to New Jersey with "his stereopticon views illustrating the advantages of protection."[80] One day after the death of President Harrison's wife, Harriman gave a solemn stereopticon lecture on protection at the Criterion Theater in Brooklyn. The *Brooklyn Standard Union* published much of his talk, which seemingly lacked Wheeler's rhetorical flair.[81]

In the late 1880s Professor T. De Quincy Tully of Ohio would give illustrated Civil War lectures in the Midwest, often as fundraisers for veteran groups.[82] While continuing to travel with the stereopticon, he had settled in Brooklyn by 1891 and became the assistant secretary of the Law Enforcement Society of Brooklyn, which was dedicated to keeping saloons closed on Sundays.[83] Based on his expertise with the lantern, the Republican State Committee employed Tully to give "an illustrated disquisition on the tariff, 125 stereopticon scenes being introduced."[84] Venues included Brooklyn's Fifth Ward Harrison and Reid Club, the Flushing Republican Club, and the Ocean Hill Campaign Club.[85]

S. W. Reese, a manufacturer of stencils and an active Republican, was busy presenting his lantern lecture in such New Jersey localities as Rahway (September 24), Hackettstown (October 27), and North Plainfield (October 29). His arguments were apparently well expressed and at one venue "convinced several Democrats that Protection was the issue to support in the coming election."[86] Early in 1892 Judge Lucius P. Deming of the Court of Common Pleas in New Haven, Connecticut, was giving illustrated lectures on travel topics related to Europe and the

Middle East. By October he had switched to political campaigning with his stereopticon, traveling through the state's cities and towns.[87] At Burnap's Hall in Windsor Locks, "he confined his remarks wholly to the tariff history of the country and explained its effects in a clear and comprehensive way so that all present could have no doubt as to how they ought to vote to continue their present prosperity."[88]

Elijah R. Kennedy was a well-known insurance broker and locally prominent Brooklyn Republican who had once served as a park commissioner.[89] Kennedy had been a successful platform orator during the 1888 campaign and also had a history of presenting illustrated lectures, including at a Labor Day weekend event in Bridgehampton, Long Island, for the benefit of the local tennis club.[90] The first day of October 1892, Kennedy was at Republican headquarters at the Fifth Avenue hotel, offering his services to J. J. Bealin, who booked speakers for New York City and environs. Pulitzer's *New York World*, which favored Cleveland, offered this snidely ironic account:

> Mr. Elijah R. Kennedy, of Brooklyn, came to offer his services to the glorious cause of high tariff and protection to American industries at $12 per night, which barely covers the cost of production. Mr. Kennedy was very swell in his get-up, not gaudy, understand, but well dressed. No unbuttoned Prince Albert for him, no string tie, but a dashing cutaway coat, fashionable scarf, patent-leather shoes. You should have seen the old war-horses look at him.
>
> Mr. Kennedy will not speak except in New York or Brooklyn and he goes around with a sort of peep-show. It is a magic lantern affair, the stylish name for it is "stereopticon," but it is a magic lantern just the same and he shows upon the canvas pictures of the tin-plate mills established since the McKinley law went into effect. He has no picture to show what a pretty price the American people had been made to pay for this tin whistle. . . .
>
> Mr. Kennedy announced that he proposed to take the hide off the Democrats in his speeches by devoting more time to the "rag-money, wildcat bank" plank, as he calls it, of the Democratic platform.[91]

Within the week Kennedy was presenting an illustrated lecture on the tariff and "red-dog" money at the Opera House in East Orange, New Jersey. "No one present went away ignorant of the inconvenience, loss and ruin resulting from the system the Democrats propose to restore," claimed the *New York Tribune*.[92]

Perhaps Kennedy's reward for traveling outside his geographic comfort zone was some flattering newspaper coverage from a prominent and reliably Republican newspaper. If so, he could hardly complain of the reportage provided by Reid's *Tribune* when several weeks later he went to Empire Hall in South Orange for the local Republican club. (See document 3 in the appendix.) This was a well-planned and elaborate event that included many displays of tinware manufactured in the United States. Kennedy, however, was clearly the main attraction. As the *Tribune* journalist reported, "Major Elijah R. Kennedy, of New York, was in command of the Republican forces, which were entrenched behind breastworks of American tinware. It was in the nature of an artillery duel, and Major Kennedy fired solid shot from a double-barreled stereopticon into the ranks of the Democracy, and followed that up with a rattling volley of statistics and arguments."[93] Appealing to local factory workers, Kennedy began with a lengthy speech in which he asserted, "The United States has applied Protection more thoroughly than has any other nation, and has been more highly prospered." The room was kept lit until his stereopticon lecture began in earnest as he used images of tinware manufactories as evidence to refute the Democratic Party's disparagement of tariffs as effective in stimulating local industries (somewhat predictably, tin plate manufacture was his prime example). He also showed photographs of women who were treated as beasts of burden in European countries that supposedly failed to use the tariff as a form of economic protection. If "seeing is believing," this photographic evidence associated the Democrats with the abuse of women and other unconscionable policies. The abomination then was not the tariff for tin plate but Democratic dishonesty.

Kennedy's enthusiastic rhetoric drew some bemused attention from the *New York Times*, which cited a "letter to the editor" that Kennedy had written to the *Tribune* in 1890. In it, Kennedy was quite critical of the McKinley tariff, particularly as it might impact Republican chances in the 1892 presidential election. Minnesota and other western states strongly opposed it.[94] Kennedy's concerns proved well founded, for Cleveland won Wisconsin and California while other Western states went into the Populist column.

Recognizing *The Tariff Illustrated* as a potent campaign weapon, Republicans and the American Protective Tariff League had six lantern lecturers on the road reprising Wheeler's innovative and successful stereopticon presentation. How many people actually saw them? The American Protective Tariff League claimed that Wheeler spoke at eighty-seven meetings: six in New Jersey, four in Connecticut, and seventy-seven in New York State. Audiences averaged 2,000 people per venue, "making fully 174,000 persons to whom the lecture was presented."[95] The other five undoubtedly did not do as well, but they too were deemed to have been well attended and effective. Even if the five of them combined only

FIGURE 5. An 1892 Cleveland-Stevenson campaign poster calls for tariff reform to reduce the costs of necessities. Courtesy the Library of Congress.

equaled Wheeler's figures, this would mean roughly 350,000 people saw some version of *The Tariff Illustrated* in the tristate area during the 1892 presidential campaign.

Believing that Wheeler's stereopticon had been key to their success in 1888, the Republicans were even ready to try out some of the techniques previously used by the Democrats. The Harlem Republican Club had a stereopticon that threw political maxims and "economic truths" onto a large outdoor canvas. They included "Whatever is manufactured at home gives work and wages to our own people" and "Never surrender to England. No pauper wages for us."[96] Sam Engel ran "a Republican free magic lantern show" in less favorable territory: in front of the John A. Logan Club's house on the Lower East Side of Manhattan.[97] Local ruffians (perhaps with Tammany encouragement) repeatedly pelted the lantern and its operator with mud, forcing Engel to shut it down.[98] Certainly the stereopticon became more integrated into the Republican playbook. At a rousing Republican gathering in Sausalito, California, "one of the principal features was Henry Hook's stereopticon cartoons and pictures of all the Republican leaders."[99]

The Democrats, who lost the 1888 election, had come to the opposite conclusions but for similar reasons. The use of outdoor advertising methods by their "wicked Stereopticon man" had not been too successful, and perhaps even counterproductive. In 1892 the Democrats rarely used the stereopticon. Conceivably it had become unremarkable and therefore an unremarked part of the urban landscape, but the absence of newspaper commentary seems telling. A major gathering of Democrats in San Francisco's Metropolitan Hall was one of the very few exceptions: after numerous speeches, the evening ended with a stereopticon entertainment. Its contents were not specified and its presence was clearly something of an afterthought.[100]

The Democrats had lost confidence if not interest in using screen practices for political purposes. Nevertheless they did recognize the potency of *The Tariff Illustrated.* The *New York Times* railed against these Republican propagandists. In early August, it went after Wheeler's tin-plate arguments with heavy irony:

> The latest addition to the Protective Tariff League's band of "spell-binders" is ex-Judge JOHN L. WHEELER, who makes his eloquence attractive by the use of a stereopticon. MR. WHEELER's idea about tin resemble those of Eli Perkins, who saw in Dakota many square miles of glittering ore bearing 65 per cent of the metal. The *Tribune* reports as follows a part of an address made by Mr. Wheeler Wednesday evening:
>
>> He killed the argument of the Democrats that there was not sufficient tin in the country to keep the mills at work for any length of time, by saying that it had been proved that there was enough tin in one mine in Wyoming alone to supply all the tin that could be used in the United States in the next hundred years.
>
> This is very interesting. The owners of the Temescal mines in California, where a few tons have been extracted with great difficulty, and those of the so-called mines in Dakota, where nothing has been produced but talk, should at once throw aside those properties and "go for" the phenomenal deposits in Wyoming. As this country uses about one-third of the world's product of this metal, one mine that can supply our demands for a century ought not to be overlooked.[101]

Another brief article in the *New York Times* mocked Elijah R. Kennedy's presentation of photographic evidence, suggesting that he was treating the audience as if it was a bunch of yokels, and made fun of the *New York Tribune*'s excessive language and eulogistic rhetoric. (See document 4 in the appendix.) The *Times* clearly enjoyed ridiculing its Republican rival in the newspaper business as much as these orators whose effectiveness had gained people's attention. If *The Tariff Illustrated* manipulated the "seeing is believing truths" of photographic evidence and played on the audience's emotions with bogus assertions, it was hardly the last time such strategies would be employed.

It is worth assessing the Republican embrace of the stereopticon and the Democratic indifference to it by situating them within a larger media context. The Democrats hardly ran an inept campaign: they won, and quite decisively. For the 1892 election, the Democrats had substantial dominance when it came to the New York press. The three principal Republican newspapers were closely aligned with the GOP—perhaps too closely for some independent voters. Two were reliable party organs (the *New York Press* and the *New York Mail and Express*), while the third had its publisher running for vice president on the Republican ticket. On the Democratic side there were many more papers, and their relationship to the Democrats was more variable. The *New York Herald* tried to be more evenhanded in its coverage of the presidential campaign. Charles Dana and his *New York Sun* did not like Cleveland: they were Tammany Hall Democrats. The *New York Times* favored the reformists. Although other Democrats favored New York State Governor Hill, the different factions in the Democratic Party managed to work together for their common goal: the defeat of Harrison. Moreover, the Democratic press was as a whole more lively. Their prose was often more entertaining to read and they used illustrations more extensively, particularly the *Herald* and the *World*.

There was little the Republicans could do about this imbalance, at least in the short run. Stereopticon lectures on the tariff were a means for the Republicans to intervene in the larger media system—an intervention that seemed much less necessary for the Democrats. Republican innovation in one area was motivated by weakness in another. Moreover, in a city that was heavily Democratic, the Democratic party apparatus mobilized those bodies and resources through the rituals of public pageantry and performance. All this was then reported, celebrated, and amplified through a sympathetic press. On Election Day eve, a reporter for the *Washington Evening Star* remarked, "The leaders at both national headquarters are absolutely in the dark as to the results of tomorrow's election."[102] The results of the next day's voting, however, gave Cleveland a respectable margin of victory—this time winning New York State by 45,000 votes (three times Harrison's margin of victory four years earlier). When the balance of political forces is considered in relation to the media overall, Cleveland and the Democrats were well positioned: in an election that seemed closely contested and lacked disruptive factors favoring one side or the other, they had more effectively tapped into the available media formation.

WATCHING THE ELECTION RETURNS

The culmination of every presidential campaign is Election Day—first voting and then waiting to learn who will be the next president. The rituals of this day are particularly well established, though some of the specifics have changed over time. Certainly the places where people follow the results have varied. In 1892 Harrison waited to learn the results in the White House while Cleveland was handed updates at his home, surrounded by a few family members and friends. Politicos waited at their party headquarters. The Tammany braves, for instance, gathered in their Wigwam on Fourteenth Street. Others attended the theater, where the management announced results from the stage between acts—or at moments when there was some decisive news to communicate.[103] This was a pregnant, transitional moment when political theater would again give way to theatrical entertainment: their momentary convergence (after voting was completed) generated a certain holiday spirit, and also an affirmation of community. Suspense and denouement could occur on both accounts, though more often the electoral outcome would not be known until the early hours of the morning. Intrepid followers of returns might then head into the streets to find additional updates, staying "till well-nigh sunrise."[104]

For many members of the electorate, the night's ritual involved going down to the headquarters or branch office of one's local newspaper of choice and watching the returns as they were posted. In Washington, DC, and other cities it was a night of male camaraderie whether in victory or defeat—the conclusion of a quadrennial ritual.[105] In New York, one reporter was struck by the fact that there seemed to be as many women as men on the streets.[106] For these boisterous, good-natured crowds, the papers gathered information primarily via telegraph and shared it with their readers, traditionally by posting bulletins on boards (thus the term "bulletin boards"). In this respect newspapers engaged in some friendly (or not so friendly) competition as to which would be the first to deliver the latest news to the public. It was a public test of their newsgathering abilities.

The 1892 election was transitional in one particular respect. The stereopticon was emerging as the preferred instrument for disseminating bulletins on election night, supplanting the standard boards. In New Haven, Connecticut, the voting results were still being posted on bulletin boards.[107] However, in Connecticut's state capitol,

> It looked last night as if every man in Hartford had come down State street way to learn how the election was going. The street in front of and on both

sides of THE COURANT building was crowded with 4,000 or 5,000 excited people eagerly watching for the bulletins which were thrown by a stereopticon [upon] a sheet attached to the federal building. As soon as the news began coming in, bulletins were put out at frequent intervals. They presented some surprises for both republicans and democrats, and the crowd was sufficiently divided in sentiment to cheer lustily every bit of news, no matter to which side it brought consolation.

During the intervals of giving news the stereopticon threw comical and taking pictures[108]—made by THE COURANT artist—upon the screen, and these amused the crowd almost as much as the bulletins, although the election news was what they hungered for.[109]

The more partisan, Democratic *Hartford Times* also showed returns using the stereopticon: "First, great majority for Cleveland; second, picture of a rooster; third, picture of Grover. Repeated at frequent intervals."[110]

In New York City, the epicenter for gatherings on Election Day evening was Printing House Square near City Hall, where most of the newspapers had their central offices. According to the *New York Times*, the newspapers were still posting the latest bulletins on their boards. "Not a newspaper in the row failed to bulletin the returns, and there was not an office which did not have about it thousands of people anxious for every little scrap of information that might give them an inkling as to the result." The problem was that only those closest to the boards could see the new bulletins; the crowds behind required an audio relay. "As soon as new figures were placed upon the boards a shout would arise from those nearest the bulletin only to be taken up by those in the rear and carried along down the row, across the park, and in every direction until the first cheer had grown into a mighty burst of sound that gradually died away in the distance."[111] The World Building (aka the Pulitzer Building) on Park Row, built in 1890, was the tallest edifice in New York City, if not the world, for its first four years.[112] This presidential contest was the newspaper's first at its new locale, and Joseph Pulitzer tried to make the most of it while addressing the challenges created by large crowds. Ladders ran up each side of the recently constructed twenty-six-story building (309 feet) to a chair on top. As results came in, the figures of Cleveland and Harrison would move up their respective ladders as each gained his electoral votes until the victor's dummy finally occupied the chair. In between waits, people chanted campaign songs.[113] At its branch office in Harlem, the *New York World* communicated results to the crowds using the stereopticon.[114] The *Herald*, which had its new main office on Broadway and Ann Street, just off

FIGURE 6. Bulletin boards traditionally adorned the facades of newspaper offices such as the *New York Journal*. On election night they were bathed in lights as citizens gathered to follow the returns. Byron Company (New York), [Park Row] ca. 1896. Courtesy the Museum of City of New York, 93.1.1.15310.

of Printing House Square, projected the latest results on a screen there and also at its branch offices at Madison Square, Broadway and Thirty-Sixth Street, and 126th Street and Seventh Avenue in Harlem.[115] Dana's *New York Sun* likewise projected results on a white screen at its relatively modest office building at 170 Nassau Street. "When THE SUN was not telling the story of the day in figures, the crowd was kept in humor by THE SUN'S cartoonist and portrait maker."[116] It used the same approach at its uptown office.[117] Although Cleveland and the Democratic Party showed little or no interest in the stereopticon in 1892, the Democratic newspapers found it useful as a way to enhance their public profile at this key moment. (In 1882 Charles Dana did a survey and found that presidential elections increased circulation more than any other news event.)[118] Already, publishers were developing a relationship between the press and the screen that would flourish in the late 1890s and early 1900s, when cinema became commonly referred to as a visual newspaper.

CHAPTER 2

The Stereopticon: Platform or New Media Form?

The previous chapter demonstrated the potency of the stereopticon as a weapon in the overall media arsenal of presidential politicking in 1888 and 1892. What was the history of the stereopticon, and where does it fit in the history of modern media? First, "stereopticon" was an American term; in Britain it was sometimes called the "optical lantern."[1] Moreover, the term "stereopticon" was often used to lay claims to a "new media" practice that combined photography with new methods of projection technology in a way that anticipated the later combination of motion pictures with projection to create cinema. Why haven't media scholars paid it more attention? For some of the reasons suggested in the introduction: because it has often been considered part of the long history of the magic lantern; because during its nineteenth-century heyday the stereopticon projector was often deployed in the service of other cultural practices and media forms such as photography and the illustrated lecture; because particular exhibitors or manufacturers promoted their lantern technologies using different neologisms and trade names such as the sciopticon; and because its identity as a media, always tentative, was eventually dispersed, overtaken by cinema on one hand and superseded by the slide projector on the other.

Did Americans living in the late nineteenth century (and should we in the early twenty-first century) look upon the magic lantern and the stereopticon as the same media form—the same cultural practice, just at different stages of development, like silent and sound motion pictures—

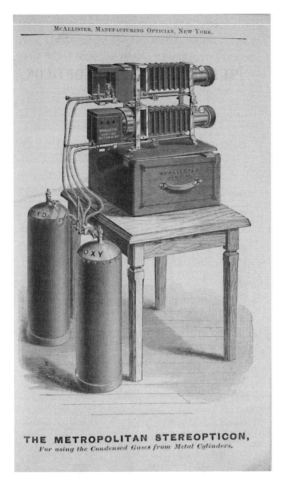

McALLISTER, MANUFACTURING OPTICIAN, NEW YORK.

THE METROPOLITAN STEREOPTICON,
For using the Condensed Gases from Metal Cylinders.

FIGURE 7. The Metropolitan Stereopticon had an
oxy-hydrogen light source and two lanterns, so
exhibitors could dissolve from one slide to the next.
Offered for sale by T. H. McAllister, circa 1890. Courtesy
Terry and Deborah Borton.

or were they distinct? For 150 years, the magic lantern's *dispositif*
involved, at its most basic, hand-painted glass slides projected onto a
screen to an audience that understood that it was seeing representations
and not inexplicable magic.[2] However, magic lantern practices were
often quite elaborate. They involved sequencing of images as well as the
manipulation of the images themselves (for instance slip slides and dissolving views). Lanternists were themselves performers who entertained

their patrons. The phantasmagoria expanded upon such practices in the late eighteenth century, facilitated by technological improvements but perhaps more importantly by developing a new set of protocols. These included the simultaneous use of multiple lanterns and the shifting of these projectors behind the screen, and so the reliance on rear-screen projection.

The phantasmagoria also enlivened traditional magic lantern practices, which were often promoted under the rubric of "dissolving views." For dissolving views two lanterns were aligned so that the image from one projector (one view) could be gradually dissolved to an image shown from the other projector. If the introduction of lithographic techniques did little to alter magic lantern protocols, the use of photographic techniques for the making of lantern slide images certainly did. They challenged media-specific notions and more. Was not the stereopticon (which used photographic slides) as different from the magic lantern (using hand-painted slides) as photography was from painting? There was a sharp disjunction, and yet both the magic lantern and the stereopticon as platforms could show one type of slide as easily as another. Moreover, lanternists continued to augment their image-generating elements to include life-model slides, chromotropes (which create kaleidoscopic effects), and even thin, miniature aquariums that could be placed between the lens and the light source. When it came to the projection of media, the magic lantern and the stereopticon were equally omnivorous.

The problem of medium specificity—what film (or cinema) can do— has haunted film scholars, but "film studies," like "media studies," is a field that relies on synecdochic figures of speech in which a part (film/ screen) refers to a much larger technological system and set of protocols involving cameras, printers, projectors, raw stock manufacture, sprocket makers, exhibitors, performers, and more. Once in place, this motion picture system was constantly revised and refined (the addition of a reframing device, the three-blade shutter, the stock company of actors, various color processes, various employments of sound, and so forth). Cinema, as we shall see, quickly became a closed or strong media form in which the motion picture projector could only show one thing: motion picture film shot with a compatible motion picture camera. If one wanted to show a photograph or a painting, it had to be put onto film, or remediated. Remediation through technological means was the assumed basis for the stereopticon but it was not, as it turned out, essential. In this sense the stereopticon—and certainly the magic lantern—might be considered a weak media form.[3]

Cold Eye Glasses and Spectacles for the Holidays.

Pearl Opera Glasses a Specialty.

ARTISTICALLY FINISHED VIEWS FOR THE MAGIC LANTERN.

Uncolored Photographic Views.

On Glass, 3¼ inches square.

Scenery, buildings, etc., in United States and Foreign Countries, Scriptural Illustrations, Revolutionary History. Copies of Engravings, Miscellaneous Pictures, etc.

50 cents each, $45.00 per 100.

STATUARY

IN GREAT VARIETY.

On Glass, 3¼ inches square.

Among which will be found the Master Pieces of Thorwaldsen, Canova, etc.

50 and 75 cents each.

Colored Photographic Views.

On Glass, 3 inches diameter. In Frame 4 × 7 inches.

Done by a new process, forming most brilliant and delicate transparencies. Scriptural Illustrations, Gems of Art. Choice Landscapes, etc., etc.

$1.50 each.

COMIC SLIDES

In Frame, 4 × 7 inches.

With Slip Movement, giving life-like motions to the figures. An endless number of subjects.

65 cents each. $7.50 per doz.

SLIDES WITH LEVER MOTION.

In Frame, 4 × 7 inches.

With these the effects are more neatly produced than with the above slip slides.

$1.75 each.

CHROMATROPES,

OR

ARTIFICIAL FIREWORKS.

In Frame, 4 × 7 inches.

$3.00 and $3.75 each.

FIGURE 8. Optical supply companies such as T. H. McAllister offered a wide variety of lantern slides, circa 1880. Courtesy Jack Judson and the Magic Lantern Castle Museum.

Whether a reformulated cultural practice constituted a new and distinct media practice or simply the revision of an old one is socially, and eventually historically, determined. The phonograph that used tinfoil in 1878 relied on a different *medium* than the phonograph that used wax cylinders in the 1890s and yet both were—in part by the determined efforts of Thomas Edison himself—still "phonographs" (though the newer iteration was often referred to as the graphophone, which began as a rival trade name). The formats or systems might vary, but each was a self-contained system—though that obviously changed at a certain point, when audio recording became more dynamic and could also be used for various platforms (sound movies, radio, and so forth). Audio recording became part of a much more open system. Perhaps almost inevitably—as with the magic lantern, stereopticon, motion picture projector, or modern (but now outdated) slide projector—there are ambiguities, which can prove messy. This messiness is embedded in the history as well.

A LEXICON OF THE SCREEN

The nineteenth century was an age of technological neologisms. Media practitioners and their journalistic promoters were quick to introduce new terminologies. Some were utilized only a few times and then disappeared, while others became popular and were adopted by the general public. "Stereopticon," "kinetoscope," "phonograph," and "telephone" were among the more successful coinages incorporated into the English (American) language for substantial periods. Yet as technologies changed, such terms almost inevitably fell out of favor—either abandoned or pushed to the margins as the technologies they named became outmoded. To gain a broad overview, this section examines the results of random word searches (RWS) for "stereopticon" and related terms such as "dissolving views," "illustrated lecture," "magic lantern," and "stereoscope." Although a RWS of other newspapers would produce some variation in word usage, my efforts for this chapter are confined to the *New York Times* for the United States. The *Manchester Guardian* and the *Observer* in the United Kingdom are examined to provide transatlantic comparisons.

A RWS of "magic lantern" and "dissolving views" in the *New York Times* shows that these two terms were already in common use by the 1850s, with "magic lantern" appearing 11 times and "dissolving views" 36 times between 1851 (the year the newspaper began publication) and

TABLE I   RANDOM WORD SEARCHES OF KEY TERMS IN AUDIOVISUAL MEDIA[a]

Figures are for number of "articles" cited in the New York Times and combined in parentheses (the London Observer and Manchester Guardian).

Terms:	Stereopticon/ magic lantern	Illustrated Lecture	Stereopticon/magic lantern with "illustrated lecture"—and both terms with "lecture" only	Dissolving Views	Optical Lantern/with Lecture	Stereoscope	Slide Projector	Slide show
1851–1859[b]	0/11 (0/75)	0 (6)	0/0–0/3 (0/0–0/21)	36 (235)	(0)	99 (256)	0	0 (0)
1860–1869	89/22 (0/95)	3 (7)	0/0–25/6 (0/0–0/9)	14 (383)	(0)	75 (369)	0	0 (0)
1870–1879	207/29 (0/130)	44 (7)	2/0–132/8 (0/0–0/4)	14 (148)	(0)	54 (39)	0	0 (0)
1880–1889	304/47 (0/130)	212 (9)	10/0–122/6 (0/0–0/28)	36 (120)	(2/0)	152 (36)	0	0 (0)
1890–1899	581/66 (0/94)	545 (33)	29/0–362/15 (0/0–0/26)	30 (35)	(30/10)	19 (25)	0	2 (0)
1900–1909	419/55 (2/107)	231 (96)	17/0–209/9 (0/0–1/11)	12 (16)	(22/6)	18 (32)	0	0 (0)
1910–1919	325/30 (1/80)	367 (99)	14/0–201/7 (0/0–0/5)	7 (6)	(10/4)	15 (29)	0	0 (0)
1920–1929	210/44 (1/61)	300 (55)	3/0–97/5 (0/0–0/7)	0 (1)	(1/1)	24 (9)	3 (1)	0 (0)
1930–1939	119/45 (0/70)	548 (60)	2/0–48/3 (0/1–0/16)	2 (10)	(1/0)	40 (8)	4 (0)	0 (1)
1940–1949	64/25 (0/32)	219 (20)	1/0–12/1 (0/0–0/3)	1 (2)	(0/0)	117 (11)	128 (0)	1 (0)
1950–1959	45/59 (0/39)	123 (79)	0/0–4/2 (0/0–0/5)	2 (1)	(1/0)	44 (9)	673 (2)	86 (1)
1960–1969	23/123 (0/60)	157 (42)	0/0–4/36 (0/0–0/10)	0 (3)	(0/0)	38 (7)	580 (46)	147 (16)
1970–1979	46/79 (2/62)	151 (67)	0/0–1/13 (0/0–0/6)	0 (0)	(0/0)	15 (6)	548 (43)	651 (83)

[a] Although the New York Times might seem a too-convenient or too-obvious source for this random word search, there are compelling reasons to use it. First, no other major New York newspaper covers the full time span of this survey. In fact, few other US newspapers cover this full period, at least in digitized form. Although long runs of the Chicago Tribune and the Hartford Courant are available, they prove less useful. Comparisons between the New York Times and other newspapers in the nineteenth and twentieth centuries indicate that the Times was particularly attentive to screen culture in general and the documentary tradition in particular. For instance, during the 1870s the term "stereopticon" received 10 hits in the New York Tribune, 37 in the Chicago Tribune, and 29 in the Hartford Courant, but 207 hits in the New York Times. During the same decade, "illustrated lecture" generated 13 hits in the New York Tribune, 13 hits in the Chicago Tribune, and 7 hits in the Hartford Courant, but 44 hits in the New York Times. The New York Times covered photography and other cultural activities much more extensively than most other papers in the nineteenth century. Moreover, this trend continued into the twentieth and even the twenty-first centuries. The New York Times offers a relatively unique consistency over a long period of time. The same appears to be the case for the Guardian and Observer. To include more newspapers in this random word search project might have created additional value at certain moments in terms of depth but would have undermined the longitudinal aspirations of the survey. Any statistical sampling of this kind has problems, and this table is offered with that awareness strongly in mind.

[b] The New York Times began publication in 1851.

[c] The fact that "stereopticon" and "illustrated lecture" appear together twice is deceiving. One document is a series of advertisements for forthcoming events, and the two terms are associated with different events ("Amusements," New York Times, 27 November 1879, 7). This is also true for the second document. Nevertheless, one brief mention reads as follows: "A lecture on 'Optics as Related to Art' was delivered at the Academy of Design last night by Prof. Ogden N. Rood. The subject was illustrated in a very interesting manner by the stereopticon" ("New York and Suburban News," New York Times, 12 March 1873, 8). So here is a false ID that actually turns out to be quite accurate, underscoring its limits in terms of both accuracy and nuance. This illustrates one of the many ways in which these figures must be used cautiously.

1859. RWS identified 51 occurrences of "magic lantern" and 28 of "dissolving views" between 1860 and 1879. Both remained common, though the term "dissolving views" became noticeably less popular. In contrast neither "stereopticon" nor "illustrated lecture" appear in a RWS of the 1850s. The term "stereopticon" quickly became popular after it first appeared in 1863, generating 89 hits during the remainder of the 1860s and 207 hits in the 1870s. Although the association of the term "lecture" with "stereopticon" was already common by the 1860s (occurring 25 times), the term "illustrated lecture" was adopted somewhat more gradually, appearing only 3 times in the 1860s and 44 times in the 1870s.

It is important to recognize that this search engine provides only an approximation of usage and generally undercounts the occurrence of such terms (though there are some terms that produce massive overcounts). Take the term "illustrated lecture." If the word "illustrated" appears on two lines with a hyphen, it will not show up in search results. Nor would the phrase "lecture illustrated by . . . " Moreover, printing imperfections mean words cannot be read by the machines. I have stumbled upon numerous such examples from the pre-1880 period, which would add significantly to these totals, but have not figured them into this article's calculations. At the same time, as text recognition software has improved, this has produced different, usually higher, counts. Ironically, since some of this has compelled me to employ a more stringent application of the RWS software in comparison to an earlier but similar effort, it can have the opposite effect of reducing the number of hits.[4] Some word variants also conceal the degree of usage. For instance, John L. Stoddard, perhaps the premier illustrated lecturer in the United States in the 1880s and early 1890s, used the term "stereoptic views," not "stereopticon views."[5] This suggests that "stereopticon" was such a popular term that it could support affectionate contractions—as "moving pictures" supported and generated the term "movies."

Although the terms "stereopticon" and "illustrated lecture" did not appear in the same *New York Times* item or advertisement before 1880, the terms "stereopticon" and "lecture" appeared together 157 times (almost half of the times when "stereopticon" appeared). This may well have been because the term "stereopticon," when employed with the term "lecture," meant "illustrated lecture" and the full coupling would have offered unnecessary redundancies.[6] Again, it was not until 1879 that the term "stereopticon lecture" appeared—in a series of exhibitions given by Reverend George H. Hepworth at Madison Avenue Church of the Disciples.[7] In contrast, "magic lantern" and "lecture" only appeared together 17 times before 1880 and typically were not directly linked. Thus John MacMullen ran a school in which he gave "Familiar Lectures on History and Geography, every Tuesday and Thursday" and "Magic Lantern and Microscopic Exhibitions every Friday."[8]

The British and the Americans may seem to speak the same language, but our linguistic differences are underscored in this study. Random word searches in the *Manchester Guardian* and the *Observer* indicate that the term "stereopticon" was not used in England and did not appear in these papers until 1903, and only then in dispatches from the United States.[9] If the British were eager to distinguish the traditional magic lantern from its more modern counterpart, they had no equivalent term. Sometimes they dropped the term "magic" and replaced it with various different adjectives: references to the oxy-hydrogen or oxy-calcium lantern began to appear in 1856 and became common a decade later. Sometimes it was just shortened to "lantern," as in "a pair of lanterns by Negritti and Zambra for exhibiting by the oxy-hydrogen light: with all the newest improvements";[10] while somewhat later the term "optical lantern" became popular. Nevertheless, "magic lantern" retained some of its prominence, being used in these British serials 300 times between 1850 and 1879. Although the term "illustrated lecture" appeared in the British periodicals 20 times in the same period, the terms "illustrated lecture" and "magic lantern" did not appear in the same item before 1880. In contrast, somewhat simplified searches found that the terms "magic lantern" and "lecture" appeared together in 34 items, while the terms "lantern" and "lecture" generated a number of additional hits over the same three decades.[11]

Subsequent random word searches continue to be broken down by decade. In the 1880s the term "stereopticon" generated 304 hits in the *New York Times*, "illustrated lecture" produced 212 hits, and the two were cited together a modest 10 times. Consistent with previous usage, the term "lecture" was linked with "stereopticon" much more frequently: 122 times (about 55 percent of the time that "stereopticon" appeared). The stereopticon was being used heavily for lectures, and these might involve wording such as "The Rev Dr. Eccleston Will deliver his new lecture on ST. PAUL'S CATHEDRAL illustrated with 50 stereopticon views."[12] Nevertheless, the term "stereopticon lecture" appeared only twice in the *New York Times* during the 1880s. The term "magic lantern" appeared 47 times, but once again it never appeared in conjunction with the term "illustrated lecture." Indeed, "magic lantern" only generated 6 hits in conjunction with the term "lecture" in the 1880s, as the magic lantern was more and more associated with non-lecture uses.

As the accompanying table shows, the term "stereopticon" occurred with the highest frequency in the 1890s (generating 581 hits), while the term "illustrated lecture" increased to 545. Moreover, the combined appearance of these two terms was higher in the 1890s than in any other decade. It is worth noting that the term "stereopticon lecture" only appeared with some regularity after 1894, generating 31 hits between 1894 and 1899. The term was being used with the greatest fluency at the very moment that modern motion pictures were appearing on the scene. Usage of the term "stereopticon" then decreased somewhat in the first decade of the twentieth century, with 419 citations, while usage of the term "illustrated lecture" dropped by more than 50 percent (from 545 hits to 231). The term "stereopticon lecture" only appeared 16 times in the first decade of the twentieth century, and these instances were all confined to its first five years.

Use of the term "stereopticon" began to fall off quite dramatically in the 1910s, a decline that was not at all evident for the term "illustrated lecture." By the 1930s, the media formation in the United States had undergone profound transformations, including but hardly limited to the arrival of synchronous-sound motion pictures and the emergence of new terms such as "documentary" in the late 1920s.[13] The term "slide projector" began to appear in the *New York Times* at the same time, generating three references in 1926–27. This included an advertisement for a "film slide projector" accompanied by a letter from Douglas Fairbanks declaring, "I think the idea of using films in place of glass slides is an excellent one."[14] Writing to the *New York Times*, one educational film professional referred to "the stereopticon slide projector."[15] Four more references appear between 1935 and 1939, including an article referring to the use of "lantern slide projectors"—rather than stereopticons.[16] Such usage suggests that writers were becoming less comfortable with the term "stereopticon," perhaps because its nineteenth-century connotations did not adequately characterize the specific configurations of the contemporaneous lantern *dispositif*. In 1940 Macy's ran advertisements selling the Keystone 35mm slide projector, and from this point on, the term "slide projector" appeared more regularly, with 127 mentions in the *New York Times* during the 1940s and 676 during the 1950s.[17] The term "slide show" became popular in the 1950s, and was used with considerable frequency from the 1970s to the 1990s. Such shifts in technology and nomenclature contributed to the rapid decline in the usage of "stereopticon," its employment only continuing after World War II in a few residual categories.

Although discourse between the American Civil War (1860s) and World War II clearly recognized that the stereopticon involved the same basic kind of projecting device as the magic lantern and was one of its descendants, it also made clear that the two possessed distinct characteristics. One reporter, writing in 1869, explained:

> The common magic-lantern is usually made of tin, has an oil-lamp inside, and is provided with a chimney to carry off the smoke. One of the two large lenses, ground to a curve of short radius and called bulls' eyes, are placed in front of the lamp, and beyond this is a common colored picture on glass. Then comes one or two more smaller lenses, throwing an image of this picture on the wall, and, as well, too, the equally diffused light of the lamp. . . .
>
> The so-called stereopticon is virtually the same thing, only instead of a comparatively weak, feeble lamp-flame, the powerful hydro-oxygen lime-light is used; in place of the common lenses, the perfected achromatic lenses as used for photographic portraiture; and finally instead of a common glass picture, a photographic glass slide like those used for the stereoscope. The stronger the light, the more perfect the lenses and the microscopic finish of the picture, the greater is the degree of the magnifying power that may be employed. In this case it is of course much greater than is possible when the common magic lantern is used.[18]

The two terms were rarely confused. "Stereopticon" was the new, dynamic, and modern term that was explicitly connected to photography and a powerful light source that entailed a degree of skill and expense. The magic lantern was associated with painted slides and related representational techniques. For instance, in 1886 a *New York Times* critic complained of "the injudicious use of the magic lantern for purposes of projecting pictures of flying Walkyries on the clouds" in the Metropolitan Opera's production of Richard Wagner's *Die Walküre*.[19] Sometimes "magic lantern" was used generically, as the underlying term, but it was more generally associated with children's tales as well as representations of ghosts and the supernatural—tied in some ways to the phantasmagoria performances that became popular in the 1790s.[20] It also included use by amateurs and children, typically in a domestic space.

Analyzing the lexicon of the screen is helpful and revealing in a variety of ways. The adoption of the stereopticon and illustrated lecture by the Republicans in 1888 and 1892 fits quite neatly in this overall pattern of proliferation. But there are sharp limitations as to what it can actually tell us about the changing nature of the lantern/stereopticon as a media form.

FROM MAGIC LANTERN TO STEREOPTICON:
A BRIEF HISTORY

The development of photography did not give lanternists immediate access to projected photographic images: this had to wait for the development of the albumen process in the late 1840s. These new photographic techniques enabled a photographic image to adhere to a glass surface, while earlier processes (daguerreotypes and talbotypes) had used either a silver-plated copper surface or paper as a base.

When John A. Whipple, a prominent Boston daguerreotypist, and William B. Jones patented an albumen process (using egg whites as an adhering agent) in June 1850, they had apparently been using it for several years.[21] The Philadelphia-based Langenheim Brothers, William and Frederick, had also been working with the albumen process and by that means came to play a central role in the introduction of photographic lantern slides.[22] During the 1840s the Langenheims facilitated the introduction of several new photographic processes in the United States. Interested in the process of paper photography developed by William Henry Fox Talbot, they became its exclusive US agents.[23] While licensing the talbotype process was not commercially rewarding, the venture encouraged them to adopt and improve the albumen process. Employing glass as a support for the emulsion, the Langenheims began making positive photographic lantern slides. In early October 1849 they declared a "new era in taking likenesses—Hyalotypes or Portraits on Glass":

> In the course of a long series of complicated experiments, undertaken for the purpose of bringing the Talbotype to the highest degree of perfection, we have not only attained our object, (as the specimens taken with our latest improvements, and now exhibited at our rooms, will show) but we have also made the important discovery, that pictures, taken with the aid of the Camera Obscura, can be permanently fixed on PLATE GLASS.
>
> These pictures possess a richness of tone, clearness in the lights and depth and mellowness in the shadows that cannot be equaled by any other production of art.[24]

The Langenheims suggested that they could be looked at directly and framed, used as ornaments in parlor windows or as candle shades, and that they were perfect for the magic lantern.[25] These new photographic slides were imagined as participating in the larger realm of photography, and the slides themselves had multiple potential uses. It was one of their many innovations in the photography field, and the lantern was only one way to display this newest innovation. The Langenheims' premise, that they were presenting various new innovations within the

FIGURE 9. Frederick Langenheim looking at talbotypes, 1850. Courtesy the
Metropolitan Museum of Art.

field of photography, was evident when they showed examples of this
work at Philadelphia's Franklin Institute later that month, for which
they received local praise.[26]

The Langenheims published "special notices" of their "NEW
INVENTION!" and the "NEW ERA IN TAKING LIKENESSES" in the
Boston Argus and elsewhere along the Eastern Seaboard.[27] Daguerreo-
typist John A. Whipple, who prided himself as an innovator in the field

of photography, may have felt upstaged and responded to this news by giving a private exhibition of dissolving views in his "Daguerreotype Rooms" at 96 Washington Street, and then opening the show to the public for a twenty-five-cent admission.[28] He presented an eclectic selection of views, but he proposed "by means of the 'Herculeanean Magnifier,' an instrument of his own invention, —to transfer to white canvass several daguerreotype pictures, embracing miniatures of the principal men of the age, of our own and other countries and views of the renowned edifices of the world."[29] Rejecting the term "hyalotype," he was soon boasting that his Grand Exhibition of Dissolving Views included "Daguerreotypes shown the size of Life."[30] Even after his move to Boston's Melodeon Theater, the projection of photographs remained only a small part of a show featuring the "Wonders of Optical Science."[31] This included portions of minute insects "powerfully magnified; such as the wing of a common fly, bill of the mosquito, a drop of vinegar with inhabitants sporting therein."[32]

After a successful Boston run, Whipple took his show on the road, in June 1850 to American Hall in Hartford and then to towns on the seashore such as Salem and New Bedford, Massachusetts, and Newport, Rhode Island. In the fall, after a return run in Boston, he exhibited in Worchester, Providence, Baltimore, Washington, DC, and—very briefly— at Philadelphia's Chestnut Street Theater, avoiding New York completely. Details about his exhibitions are limited, but if he continued to show photographic slides they were in the context of a scientific demonstration. By the summer of 1851, someone had acquired the components of his exhibition and he refocused his energies on photography.[33]

Meanwhile the Langenheims concentrated on their photography business and prepared for a larger effort to market their hyalotypes, tied to the London Crystal Palace Exhibition, which opened in May 1851. Perhaps this involved technical refinements as well as the gathering of a wide selection of images, including views of Niagara Falls. These hyalotypes competed with all the latest novelties and received extensive praise:[34]

> The new magic-lantern pictures on glass, being produced by the action of light alone on a prepared glass plate, by means of the camera obscura, must throw the old style of magic lantern slides into the shade, and supersede them at once, on account of the greater accuracy of the smallest details which are drawn and fixed on glass from nature, by the camera obscura, with a fidelity truly astonishing. By magnifying these new slides through the magic lantern, the representation is nature itself again, omitting all defects and

incorrectness in the drawing which can never be avoided in painting a picture on the small scale required for the old slides.[35]

Here William Langenheim presented their new slides clearly within a magic lantern framework. Views were of buildings and landmarks in Philadelphia (US Custom House, Penitentiary of Pennsylvania), Washington, DC (the Smithsonian, the Capitol), and New York (Croton Aqueduct) as well as portraits of well-known Americans.

Simultaneous with their success in London, Frederick Langenheim opened the Polytechnic Lecture Rooms on the second floor at 171 Chestnut Street, above Fifth Avenue in Philadelphia. During the day it was his studio, and he kept busy taking photographs of various types, while in the evening he gave exhibitions, screening the brothers' hyalotypes using the "physiorama."[36] (See document 5 in the appendix.) One notable aspect of this presentation was Langenheim's effort to show motion on the screen, presumably by projecting a succession of photographs of Niagara Falls (or perhaps alternating between two or three). A reporter for the *Pennsylvania Freeman* had decidedly negative reactions to this attempt, finding that "it appeals less to our sense of the sublime" and "more to the love of the ludicrous."[37] Was the illusion unsatisfactory, or did it produce an effect of excessive realism? In any case, this interest in creating the illusion of motion using photographs would be picked up by two other Philadelphia innovators: Coleman Sellars, who patented the "kinematoscope," an improvement on the stereoscope that showed movement through a succession of images, in 1861; and Henry Renno Heyl, who presented his "phasmatrope," projecting a succession of images using a magic lantern, in 1870.[38]

Although the Langenheims did not pursue their efforts at creating movement through the projection of photographic images, they did begin to sell lantern slides. These early positive pictures on glass slides were mounted in rectangular wooden frames that were 3 5/8 × 6 7/8 inches with a 2 3/4 inch or 3 inch circular opening for the image. Many were hand colored, and they cost four or five dollars apiece. Yet this proves telling. The Langenheims thought of themselves as photographers who took and sold images rather than magic lantern exhibitors. They apparently did not take their physiorama on the road. Viewing their achievements as just one of many innovations in the photography field, they used the magic lantern to show off their photographs rather than using their photographic slides to transform magic lantern practices. In short, they conceived of the lantern as a platform (one of many), not as a distinct media form.

The Stereopticon

If the stereopticon was characterized as involving the projection of a photographic image by a modern lantern with a strong light source and quality lenses, why did it take a decade for a name such as "stereopticon" (though not necessarily that exact appellation) to come into being? It is roughly the same time lag between the appearance of what was recognized as the modern documentary (*Nanook of the North*, 1922) and the coining of the term in Anglo-American discourse. As we have seen, the Langenheims offered at least two possible designations for this new conjunction, but neither was picked up. Perhaps this was not only the conceptual limitation of seeing projected lantern slides as part of the still dynamic and rapidly changing media of photography but a failure in effective branding. Other changes that ultimately contributed to the conceptual shift involved advances in photographic techniques and in media culture more generally. Although oxy-hydrogen lanterns were being offered for sale by London opticians as early as 1851, they remained a rarity.[39] For instance the adaptation of the oxy-hydrogen or calcium light to the lantern was first mentioned in the *Manchester Guardian* in late 1855.[40]

Progress in photographic processes likewise moved back and forth between Europe and the United States. The move from daguerreotypes to more modern photographic images for the stereoscope was not straightforward. Philadelphia photographer Marcus Aurelius Root, author of *The Camera and the Pencil: or, The Heliographic Art* (1864), offered a brief history of photography's application to the magic lantern: the Langenheims adapted "Mr. Niepce's process of making negative pictures by using albumen in combination with iodide of potassium" and "obtained the *first positive pictures on glass* to be viewed by transmitted light, in 1848." In 1851 the Paris-based instrument maker Louis Jules Duboscq, who is credited with the invention of stereoscopic photography, was also at the Crystal Palace Exhibition, where he saw the Langenheims' "photo magic lantern pictures," which were "the first he had ever seen." He subsequently arranged to adapt their process for the making of stereoscopic glass slides "to supersede the daguerreotype pictures."[41]

Photographers in France and England soon enjoyed a booming business in making glass slides for the stereoscope, but this innovation happened somewhat later in the United States. It was again the Langenheims who responded to European developments by making the first stereoscopic glass slides in the United States during the summer of

FIGURE 10. The Langenheims' stereoscopic slide *Winter, Niagara Falls, Table Rock, Canada Side* (1855). Designed for use in the stereoscope, these slides could be cut in half and sold for use in the stereopticon. Projected lantern-slide photographs gave a strong sense of depth, which was often mistaken for a stereoscopic effect. Courtesy the Cooper-Hewitt, Smithsonian Design Museum.

1854.[42] Although the Langenheims' stereoscopic slides were being marketed in Washington, DC, by 1856, the production and sale of stereoscopic glass slides was still getting started in New York City two years later, with landscapes on paper selling from six to nine dollars per dozen and landscapes on glass from fifteen to thirty dollars.[43] Perhaps the success of the stereoscope muted the impact and appreciation of projected photographic slides, for stereo views proved easy to access and a powerful instance of what Francesco Casetti has described as "relocation"— magically transposing three-dimensional spaces across vast distances and into the domestic sphere of the parlor.[44] The wet plate collodion process, introduced by Frederick Scott Archer in 1851 and widely adopted over the next decade, was another factor in the increasingly robust business in photographic slides.

The French-born but London-based photographer Antoine Claudet tried to project individual halves of a stereoscopic slide and retain or re-create three-dimensional effects in 1857. The resulting achievement, which he called the stereomonoscope, received significant attention in the press and among scientific journals. Claudet believed (wrongly) that projecting a photographic image onto ground glass was the key to retaining a three-dimensional sense of depth. In fact, although projecting a single photographic image does not produce that actual effect, viewers do experience a visceral sense of depth that is much stronger than if they viewed a photograph on paper or a metal surface.[45]

Chemist John Fallon of Lawrence, Massachusetts, apparently acquired one of Claudet's lanterns and, after refiguring and discarding elements, offered what was referred to as an "improved stereopticon." According to one press report, "It was developed into something so perfect that his friends desired that others might have the pleasure which he enjoyed. He has sent it forth on a charitable mission, and for churches, Sabbath schools, and sanitary commissions its charities can be counted by thousands. In Massachusetts, such men as Prof. Agassiz, Longfellow, Hillard, Holmes, Rev. Dr. Park, and many other leading representative men 'assisted' with delight at many of the exhibitions, and the first two aided in delineating the scenes."[46] "Delineators" provided commentary for the images, pointing toward the illustrated lecture as an emergent mode.

After some informal, little-publicized screenings, Fallon's stereopticon had its commercial debut in Philadelphia under the direction of Thomas Leyland, a Fallon associate from Lawrence, Massachusetts, and Peter E. Abel, who was actively involved in the local theatrical business.[47] Their stereopticon program premiered at the Concert Hall on December 22, 1860—less than two months after Republican presidential candidate Abraham Lincoln had won the election. A week of afternoon and evening screenings followed. Newspaper advertisements promoted "Gigantic Stereoscopic Pictures" that surpassed "anything hitherto presented to the public," as the images were produced "with surprising and almost magical accuracy."[48] The *Saturday Evening Post* declared, "It produces in a wonderful degree the impression that you are gazing upon the real scenes and objects represented."[49]

The Fallon team ventured to the home of the Langenheims and the center of photographic activity in the United States, where they found an enthusiastic audience. One might think that this was simply a revival of the Langenheims' efforts and so nothing new, but evidently this was not the case. There were a number of contributing factors. As Kentwood Wells has pointed out, John Fallon did not present his lantern system himself but delegated this task to two people who had experience in the entertainment field.[50] They were operating within the field of screen entertainment rather than that of photography. Moreover, the practice of making photographic images on glass had been further developed, aided by the demand for stereoscopic slides, which then could be easily cut in two and used for the stereopticon. Better slides and a new high-tech lantern provided the technological basis for this emergent media form. But there was another factor as well: the assemblage of slides into a coherent program with sound accompaniment. Unlike Whipple, who showed many types of slides, Leyland only showed one kind: photographic ones. Moreover, it was at this moment that the informal spiel that accompanied lantern shows was taking the shape of—and was associated with—an illustrated lecture. Here a random word search proves revealing. For while the term "illustrated lecture" can be found on rare occasions going back to the early nineteenth century, it is quite rare until about 1857–58 and does not signal a vital, coherent practice until roughly 1879–80. The terms "stereopticon" and "illustrated lecture" entered mainstream discourse at virtually the same time: they interacted and supported each other, ultimately creating a dynamic media form that gave shape to the documentary tradition. In this respect Abel and Leyland were in the right place at the right time. If the Langenheims introduced an important innovation in the photographic field, Fallon, Abel, and Leyland were able to reposition and refine this practice within the framework of screen entertainment, giving it a new prominence, a new vitality, and even a new identity that we can identify as a new media form.

After their initial success showing the stereopticon at the Concert Hall, Abel and Leyland used the next five weeks to prepare for a more extended run at a new Philadelphia location. Reopening at the Assembly Buildings, Tenth and Chestnut Streets, on February 4, 1861, their stereopticon exhibition ran for twelve weeks, through April 27.[51] This run began with a variety of images that offered little narrative continuity, but gradually the programs gained greater coherence.[52] On Thursday, April 4, it was announced that the "evening's programme comprises a number of superb views on the river Rhine, and amongst the mountains and cities of Switzerland and Germany. The majority of these are the most perfect specimens of photographic art ever presented to the spectator."[53] Photographic slides of sculptures, which emphasized the images' illusion of depth, were also featured. Musical accompaniment and a delineator (as the proto-lecturer was then being called) were becoming more important to their exhibitions: on March 29, a special complimentary benefit was given for the delineator (who nonetheless remained unnamed).[54] By April, Abel and Leyland announced different topics for each evening's screening: Monday, Egypt and the Holy Land; Tuesday, France, Spain, &c; Wednesday, England, &c., and so forth.[55] By the last week in April they were offering "Views from the Seat of

War."[56] (The Civil War had begun ten days earlier with the attack on Fort Sumter on April 12.) *Arthur's Home Magazine* hailed this "triumph of science and art combined" and declared, "No picture or dioramic view is comparable with the 'Stereopticon' in giving a just idea of scenery or architecture. You seem to stand in the very place that is represented, and to see everything just as it exists, in all its true portions."[57]

After Philadelphia, Abel and Leyland took their stereopticon to Library Hall in Newark, New Jersey, opening on May 1 for at least a week.[58] They subsequently exhibited at the Boston Museum for two weeks in mid-July.[59] Competition quickly emerged: James W. Queen, a Philadelphia optician, was selling an improved version of the stereopticon by the beginning of April.[60] On May 27, one month after Abel and Leyland left Philadelphia, H.P. Sanderson presented his stereoscopic exhibition *The Great Rebellion* at the same Assembly Buildings—and continued with only brief interruptions into October.[61] Soon various stereopticon showmen were giving programs in Trenton and elsewhere, usually showing war-related images. The term "stereopticon" was catching on.

If we compare the diffusion of the stereopticon to that of cinema less than thirty-five years later, there is one notable difference: the stereopticon did not appear in some major cities, most notably New York, until two years after the Philadelphia debut. Was the war a factor? Did the Langenheims' and Whipple's previous achievements in producing photographic lantern slides cause some kind of interference? Or was the stereopticon less an invention or even an innovation than the timely naming of a new media form as it was beginning to congeal? For instance, the *New York Times* first employed the term "illustrated lecture" in its issue of August 4, 1861, to refer to Rafael J. De Cordova's presentation at Hope Chapel, a theater at 720 Broadway near Waverly Place, which he had renamed De Cordova's Lyceum. De Cordova was a well-known humorist and platform orator; beginning on July 24, however, he turned to a more serious subject. He recited his new historical poem *The Rebellion and the War*, which was "illustrated by Dissolving Views of the Principal Events of the Campaign."[62]

While De Cordova possibly used photographs in some instances, his views were generally "after designs by eminent artists and exquisitely done."[63] (See document 6 in the appendix for his list of images.) De Cordova soon abandoned his Lyceum Theater, and while he occasionally presented *The Rebellion and the War* on the road, he lectured (without visual accompaniment) primarily on more humorous topics such as courtship and marriage. Did his program on the war act as a deterrent for those exhibiting Fallon's stereopticon? Or was Fallon, like Whipple, hesitant to take on the nation's emerging entertainment capital, New York City? There are no easy answers.

In any case, Fallon's stereopticon appeared in Providence and Portland, Maine, before opening at Toro Hall in Hartford on December 23, 1862, where the effects were declared to be "brilliant and startling, and the representations singularly truthful."[64] Finally, exhibitor T. Leyland took the exhibition to Brooklyn and debuted this "scientific wonder of the age" at the Athenaeum on April 14, 1863. Although audiences were embarrassingly small at first, the city's leading citizens (including Mayor M.B. Kablefleisch and Charles J. Sprague) urged Fallon and Leyland to remain "so that all may enjoy its beauties and profit by its instructions."[65] It ultimately ran almost continuously for six weeks with a twenty-five-cent admission fee. The evening's debut consisted of "a choice selection of landscapes, architectural views and sculptures gathered from travels in the most illustrious parts of Europe, Asia and our own country."[66] These views of distant lands again involved an act of relocation—in this case, a relocation of distant geographic space to the theater or metaphorically taking the spectator to the distant locale, turning the patron into a virtual traveler—a tourist.[67] One reviewer remarked, "You can imagine yourself borne away on the enchanted carpet of the Arabian tale, and brought where you can look down upon the veritable Paris, and Rome, and Egypt."[68] The mistaken belief that "half of a stereoscopic view could be made to present a solid [i.e., stereoscopic] effect" persisted, and this was related to the popularity of showing stereopticon views of sculpture.[69] As before, Leyland soon made almost daily program changes, devoting each illustrated lecture to a specific country or region.[70] These evening shows—with Wednesday and Saturday matinees at a reduced fee—were "attended by the learned and scientific portion of society as well as others."[71]

While strong ties between cultural elites and the stereopticon were being forged in Brooklyn, P.T. Barnum hastened to appropriate the invention for his own amusement purposes in Manhattan. On May 4 the "Great English Stereopticon" opened as the principal attraction at his American Museum with "photographic views of scenery, celestial and animated objects, buildings, portraits, &c, &c."[72] For this "new pleasure," which Barnum claimed to have cost thousands of dollars, "the picture stands out upon a curtain with the same perspective that is seen in nature, and thousands of people can see it at the same time." After two weeks the stereopticon was being shown between acts of

Dion Boucicault's drama *Pauvette*.[73] This was hardly a radical departure from previous programming, given that Barnum had frequently shown "dissolving views" in the 1850s.[74]

Fallon's "great work of art, the stereopticon" opened in Manhattan on June 15 at Irving Hall, where it ran for five weeks. Returning the following May, the showman gave exhibitions every evening (with matinees on Wednesdays and Saturdays) for seven weeks. He had 1,000 slides in his collection, and programs changed each week. The initial program, *Celebrated Places and Statuary*, included portraits of various Union Army generals.[75] A subsequent program offered local views—images of New York Harbor, a recent fair, and the new Worth Monument.[76] The final week was devoted to a program on the war, *The Army of the Potomac*, which used photographs taken by Alexander Gardner—official photographer for the Army of the Potomac—and a corps of his associates. As chapter 1 explained, many of the men who delivered their version of *The Tariff Illustrated* had prior experience presenting lantern lectures on the Civil War—a subject, perhaps a genre (a quite early version of the war documentary), that emerged during the Civil War and flourished for almost fifty years after its bloody conclusion.

A combination of factors contributed to the sense that the stereopticon was a new and important media form. Its powerful illusory effect was similar to the experience that spectators would later have with the first projected films—the sense of being transported to a different place and/or time. Commentators were impressed by the realism and the immediacy of the image—the sense of "being there." These "wonderful exhibitions" produced "brilliant and startling" effects as well as representations that were "singularly truthful." "The Old World and the New are brought in all their beauty and grandeur to our very doors."[77] These are very similar to the kinds of responses by those who first saw projected motion pictures in 1895–97 in the sense of immediacy, of unprecedented realism, of disorientation. Tom Gunning and others see this as a feature of modernity, and what is worth noting is the extent to which Americans experienced similar sensations in the 1860s (and the 1790s with the phantasmagoria as well).[78] If the cinema at its beginnings is linked to the shock of modernity, the same can be said for the stereopticon (paralleling the many shocks of a brutal war).

The formation and articulation of a new media form around the term "stereopticon" had one important additional factor: the Civil War. Stereopticon presentations on the war were ubiquitous and served multiple purposes. Certainly they engaged a profoundly political issue, about the status of the nation and the future of slavery. They were pro-Union—De Cordova's program started off with images of the Star-Spangled Banner and was presumably accompanied by patriotic music. Moreover, they consistently assumed a Northern point of view, showing for instance Southern aggression with the attack on Fort Sumter, Union soldiers marching off to battle, and martyrs to the cause. In this respect they often constructed a narrative about a war, which provided viewers with a perspective and framework for understanding the present moment. They also bridged a spatial gap by bringing spectators into more direct contact with events unfolding hundreds or more miles away.

The war's immediate cause was the outcome of a presidential election—Republican Abraham Lincoln's victory, which led to Southern secession—but this meant that there was little opportunity to use the stereopticon for purposes of politicking for four years. When Fallon's stereopticon screened at Irving Hall on July 4, 1864, the *New York Times* noted, "Many important additions have been made to the *repertoire* of views, especially views of the present struggle for Freedom. Patriotism can find no better place for an evening's entertainment and instruction than the Stereopticon."[79] But this was a special occasion—Independence Day. The Civil War as a subject for the screen seemed to almost disappear as the 1864 election approached. Before Fallon's stereopticon left Irving Hall in New York at the end of September 1864, just as the election was heating up, a rare and fairly elaborate review praised its depictions of statuary and its photographic mastery such that "the exhibition is enabled to change a night scene to the same at sunrise or at mid-day, or to produce with absolute fidelity to natural law, the semblance of the moon breaking through masses of cloud and shedding silver rays over earth and sea."[80]

It has been almost impossible to find advertisements or notices for stereopticon exhibitions in October and early November 1864, when presidential politicking was at its height. One exception involved a long-running "Grand Stereopticon Exhibition" at the Assembly Buildings in Philadelphia. Offering a tour of the world and a ghost scene, it seemed to avoid war-related topics. This choice of subject matter apparently continued even in mid-October when it was suddenly paired with Pauline Cushman, an actress who recalled her ordeal as a Union spy. Captured by the Confederates, she was rescued a few days before her scheduled execution.[81] Another exception took place at Clinton Hall in Ithaca, New York: *The Stereopticon! Or Mirror of the Rebellion* was shown on Saturday evening, October 29, 1864, just ten days before the presidential election. But in an effort to avoid political partisanship, its

FIGURE 11. Outdoor advertising using the stereopticon
emerged as a profitable and popular practice in 1871.
This method was rapidly adopted for the reporting of
election returns and presidential politicking. From a
T. H. McAllister catalog, circa 1890. Courtesy Terry and
Deborah Borton.

last two slides were of Major General McClellan, the Democratic candidate for president, and his opponent, Abraham Lincoln.[82] At a time
when speeches and torchlight parades were the most visible evidence of
politicking, the stereopticon was muted and only returned to popular
use in January 1865.

Lectures with the stereopticon, precursors of the documentary, were
delivered almost exclusively in public indoor spaces: halls, auditoriums,
churches, and commercial establishments. Then, around 1871, a new
type of exhibitor began to use the stereopticon for outdoor advertising,
throwing images onto the painted wall of a building at night. In Chicago it was reported that a Mr. Van Dusen "exhibits in the open air, by
means of mammoth views, interspersed with business cards. The views
are so pretty that the public is willing to stand the advertisement in
order to see the whole of the views. The idea is novel."[83] By mid-1872,

nighttime advertising with the stereopticon had become popular, as "pictures and business cards are alternately thrown on a large screen."[84] The projection technology associated with the stereopticon—a strong light and sharp lenses—were essential for a viable image, demonstrating yet again how the term referenced a certain kind of projection technology. The stereopticon assumed a dual identity—associated either with the illustrated lecture or a more variegated and silent projection of images that could be used to sell products—and candidates.

THE STEREOPTICON AND PRESIDENTIAL POLITICS, 1872–1884

The outdoor stereopticon was first applied to the realm of politicking as electoral campaigns were coming to a close: it was used to report election returns in the fall of 1872 as the Democrat/Liberal Republican candidate, former New York congressman and newspaper editor Horace Greeley, ran against the incumbent Republican, President Ulysses S. Grant. The *New York Herald*, one of the nation's most prominent newspapers, bathed the area around its building on Broadway and Ann Street in a blaze of calcium light. The sea of faces—those of millionaires, small businessmen, muscular roughs from the slums, and those betting on the outcome—watched "the election returns as they were being rapidly transferred to the pieces of canvas prepared for this purpose, covering a good share of the lower story of the Broadway façade."[85] The *Herald* was to continue this method of posting election results on its bulletin boards into the 1880s. The *New York Times*, which had offices one block away at 41 Park Row, chose not to directly compete with the *Herald*. It collaborated with Mr. Keeler's Stereopticon Advertising Company, which was projecting its images onto a large canvas at Twenty-Third Street and Broadway. The *Times* ran a telegraph line from its offices on Printing House Square to Keeler's offices so the results could be quickly communicated.[86]

The 1872 elections did not happen on the same day everywhere in the country. Several states, notably Pennsylvania, Indiana, and Ohio, held elections for governor, Congress, and its state houses almost a month earlier, on October 9—though these were read in the context of the presidential election to follow.[87] This gave the *Times* an opportunity to try out its system in preparation for the presidential elections the following month even as it served as an occasion for an informal campaign rally. The *Times* declared the event to be a huge success as people gathered in Madison Square and politicians came out of their headquarters at the Fifth Avenue Hotel to follow the news. As accounts of Republican victories were projected onto the canvas, "the shouts and handclapping must have frightened the horses and aroused the people on Sixth-avenue, who had not yet heard of the new enterprise. Pennsylvania news grew better and more decidedly victorious, until the gladness of the spectators knew no bounds, and they gave cheer after cheer for Grant, [Republican vice presidential candidate Henry] Wilson and the NEW YORK TIMES."[88] (See document 7 in the appendix.)

The *New York Times* and the Stereopticon Advertising Company reprised their success on election night, November 5. The crowd, which heavily favored Grant, was energized by the posted results and entertained by "cartoons of the leading incidents and advocates of Liberalism, which were executed on the spot" by the *Times* special artist.[89] This collaboration proved so successful that the Stereopticon Advertising Company subsequently integrated news bulletins from the *New York Times* into its regular repertoire.[90] While the company showed election returns at the same location during the 1876 election, this was given little press attention, as most people went downtown, where they could move among the bulletins posted on the boards of various newspapers.[91]

The political deployment of the stereopticon within the framework of outdoor advertising expanded in the 1880s. For the 1880 election, which pitted Republican Congressman and Civil War General James Garfield against the Democratic candidate, the general and Civil War hero Winfield Hancock, the stereopticon advertising site at Broadway and Twenty-Third Street continued to be popular. On October 11 the Republicans organized a massive demonstration, and some 40,000 men marched up Fifth Avenue. When they reached Madison Square, "a large portrait of General Garfield, bearing under it the words, 'Our next President,' was displayed on the stereopticon at that point and was hailed with a storm of cheers. This was then followed by a portrait of General Grant, who was designated 'Our Guest' and this was also cheered."[92] The parade's reviewing stand was located on Twenty-Fourth Street and Madison Square, only a block above the stereopticon display. Given that previous election-night reporting of returns had been more of a political demonstration than a simple public service, the stereopticon's use in conjunction with political rallies was only a modest innovation.

More independent uses of the stereopticon for political campaigning were occasionally reported in the press, again within the framework established by outdoor advertising. On October 22, 1880, the president of Edge Moor Iron Company of Delaware wrote to the editor of the *New York Tribune*:

> Sir: Amongst the various ways in which our "Republican League" is placing the tariff question before the workingmen of Wilmington and vicinity is by the use of a stereopticon. At the crossing of two of our principal streets we have a screen 30 feet by 25 feet, and nightly give them short, terse sentences bearing upon the question, which the crowds are able to read as much as two blocks away. We propose to address ourselves on one evening of the coming week to the wives and mothers, in an endeavor to get them interested in a question which so vitally affects them, and the object of this letter is to ask the help of THE TRIBUNE in the preparation of suitable sentiments for the occasion. We should like you to give us, say half a dozen, and if they were published in Monday's issue of your paper they would be in time for us and we could slip them. We can present as much as sixty lines of printed matter. Yours truly, Wm H. Connell, President.[93]

The outdoor stereopticon was beginning to be used to communicate political messages and slogans.

Not surprisingly, the stereopticon continued to be employed in conjunction with large-scale demonstrations and parades during the 1884 presidential campaigns. The *New York Times* was supporting New York State Governor Grover Cleveland, who would defeat former Maine Senator James Blaine to become the first Democrat to win the presidency since 1856. When the Democrats marched up Fifth Avenue to Madison Square, "the stereopticon at the junction displayed the fatal word in handwriting resembling Gail Hamilton's, and the crowds outside the lines joined generally in the cry."[94] This cry was "Burn-burn-burn this letter!"—a quotation from a damning letter that was not burned and revealed Blaine's corrupt arrangements with a railroad corporation. Then when the Blaine forces marched up Fifth Avenue a few days later, "the advertising stereopticon on the roof of the building at the junction of Broadway, Twenty-Third Street and Fifth-avenue, excited alternate laughter, cheers and hisses by presenting a great variety of campaign views."[95]

The use of the stereopticon for political purposes gradually became more common and more robust between 1872 and 1884. Yet its role remained minor—designed to add color and a festive air. Its chief counterparts were campaign buttons, banners, and posters, and it was not a significant component of the media formation that could influence the outcome of a presidential election. Elections were not to be won by better campaign hats—or by better stereopticon slides projected onto the side of a particularly well-placed building. The stereopticon was ancillary; its greatest value perhaps lay in its superfluous excess. This changed

FIGURE 12. Showing congressional election returns on the stereopticon in Columbus, Ohio, the night of October 14, 1884. *Frank Leslie's Weekly*, October 25, 1884. Courtesy Jack Judson and the Magic Lantern Castle Museum.

quite dramatically with the 1888 and 1892 elections, as the Republicans made extensive use of *The Tariff Illustrated*. Perhaps the issue-centered debate around the tariff created a sobrietous context for the appropriate lantern lecture to be introduced: Judge Wheeler's unexpected offshoot of supersaturated political oratory designed to compensate for the Democrats' press supremacy in New York City. Moreover, Harrison's defeat in 1892 did not cause Republicans to lose interest in the screen. Rather, they became even more inventive the next time around. For the 1896 presidential election Republicans sought out other new possibilities that might work to their advantage. Although the illustrated lecture would play a modest role in the 1896 presidential campaign, a number of key Republicans believed that the emerging phenomenon of projected motion pictures held out interesting possibilities.

CHAPTER 3

Cinema, *McKinley at Home*, and the 1896 Election

The nation's financial system was beginning to unravel even before Grover Cleveland's March 1893 inauguration. US railroads had over-built and were financially overextended: the Philadelphia and Reading Railroad went bankrupt in late February, and by the time the panic was over more than 500 banks and 15,000 businesses had followed. The unemployment rate reached 25 percent in Pennsylvania, 35 percent in New York, and 43 percent in Michigan. Desperate workers reacted with massive strikes in the Midwest—strikes that in the end were unsuccessful and further crippled the economy. Cleveland's response as well as the resources he had available to ameliorate the crisis were completely inadequate. Perhaps unfairly, the Republicans were able to blame him for the protracted devastation that lasted for the next four years: the second term of his presidency was shattered even before it began. In the 1894 congressional elections, Democrats outside the South lost all but a dozen seats in the House of Representatives. Republican congressmen outnumbered their Democratic counterparts more than two to one. The Democratic Party was in complete disarray.

In looking toward the 1896 presidential elections, Republicans enjoyed many political advantages: the greatest potential danger was that opportunity could breed greed and factionalism. On the Wednesday before Memorial Day 1895, Chauncey Depew, president of the New York Central Railroad, hosted a modest dinner at his house on Manhattan's West Fifty-Fourth Street. His guests included three preem-

FIGURE 13. Assisted by Secretary of the Treasury John G.
Carlisle as well as Congressmen Michael Harter (D-Ohio),
Charles Tracey (D-New York), and William Lyne Wilson (D-West
Virginia), Grover Cleveland tries to restore prosperity. *Puck,*
September 20, 1893. He did not succeed. Courtesy the Library of
Congress.

inent contenders for the 1896 Republican presidential nomination:
across from him sat current New York Governor and former Vice President Levi P. Morton, on his right was former President Benjamin Harrison, and on his left was Ohio Governor William McKinley (he had
first won the governorship in 1891). Various power brokers were also
in attendance. Business tycoon Cornelius Vanderbilt sat across from

McKinley, and General Horace Porter, president of the powerful Union League, sat on McKinley's left. Senator Thomas H. Carter of Montana, chairman of the Republican National Committee (RNC), sat next to Cornelius N. Bliss, treasurer of the RNC and the new president of the American Protective Tariff League. The banker Darius Ogden Mills, Whitelaw Reid's father-in-law, sat across from Theodore Roosevelt, president of the Police Board. Half a dozen senators and ex-senators, New York City Mayor William Lafayette Strong, and other prominent local politicians filled out the list. With the leaders of most Republican Party factions present, Depew made it forcefully clear that they were attending a "harmony dinner."[1]

The dinner started at nine o'clock and ended at midnight. During the next day's commemorative ceremonies at Grant's Tomb, Governor Morton fainted in the midst of his speech, damaging his candidacy. That evening, General Horace Porter held a second dinner at his nearby abode on Fortieth Street and Madison Avenue: Depew and Vanderbilt were there. So was Bliss, Mayor Strong, Roosevelt, and half a dozen other dinner guests from the night before. But Porter had invited only one of the presidential contenders: William McKinley. Porter, it had been widely assumed, was pro-Harrison. His dinner revealed that this was no longer the case.[2] It is perhaps not too much to suggest that in less than twenty-four hours, McKinley had emerged as the front-runner for the Republican presidential nomination.

New York was not only a pivotal swing state when it came to presidential elections; it was also the nation's financial capital, its media and communications capital, and its entertainment capital. When anyone who was anybody made it anywhere in these United States, they moved to New York City. It is therefore worth noting that at this second dinner, McKinley's younger brother Abner accompanied the Ohio governor and newly anointed front-runner. Presidential historians have often written about Mark Hanna as the businessman-politician who skillfully managed McKinley's bid for the presidency. While there is considerable truth in this, Abner or "Ab" McKinley also played a crucial role while adroitly remaining behind the scenes.[3] Abner and his older brother William had been law partners in Canton, Ohio, between 1872 and 1884. The younger brother then moved to New York "to push the invention of . . . a telegraphic machine, operated like a typewriter at one end, and delivering a message at the other end of the wire in perfect printed characters."[4] Although reportedly "indorsed by the best telegraph experts in the country," the large telegraph companies had not been interested. In one final effort, Abner McKinley's company tried to launch the business independently.[5] In the end this new media start-up did not succeed, and it would be more than forty years before the telex became operational. Abner McKinley remained in New York, a patent attorney and reasonably successful businessman, looking for an opportunity that might bring him immense wealth. By early 1896 he was involved in the financing of another new media venture, one that might make him rich and—though this was never said explicitly—help catapult his brother to the presidency: projected motion pictures.[6]

William McKinley had gradually emerged as a preeminent figure in the Republican Party. A US congressman from Ohio from 1877 to 1891, he lost his congressional seat shortly after engineering the 1890 McKinley Tariff Act, in part because the Democratic state legislature had gerrymandered his district. He was subsequently elected governor of Ohio in 1891 and 1893, serving from January 1892 to January 1896. As a speaker he campaigned extensively for fellow Republicans in both the 1892 and 1894 elections—years he was not himself running. In the 1894 midterm elections he conducted something of a whistle-stop tour, speaking on behalf of Republican candidates: he covered sixteen states and spoke 371 times.[7] Effective opposition to his 1896 presidential run never emerged within the party, and at the Republican National Convention in St. Louis, June 16 through 18, 1896, McKinley easily received the nomination for president on the first ballot.[8]

Although McKinley's strong stand on the tariff was well established, "Free Silver" or bimetallism had emerged as the preeminent issue of the 1896 election. The Free Silver movement wanted the government to be free to coin unlimited silver and reestablish the value of silver to gold at sixteen to one (it was then about thirty to one). If silver-backed dollars became legal tender, the money supply would increase and prices for agricultural goods would rise, helping poor farmers and expanding the economy. At least that was the argument. On the other side were those who believed in the Gold Standard and "Sound Money." The issue cut across Republican and Democratic party lines. Cleveland and the Bourbon Democrats supported the Gold Standard. McKinley sought to straddle the divide for a time but finally came down on the side of Sound Money, which he linked to a protective tariff as well as the Gold Standard. When he did so, many pro-Silver Republicans from the western states, including RNC Chairman and Montana Senator Carter, walked out of the convention. If the West was likely lost to the Republicans, McKinley's team sought geographical balance by choosing

FIGURE 14. An 1896 Bryan-Sewall campaign poster calls for the unlimited coinage of silver. Courtesy the Library of Congress.

Garret Hobart as his running mate. The leading Republican politician of New Jersey, Hobart had an affable personality and strong ties to Wall Street and corporate America.

The Democrats held their convention in Chicago one month later, from July 7 to 11. Pro-Silver delegates were in control of the proceedings but needed to boost their numbers in order to attain the two-thirds majority required to nominate a candidate. To that end the credentials committee made several rulings, one of which was to seat an insurgent delegation from Nebraska headed by William Jennings Bryan, thereby replacing a Gold Standard delegation with one that was Free Silver.[9] The following day, Bryan, "The Boy Orator of the Platte," gave his renowned "Cross of Gold" speech, asserting that "we are clad in the armor of a righteous cause, and this is stronger than the army of error which is being led against it." When New York Senator David B. Hill proposed an amendment to the Democratic platform "commending the honesty, fidelity and economy of the Cleveland administration," it was defeated by a vote of 564 to 357.[10] This vote not to commend was understood as a repudiation of Cleveland and the conservative wing of the party. If the Republicans successfully blamed Cleveland and the Democrats for the economic calamity of the past few years, this Democratic Convention made clear that they had broken with a failed administration in spirit as well as policy.

Bryan became the Democratic nominee for president on the fifth ballot as some Gold Standard Democrats left the convention hall even before the votes were counted.[11] It is often said that it was Bryan's oratorical tour de force that won him the nomination. Not only did he personally inspire the Free Silver delegates, but they must have also recognized that his oratory skills would be essential if the Democrats had any hope of winning the election. He chose Arthur Sewall, a shipbuilder and industrialist from Maine, as his running mate. Sewall was a local Democratic politician (like Hobart) whose business background might mollify nervous voters who were concerned that Bryan might be too radical.

THE NATION'S MEDIA FORMATION

In 1896 as in 1892, the press retained its dominant role in the nation's media formation (perhaps even having enhanced that position in the intervening four years). While the nation's newspapers remained the only mass media, their political alignment underwent a profound shift—one that could not have been predicted far in advance. The reaction of the traditionally Democratic newspapers to Bryan's nomination and the Democrats' Free Silver/pro–income tax platform was immediate. The *Brooklyn Eagle*'s front-page lede declared: "REVOLT OF THE PRESS. Democratic Newspapers by the Score Declare They Will Not Support Bryan. Words of Bitter Scorn for Ticket and Platform."[12] Charles Dana's *New York Sun* rejected Free Silver coinage as a "national dishonor and a monumental anachronism" and declared, "The presidential candidate of every Democrat who favors honest money . . . should be, without hesitation, evasion or sop to prejudice, William McKinley."[13] It characterized Bryan as a charlatan who "jumped in with the Populists, Socialists, and all sorts of folks who hunger for new fads and new political theories."[14] *Puck* turned its satiric humor on Bryan while the *New York Herald* immediately endorsed McKinley. In effect so did the *New York Times*, which asserted:

> The Chicago candidate fits the platform. He must at any cost and by whatever means are most effective be beaten. Better McKINLEY were his tariff record a hundred times worse than it is, than the disgrace and disaster of BRYAN's election. . . .
> The convention is Populist, the platform is Populist, the candidate is Populist. There is nothing Democratic in any of them, and no true Democrat can

support them directly or indirectly. THE TIMES cannot and will not. THE TIMES repudiates the convention, its platform, and its candidates. It will use all the power it possesses to expose their true character and to defeat them.[15]

Later, the *New York Times* halfheartedly endorsed Senator John Palmer of the National Democratic Party (the so-called Gold Democrats) even as it remained pro-McKinley. The *Brooklyn Eagle* took a similar position. All agreed: Bryan was an abomination and outside civil society.

Although the fiercely Democratic *New York World* was anathema to Republicans, its publisher, Joseph Pulitzer, insisted on endorsing McKinley over the objections of many of his editors.[16] This gave an opening to Pulitzer's newest rival: William Randolph Hearst and his *New York Journal* became the only mass-circulation daily in New York City to support Bryan. Similar shifts occurred throughout the Northeast and Midwest as traditionally Democratic newspapers such as the *Buffalo Courier*, the *Philadelphia Record*, and the *New Haven Register* rejected Bryan's candidacy. Of course, the traditional Republican newspapers—in New York and Brooklyn, the *New York Tribune*, the *Mail and Express*, the *New York Press*, and the *Brooklyn Standard Union*—remained enthusiastically pro-McKinley.

Many Americans were in desperate financial circumstances, and it was unclear how high the tidal wave of enthusiasm for Free Silver might rise and when it would crest. Assuming McKinley and the Republican Party were not overwhelmed by a silver tsunami, the Northeast seemed fairly certain to go for McKinley. New York, New Jersey, and Connecticut were not in play, which did not mean they could be overlooked. Likewise the South and the West seemed to be lining up in Bryan's camp. In terms of electoral votes, victory for either candidate rested in Illinois, Indiana, Iowa, and other states in the region (Wisconsin, Minnesota, and so forth). How to coordinate the various state committees and local clubs in order to manufacture the necessary sentiment that would ensure a McKinley victory was the task. Mark Hanna, who had become chairman of the Republican National Committee in June 1896, responded to this challenge by having two Republican campaign headquarters: one in New York, the traditional nerve center of Republican activity, and a second in Chicago, at the heart of the electoral battlefield. Asked where the "real headquarters" would be, he retorted that it would be wherever he was: Chicago, New York, his private railway car, or at home in Canton, Ohio, where he would be connected by long-distance telephone.[17] The long-distance telephone was a telecommunications innovation for the 1896 campaign.[18] Democratic headquarters, based in Chicago, also used it, and the service was installed in the homes of both Bryan and McKinley.[19]

Given that McKinley and Bryan were the most gifted speakers of their respective parties, political oratory was certain to play an important role in the presidential contest.[20] Nevertheless, for most Americans the press would be the lens through which their rhetoric and presidential qualities would be judged. McKinley remained at his home in Canton and conducted a "front porch campaign"—a way to act presidential and avoid any direct comparison with Bryan as to oratorical skills. Assured of strong support from the press, he could count on favorable coverage of his speeches to visiting delegations of supporters. In contrast, since many newspapers would use every opportunity to distort, malign, and selectively ignore Bryan's efforts, the candidate recognized that "we have not so many daily newspapers through which we can talk and therefore we have to do more talking ourselves."[21] In response, Bryan pioneered the whistle-stop campaign, traveling by train around the country in an effort to bypass the press and talk directly to the people. In the end he gave between four hundred and six hundred speeches.

The Republicans leveraged their advantages in every way possible. Mark Hanna visited the executives of large corporations, who were terrified by Bryan's radicalism and made extremely generous campaign contributions. The Republican National Committee received and expended more than $3.5 million, compared to Bryan's campaign chest of $300,000.[22] But the RNC was only the tip of the financial iceberg. Cornelius N. Bliss, the RNC's treasurer, was also president of the American Protective Tariff League, another major source of pro-McKinley propaganda. The league was quick to dredge up Bryan's anti-protection tariff statements, which he had made while a congressman in the early 1890s, and share them through its journal, the *American Economist*. Indeed, McKinley was a prominent league member. Both the RNC and the American Protective Tariff League printed many millions of copies of speeches, pamphlets, and other Sound Money materials. The Democrats relied heavily on printed information as well—particularly copies of Bryan's "Cross of Gold" speech, but had serious restrictions when it came to funding speakers. The Republicans had plenty of funds for speakers of all types. Theodore Roosevelt, president of the Police Board, went on two western trips and spoke frequently in New York City and the surrounding area. The RNC easily absorbed the many costs, such as renting halls and transporting speakers.

THE STEREOPTICON AND ILLUSTRATED LECTURE IN THE 1896 CAMPAIGN

The progenitor of what we can now recognize as the campaign documentary, John L. Wheeler, died in December 1893. The American Protective Tariff League did not try to replace him but rather abandoned the illustrated lecture as a tool for education. Those speakers who had given their own versions of *The Tariff Illustrated* likewise abstained. Harrison's failure to win New York, New Jersey, or Connecticut must have suggested the limited effectiveness on such presentations. These lantern lectures had been deployed in the previous two election cycles, and those working out of the RNC's New York headquarters must have recognized the inevitability of diminishing returns, particularly for the tristate area. In 1888, when it was a novel form of political propaganda, Wheeler's presentation had seemingly worked. When recycled, it became stale and less effective.

Republicans, nevertheless, did not entirely discard the use of stereopticon lectures. A few Republican speakers went on the campaign trail with illustrated lectures in other parts of the country. In the crucial swing state of Illinois, William Dickson ("W. D.") Boyce, the Chicago-based owner of the nation's largest weekly newspaper and future founder of the Boy Scouts of America, achieved a high level of visibility.[23] Boyce gave his illustrated lectures in the Chicago area on a daily basis, usually before large audiences and often as part of a larger Republican campaign rally. His appearances were extensively covered by the pro-McKinley *Chicago Tribune* and *Chicago Inter Ocean*. (See document 8 in the appendix.) While many elements of Boyce's illustrated lecture were indebted to previous efforts by Wheeler and his epigones, his "introduction of the stereopticon as an adjunct of the campaign speaker" was greeted as "something that had never before been attempted in politics."[24] It was promoted as a novelty and media innovation. Boyce was an active and well-connected Republican who certainly knew about the deployment of *The Tariff Illustrated* in the New York area in the previous two elections. He might have even been given some of the materials, but he also knew that it would work best when presented as something fresh and original. In any case, it was new to the Midwest. There were, of course, important differences from Judge Wheeler's presentation. First, Boyce used photographic images to remind his audiences of the closed factories and hungry families that resulted from the 1893 panic and Democratic misrule. The topic of tin plate was discarded. There was also much less talk. Boyce claimed to feel insecure as a speaker and his comments were notably brief. In fact, his cartoons were designed to make his presentations much more participatory, calling for vocal responses from the audiences. Boyce placed less emphasis on sustained argument and more on showmanship. He also introduced a new gimmick. "A feature of the evening was an illustration of the advancement in photography," the *Chicago Inter Ocean* explained. "Ildo Ramsdell, who had charge of the W.D. Boyce Company illustrating department, took by flashlight a picture of the audience, developed it, and transferred it onto a stereopticon slide in twenty-two minutes. At the close of the exhibition the picture was projected upon the canvas and the audience was given an opportunity of seeing themselves."[25] As will be evident in what follows, this rapid-fire novelty resonated with other elements of the McKinley campaign.

The 1896 campaign, in comparison to the previous election, gave greater prominence to personalities. Boyce seemed to be promoting himself and McKinley almost as much as Republican policies. Correspondingly, T.E. Shields delivered illustrated lectures on the life of McKinley "from the cradle to the White House." He used "fifty stereopticon views, made from copies of original photographs owned by Maj. McKinley," for his presentation.[26] Shields's emphasis on personality-driven politics contrasted to earlier issue-centered illustrated lectures, and this difference was evident in other parts of the campaign as well.

The Democrats once again displayed little interest in using the illustrated lecture for campaign purposes. Searches of digitally archived newspapers offer no evidence of such activity. Even the relatively small Socialist Labor Party had Max Forker of New York travel to cities such as St. Louis to give campaign-related stereopticon screenings.[27] However, Democrats as well as Republicans made use of various new media forms. This involved the phonograph and telephone as well as projected motion pictures. As one might expect, the Republicans were more expansive. Why? First, their dominance in the press was unexpected and occurred relatively late, so they had necessarily developed their strengths in other areas. Second, they enjoyed bountiful finances that could readily be deployed. Third and perhaps most importantly, they were attuned to the possibilities of innovative technologies. Most of the companies working with new media had Republican ownership and executives.

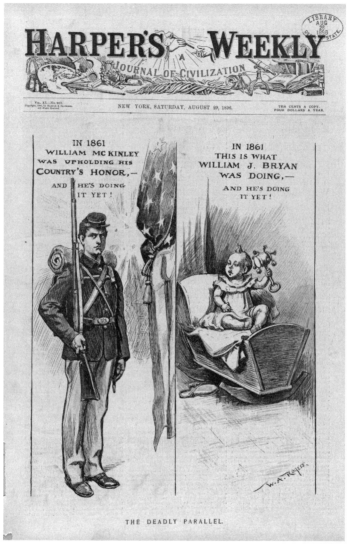

FIGURE 15. The pro-Republican *Harper's Weekly* asserts an ethical binary for its cover illustration, August 29, 1896. In contrast to Bryan, McKinley is shown as a man of courage, honor, and experience. Courtesy the Library of Congress.

THE AMERICAN MUTOSCOPE COMPANY AND THE
MCKINLEY CAMPAIGN

Abner McKinley's investment in an unnamed invention of great possibility referred to the most ambitious of the new motion picture enterprises: the American Mutoscope Company, which would become the world's preeminent motion picture enterprise by 1897–98. Given the younger McKinley's interest in new media technologies, his involvement is hardly surprising. He must have been attentive to anything coming out of Thomas A. Edison's laboratory in West Orange, New Jersey. In 1894–95 Edison's peep-hole kinetoscope had drawn considerable media attention to strongman Eugen Sandow and heavyweight boxing champion James Corbett, boosting their reputations in the public imagination. Businessmen, particularly in the entertainment field, quickly understood that showing films in the peep-hole kinetoscope was an effective means of advertising and promoting performers and shows. This potential became even more evident with the introduction of commercially successful projected motion pictures in New York City, following the debut of Edison's Vitascope at Koster & Bial's Music Hall on April 23, 1896. *The John C. Rice-May Irwin Kiss*, a short film of two popular musical comedy performers engaging in a protracted kiss, was shot at Edison's Black Maria studio in mid-April. Screened theatrically in late spring, throughout the summer, and beyond, the picture proved immensely popular and turned the aging Rice into a kissing star.[28] What might such a film do for the rather staid and physically absent McKinley? Here was a chance to move politicking into the nation's theaters and mix politics with entertainment.

William Kennedy Laurie Dickson, coinventor of Edison's initial motion picture system, had been in charge of film production at the Edison Manufacturing Company until he left in early April 1895. He quickly became a key member of the American Mutoscope Company, which developed its own motion picture system using 68mm/70mm film that was shot and projected at a high rate of speed. Its projector produced a screen image that was superior to that of any of its competitors and was called the "biograph." For this reason the company was widely referred to as the Biograph company and would soon be officially renamed the American Mutoscope & Biograph Company. In late September and early October, Biograph had only one projector, which was attached to Sandow's Olympia, a touring vaudeville company organized by Charles B. Jefferson (son of the iconic American actor Joseph Jefferson) and headlined by strongman Eugen Sandow.[29] Once again Dickson was in charge of production, taking films of Sandow displaying his muscular physique and of Joseph Jefferson in brief excerpts from his all-American theatrical classic *Rip Van Winkle*. These were among the pictures that were screened at the biograph's debut in Pittsburgh on September 14.

Several prominent Republicans, including ex-President Benjamin Harrison, had invested in the American Mutoscope Company. Abner McKinley was certainly not a passive financier; he had some ideas as to how a top-of-the-line motion picture system might benefit his brother's campaign. Perhaps he also appreciated how brother Bill and the Republicans could help the fledgling business. The younger McKinley was evidently in Pittsburgh on Sunday for the biograph's public debut, since he arrived in Canton the following morning, September 15.[30] Abner remained in Canton for several days, and this stay was important for at least two reasons. First, he needed to be present for a visit by the Somerset County Republicans. He and his wife had a family home in the town of Somerset, Pennsylvania, and they often spent summers there. It was a social obligation. Second, and more importantly, a Biograph camera crew headed by W. K. L. Dickson stopped in Canton on September 18 to take films of Republican political demonstrations and McKinley at his home in "a re-enactment of the notification for the benefit of the people who wished to see the new Republican nominee."[31] Abner must have overseen this undertaking, making sure they had proper facilities and that his brother found the time to be filmed. Dickson and his assistant, Billy Bitzer, even had lunch in the McKinley kitchen, presided over by the candidate's invalid wife.[32] Only on September 20 would Abner head back to New York, with a stopover in Somerset.[33] Meanwhile, Biograph producer Dickson and his team continued on their travels, which included the filming of West Point cadets, Niagara Falls, and the flagship train of Chauncey Depew's New York Central Railroad, the Empire State Express. These provided the kinds of subject matter that would be used to frame the scene of McKinley at home: symbols of American military might, American culture, American technology, the nation's natural grandeur, and Republican parades.

After its week in Pittsburgh, Sandow's Olympia moved on to Philadelphia and then Brooklyn. For the Biograph company these stops were the equivalent of out-of-town tryouts—a shakedown for its exhibition service until the necessary films could be taken and prepared for screening. Meanwhile, Sandow's Olympia was failing to cover its costs, perhaps not surprisingly, since many potential patrons were then more concerned with political theater, and the fees for its all-star cast were substantial.[34] Its closing frame was October 5–10 at New York's Grand Opera House, where the biograph went virtually unnoticed by the press. Such negligible coverage was easily attained since quite a few motion picture exhibition services were then playing in New York theaters: the vitascope (at two of Proctor's theaters), the kineopticon (at Pastor's), the Lumière cinématographe (at Keith's Union Square), the centograph (at Miner's Bowery Theater), and so forth. These competitors, of course, only underscored the importance of making a big splash in order to gain media attention. Abner McKinley had been arranging exactly such a surprise for some time.

The biograph had its "official" premiere on Monday evening, October 12, at Hammerstein's Olympia Music Hall on Broadway between Forty-Fourth and Forty-Fifth Streets, New York City. The theater was new, having been built the previous year.[35] This carefully staged event involved the kind of cross-promotions that had worked so successfully for Dickson and his earlier motion picture efforts.[36] *McKinley at Home* was shown for the first time as part of this event, which was both a political rally and the biograph's formal public unveiling. That morning, the *New York Herald* initiated the feedback loop between this political event and newspaper coverage by running four line drawings "From Instantaneous Photographs Taken for the Biograph. To Be Exhibited at the Olympia Theatre, Under the Auspices of the Republican National Committee." These images were said to illustrate "Incidents in Major McKinley's Life in Canton, Ohio."[37]

It has often been assumed that the film program was accurately represented by the evening's playbill, which lists nine films in this order: 1) *Stable on Fire*, 2) *Niagara Upper Rapids*, 3) *Trilby and Little Billee*, 4) *Joseph Jefferson, in Toast Scene from Rip Van Winkle*, 5) *A Hard Wash*, 6) *Niagara, American Falls*, 7) *Empire State Express*, 8) *McKinley and Hobart Parade at Canton, O.*, and 9) *Major McKinley at Home*.[38] This was probably the initially intended order, but reviews suggest that the impact of *Empire State Express* on the audience was so intense that it overpowered the final two McKinley campaign films. A private screening at the Olympia on Sunday evening, October 11, probably led to last-minute changes. "The finest of all these pictures was one of the Empire State Express going at sixty miles speed," remarked the *New York Times*. It had a powerful, visceral effect on the audience, which threatened to make *McKinley at Home* anticlimactic as a follow-up. As

FIGURE 16. Line drawings based on frames from *McKinley at Home*, shot September 18, 1896. *New York Herald*, October 12, 1896.

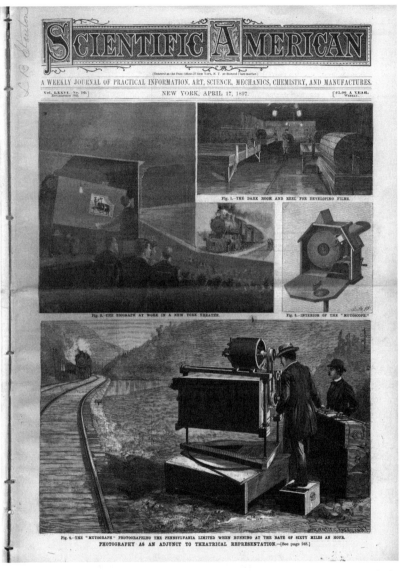

FIGURE 17. Republicans invested heavily in the American Mutoscope Company, which vigorously promoted McKinley in the closing weeks of the 1896 presidential campaign. The filming and projecting of one of its most successful films, *Empire State Express*, is here featured on the front page of *Scientific American*, April 17, 1897.

FIGURE 18. The official premiere of the biograph took place at Hammerstein's Olympia under the auspices of the Republican National Committee. Byron Company (New York, NY) Theatre, Olympia, B'way, 44th & 45th Sts., Hammerstein's, 1895. Courtesy the Museum of the City of New York, 41.420.512.

a result, *Empire State Express* was moved down to conclude the program: "The cheers that greeted the picture and its repetition were as great as those for McKinley."[39] The biograph projector was designed so that only the final film could be repeated, further suggesting that *Empire State Express* was the picture that actually concluded the film program. (However, it seems likely that at some point a second print of *McKinley at Home* was discreetly added to the program reel so it too could be repeated.

Biograph's program at the Olympia consisted of a number of individual "attractions," and to this extent conforms to the "cinema of attractions" paradigm made famous by Tom Gunning, in which film programs use a variety format and are composed of discrete films "supplying pleasure through an exciting spectacle—a unique event, whether fictional or documentary that is of interest in itself."[40] But such a label conceals as much if not more than it reveals. The filmmakers' careful organization of one-shot films produced a highly effective political rhetoric. In constructing this film program, Biograph's showmen were less interested in principles of variety and more concerned with those of associational editing. The final part of the program has more affinity to Sergei Eisenstein's concept of "montage of attractions" than it does to "cinema of attractions": Eisenstein saw montage of attractions as a new editing technique "in which arbitrarily chosen images, independent from the action, would be presented not in chronological sequence but in whatever way would create the maximum psychological impact."[41] In this respect, "the filmmaker should aim to establish in the consciousness of the spectators the elements that would lead them to the idea he wants to communicate. He should attempt to place them in the spiritual state or the psychological situation that would give birth to that idea."[42] As an exhibition service, Biograph programmed, sequenced, and edited these single-shot films into a larger unit. And it did so to powerful, calculated effect—even using a test audience.

Biograph's program for the Republican National Committee built gradually. The relationships between the opening short films were almost poetic. A fire scene was followed by a water scene (of Niagara Falls), which was followed by a hot kissing scene. The stage kiss from *Trilby* was followed by a stage toast from *Rip Van Winkle*. An African American woman giving her baby a vigorous bath was followed by another water scene of Niagara Falls. Biograph had probably not previously shown the two Niagara Falls films, but it had screened the other four. Most of the pictures had antecedents in films by rival companies, although very few members of the audience would have seen them. *Trilby and Little Billee* was Biograph's answer to *The John C. Rice-May Irwin Kiss*, the most popular film subject of the previous five months. *Joseph Jefferson, in Toast Scene from Rip Van Winkle* employed a medium shot—a closer view that echoed the intimate framing of the Rice-Irwin film. Likewise the Edison company had already filmed Niagara Falls, the results of which were mixed but still widely screened. Biograph's versions were far superior in quality. The first half of the program thus allowed spectators to assess and appreciate the technical achievements of the biograph and its films—its large, steady image and comparative lack of flicker. The program to this point was light in tone, even playful. It was a preparation for what followed.

The second half of the program generated much greater intensity, just as the earlier film of the rapids leading to the falls was followed by the powerful scene of Niagara Falls itself, thereby creating a retrospective pairing. Narrative progress was implied, but now the water was at its most forceful and dramatic, offering a majestic view and potent symbol of America's natural grandeur (significantly, the film was titled *Niagara, American Falls*). These two Niagara films anticipated two subsequent pairings: the pictures of the McKinley and Hobart parade as followed by McKinley at his home as well as the repeated projection of *Empire State Express*. The powerful movement of the falls was replaced by the stream of Republicans marching in the McKinley-Hobart parade. At least one reviewer made this connection, though offering a less obvious, audio-related association. According to the *New York Times* reporter, "McKinley paraders tramped through Canton streets, and a New-York assemblage applauded them to the echo. Niagara Falls made a realistic pouring picture, but their noise in the original could not be much louder than the cheers that greeted the picture of them."[43] In the mind of this reviewer, and undoubtedly other spectators, there was a dynamic relationship between these two single-shot scenes.

Certainly the audience's response to the paired campaign films was widely covered. According to the Republican *Mail and Express*,

> The scene of the McKinley and Hobart parade at Canton called forth great applause, but when a few minutes later the audience caught sight of the next President himself, "in the flesh," pandemonium broke loose for five minutes. Men stood up in their seats and yelled with might and main, and flags were waved by dainty hands that would fain cast a vote on November 3, for the good cause. To satisfy the audience the Major was brought forth again with like result. There he stood on his much-betrampled lawn at Canton, talking with his son [*sic*]. Leisurely he read a telegram of congratulations, and then turning he came toward the excited audience, until it seemed as though he were about to step down into their very midst. But at that moment came the edge of the curtain, and he vanished round the corner to address a delegation of workingmen.[44]

The New York Tribune likewise reported,

> The biggest part of the enthusiasm began when a view of a McKinley and Hobart parade in Canton was shown. The cheering was incessant as long as the line was passing across the screen, and it grew much greater when the title of the next picture appeared: "Major McKinley at Home." Major McKinley was seen to come down the steps of his house with his secretary. The secretary handed him a paper which he opened and read. Then he took off his hat and advanced to meet a visiting delegation.[45]

As the *New York Times* made clear, it was as if the audience has been transported to Canton *and* at the same time McKinley had been transported to Hammerstein's Olympia: "McKinley stepped out of his house

FIGURE 19. Frames of *McKinley at Home* and *Parade, Canton, Ohio*, taken on September 18, 1896. From the *Biograph Picture Catalog*. Courtesy the Museum of Modern Art, New York.

in Canton, and strolling down his lawn, seemed to smile in appreciation of the roar that greeted his appearance."[46]

Showing a film of the Empire State Express train was a brilliant conclusion. After all, New York *is* the Empire state, and so New York was metaphorically moving full speed ahead for McKinley. It might also be seen as Biograph's version of the advancing prow of the battleship that concluded Sergei Eisenstein's *Battleship Potemkin* (1925). The Empire State was moving full speed ahead for McKinley. Or, like the express train, the Republican candidate was an unstoppable force. And yet— here American film programs were already ambiguous and open to mul- tiple, often mutually inclusive interpretations—the train was also like the Biograph motion picture system: an impressive technological marvel that was hailed for the absence of flicker and "jump" noticeable in its competitors. The repetition of *Empire State Express* moved the pro- gram beyond McKinley (without, however, leaving him behind) to reas- sert and equate the power of American technology and industry with the Biograph motion picture system—even as the superior technology was linked to the Sound Money politics of the Republicans.

The fortunes of Biograph's high-quality exhibitions and the business- man's candidate were linked. "No good Republican or upholder of sound money doctrine can afford to miss the lifelike representation of their champion on the lawn of his home at Canton," declared the *Mail and Express*.[47] Theatergoers who had been distracted by politics were brought back into the vaudeville house as paying customers. Indeed, for the next two weeks, Republicans poured into Hammerstein's Olympia, wanting a glimpse of their candidate "in the flesh." McKinley's front porch served as a modest counterpart to the Olympia's stage, which it seemed to momentarily replace. McKinley's virtual self served as a surrogate for his absent self. His absent presence could miraculously appear on stage (on screen) at the front of the theater, acting as a relay between the man in Canton and the spectators in the theater. This was an astute way to pro- mote McKinley and the Biograph exhibition service at the same time.

Oscar Hammerstein was another early investor in the American Mutoscope Company,[48] and one wonders, given the similarities of their titles, if Sandow's Olympia was intended to play at the Olympia Music Hall before the company was disbanded. If so, Hammerstein needed to assemble a new vaudeville bill, which included the biograph. The strongman Samson—Sandow's former teacher and current rival—may have been a last-minute substitute. On the other hand, several of the performers had been held over. This included Ludwig Amann, the impersonator who "prepared the way for enthusiastic outbursts by giv- ing lifelike representations of McKinley and Palmer."[49] He had been performing these impersonations for almost a month, and his act was well suited for this avidly Republican crowd. From the outset, Amann's "likeness of Mr. McKinley was received with great cheering, and the likeness of Mr. Bryan with some applause and much more hissing."[50]

The biograph's debut at Olympia Music Hall seemingly was a mixture of careful planning and last-minute improvisation. Hammerstein's advertisements in the Sunday newspaper mentioned the biograph but offered no hint of what was about to occur. Indeed, the theatrical sections of several weekend newspapers failed to mention it as among the coming week's entertainers.[51] This may have been a calculated effort to conceal the Republicans' *coup de theatre* from the Bryan Democrats in order to ensure that they did not match, preempt, or otherwise disrupt it. As in any struggle—whether military or political—surprise was an important element. Or was it due to last-minute haste and Hammerstein's uncertainty as to the biograph's reception? A preview screening on Sunday evening undoubtedly generated greater confidence and excitement.[52] A reliably Republican newspaper finally revealed Biograph's coup on the very afternoon of the event. A lengthy announcement in the *New York Mail and Express* began,

MAJOR M'KINLEY'S SHADOW

A NOTABLE GATHERING OF NOTABLE REPUBLICANS WILL WITNESS ITS PRODUCTION TO-NIGHT IN THIS CITY

Major William McKinley will appear tonight in New York before a great throng of people, which will include members of the Republican National Committee, and in all probability, Mr. and Mrs. Garret A. Hobart. Major McKinley will not make a speech. He will talk with a friend, and then retire to his dwelling, which it may be remarked, will appear with him.

The new wonder in instantaneous photography and enlarged reproduction of photographic plates, called the biograph, is the medium through which the distinguished statesman will make his appearance, apparently on the lawn of his house in Canton, full life size, and in action so perfectly natural, that only the preinformed will know that they are looking upon shadow and not substance.[53]

McKinley, who was rooted in Canton, Ohio, was to make an almost miraculous visit to New York City and be greeted by his vice presidential running mate. Moreover, the candidate's beloved homestead would travel with him.

Although the *New York Dramatic Mirror* reported that Garret Hobart was in the audience, he probably did not attend, since other newspapers failed to mention his presence.[54] With McKinley's motion picture image now acting as an effective intermediary, the need for a prominent politician to represent him was greatly reduced. In this respect vice presidential candidate Hobart's presence was suddenly less necessary. The normally Democratic *New York Times* gave an extensive, firsthand account of the evening and the many prominent people in attendance.[55] (See document 9 in the appendix.) The mix was telling. Some were Republicans associated with New York Senator Thomas C. Platt, who had opposed McKinley's nomination, which suggests that the event served as a public display of party unity. The crowd of patrons associated with the New York Central Railroad—*Empire State Express* was a film they had sponsored—was also more connected to this event than one might assume, given that the corporation's president, Chauncey Depew, was a Republican power broker. Several prominent Republicans, such as Horace Porter and Charles W. Hackett, were also railroad executives. Although Abner McKinley went unmentioned, he almost certainly attended but stayed discreetly in the background. Some besides Hobart did not attend: Marcus Hanna and Theodore Roosevelt were both busy campaigning in Chicago.[56] Depew was presumably absent that evening, though the famous storyteller and railroad executive doubtlessly saw the films on another occasion. Despite such no-shows, the event brought together an array of powerful business and political elites, who were often one and the same. To follow McKinley with an image of the onrushing Empire State Express was certainly fraught with meaning.

For those who could not afford the time or money to travel to Ohio to see the Republican candidate, the opportunity to see McKinley's virtual self at Hammerstein's Olympia continued for a second week; attracting large crowds, it invariably roused "the greatest enthusiasm."[57] Republicans and the New York Central Railroad continued to flood the music hall with supporters. The Republican Club bought the whole tier of box seats for the October 21 performance, while the New York Central Railroad purchased two hundred seats for the following evening.[58] The New York Central Railroad promoted itself and its Republican candidate at the same time—with the American Mutoscope Company the indirect beneficiary of both causes.

Biograph left Hammerstein's theater unexpectedly after a two-week run (October 12–24) and promptly reopened at Koster & Bial's Music Hall on October 26—again with little advance notice.[59] This change in venue has an intriguing backstory, all the more so since Hammerstein's theater would provide a home for pro-Bryan forces on election night. Oscar Hammerstein was not simply locked in a bitter rivalry with John Koster and Albert Bial around their competing music halls (competing for talent as well as patrons); Hammerstein had once managed Koster

& Bial's and was in a bitter dispute over a debt that Bial still owed him.[60] Was some arrangement worked out so that Hammerstein would stop offering vaudeville and no longer compete directly with Koster & Bial's, in exchange for some form of financial reimbursement? Did Koster and Bial get the biograph as some part of this negotiation? In any case, Hammerstein abandoned vaudeville a week after the biograph's departure and reopened the Olympia Music Hall as the Olympia Auditorium.

Koster & Bial's promoted the biograph and the Barrison Sisters as their headline acts. By today's standards at least, this was a rather unlikely pairing. Scandal and controversy was swirling around the five Barrisons, who did a fair amount of indecent stripping onstage—though not quite enough to get them thrown into jail. (Apparently they stopped well short of what they had been doing in Europe.) Although no one seemed to object to McKinley's image sharing the stage with the almost-naked Lona Barrison, it was perhaps fortuitous that Biograph had no official relation with the Republican Party. On the other hand, it makes clear the extent to which both politics and music hall entertainment were still largely homosocial activities. It is also worth noting that Koster & Bial's variety program also featured the African American comedians Bert Williams and George Walker in their first appearance on the vaudeville stage.[61] But were there black Republicans in the music hall's seats? In a disconcerting way, these two burnt cork comedians had their motion picture counterpart in Biograph's *A Hard Wash*.

The *Mail and Express* declared, "The Biograph will have its first thoroughly adequate and complete presentation in New York at Koster & Bial's."[62] What would make the Koster & Bial's screening superior to the Olympia's is unclear, though it was mentioned that *Empire State Express* would be shown in color. Not surprisingly the *New York Herald* reported, "The Biographe's view of Major McKinley was an immediate hit."[63] As Election Day approached, political demonstrations reached a fever pitch, inside as well as outside the theater. The biograph "took best" with the audience on the day before the election. However, one "new thing" occurred "in that portion of [the exhibition] where a picture is shown of Major McKinley walking down the lawn in front of his Canton home, in earnest conversation with a friend."[64] A Bryan supporter jeered at the image. "Mr. Bryan's friend hissed in his feeble way, and then there came a sudden thunderclap of cheering which echoed the applause of Saturday's parade, and continued for several minutes," reported the *Mail and Express*. "The picture was shown again to the patriotic audience, and the popocrat was observed to escape hurriedly past the box office, where they do not furnish return checks."[65] McKinley's silent, virtual self was once again one of the candidate's most effective surrogates and turned an evening at the theater into a campaign rally.

What did Biograph's McKinley program achieve in the three and a half weeks between its unveiling and the election? Opening night was an entertainment for the party faithful and big donors to McKinley's campaign. In the stress of the campaign, it offered them reassurance, a sense of camaraderie and momentary release from business and political anxieties. It was also designed to generate enthusiasm and so to inspire those present to donate still more money to the Republican campaign in its closing weeks: Cornelius N. Bliss, treasurer of the Republican National Committee, was not just there to see some films. We might also calculate attendance: Hammerstein's Olympia Music Hall had a seating capacity of 3,815. Koster & Bial's Music Hall had 3,748 seats.[66] With matinees and evening programs, these theaters might have averaged 5,000 patrons a day. With no Sunday entertainments, this meant a run of twenty or twenty-one days. Perhaps 100,000 tickets were sold, with some patrons inevitably repeats. With ticket prices between 25¢ for gallery seats and $1.50 for those in the orchestra, the venue appealed to those with disposable income. And clearly most of those in attendance were anti-Bryan if not strictly pro-McKinley. This number roughly equaled the number who walked in the McKinley Sound Money Parade on October 31.[67] Perhaps the voters whom Biograph's program was most likely to influence directly were Gold Standard Democrats wavering between voting for Palmer or McKinley. Enjoying a certain amount of press coverage, these screenings underscored Republican energy and innovation. Clearly McKinley and the Republicans were up to date: they knew how to move boldly and to connect with new technological innovations of the highest quality. These screenings demonstrated a "can-do" attitude that was needed in order to renew the nation's economic prosperity. The direct impact of the program was limited because Biograph was only able to service one venue due to a shortage of projectors. Although Abner McKinley must have hoped to present *McKinley at Home* in other major cities, this constraint was less critical to the electoral outcome given the unprecedented support the Republicans enjoyed from newspapers. Rhetorically powerful, the Biograph's McKinley program contained compelling symbolic value.

CAMPAIGN-RELATED FILMS AT THE EDISON
MANUFACTURING COMPANY

The first campaign-related motion picture was not made by the American Mutoscope Company but by the Edison Manufacturing Company. This was *Blackton Sketches, No. 2*, also known as *Political Cartoon*. Shot in early August, it showed the cartoonist and lightning sketch artist J. Stuart Blackton "drawing pictures of McKinley and President Cleveland."[68] Such a sketch aligned the Republican candidate with the Democratic president, implicitly suggesting that Cleveland supporters who favored Sound Money should now back McKinley—and that McKinley would be Cleveland's successor to the presidency. This was one of three lightning sketches that Blackton made for Edison and the Vitascope Company, which began to screen films in Proctor's two New York vaudeville houses in early September. *Inventor Edison Sketched by World Artist*, shown during the second week of its run, proved immensely popular and may have precluded the inclusion of *Political Cartoon* in these theaters. It is also likely that associating McKinley with Cleveland could have been seen as problematic from various political perspectives.

Certainly Edison personnel seemed to be, like their Biograph brethren, pro-McKinley. They made *Pat and the Populist* (September 1896), in which "Pat ascends a ladder with a hood of bricks. Is approached by a Populist politician. Shows his displeasure by dropping bricks on the politician."[69] Pat is clearly a working-class Irishman—the kind of traditionally Democratic voter that Republicans hoped to win over to their candidate. In this film, he had already switched! (While German Americans left the Democratic Party in large numbers as a result of Bryan's candidacy, the Irish tended to stay despite Republican efforts.)[70] The Vitascope Company screened *Pat and the Populist* in Proctor's vaudeville theaters the very week that Biograph first showed *McKinley at Home*—suggesting a rather unified pro-McKinley outlook on the vaudeville front. However, the kind of carefully constructed, politically potent film program that Biograph deployed was nowhere in evidence. By this time the vitascope had been at Proctor's theaters for more than a month, and the Vitascope Company was simply adding new or unfamiliar views each week. It would be unfair to suggest that the ordering of these films was entirely random, but their succession was seemingly based on principles of variety. The program fits comfortably within a cinema of attractions paradigm, and for reasons that made good commercial sense: when *Pat and the Populist* was shown as a brief, self-contained comedy, it was unlikely to deeply offend a pro-Bryan patron.

The Edison Manufacturing Company and the Vitascope Company faced a somewhat fraught situation in respect to the 1896 political season. First, they were supplying films to a much wider network of licensed exhibitors, many of whom were in states where Bryan was extremely popular. These showmen were eager for motion pictures of Bryan. Second, the Biograph and Edison interests quickly established a competitive rivalry, which was evident in their choice of similar yet competing subject matter. For instance, Biograph had its kiss film (*Trilby and Little Billee*) to counter Edison's *The John C. Rice-May Irwin Kiss*. After the American Mutoscope Company formed an alliance with the New York Central Railroad Company (filming its prestige train, the Empire State Express), the Edison Manufacturing Company affiliated with the Leigh Valley Railroad (filming its famed train, the Black Diamond Express, soon after the election). Hypothetically Bryan should have been the Edison candidate![71] And whatever the political sentiments at the Edison and Vitascope companies, he was.

When Bryan left Philadelphia on his whistle-stop tour on September 23 he was accompanied by Johnston Cornish, national committeeman of the Democratic Party and then running for Congress, and State Senator William Daly, who had been a delegate to the Democratic National Convention and chair of the Democratic State Convention in 1896. On their way to Brooklyn, they made several stops in New Jersey, first at the small town of Washington, where Cornish had been a popular mayor. When they reached Morristown, Bryan told his audience that "a financial system that commends itself to the wealthy only is a curse to any land."[72] The candidate paused briefly in Orange, New Jersey, where, as he later recounted, "Mr. Thomas A. Edison took a picture of the crowd and moving train, the views secured have since been exhibited throughout the country by means of the vitascope."[73] There must have been considerable coordination between Bryan's campaign and James H. White, who was in charge of film production at the Vitascope Company and would soon head Edison's Kinetograph Department. The film was marketed as *Bryan Train Scene at Orange*, "showing Mr. Bryan addressing a crowd of people from the rear platform of a moving train."[74] Bryan clearly took some pride in this coup, which occurred a mere five days after Biograph filmed McKinley. It may also be worth noting that just as Bryan toured the nation at a frenetic pace, the Edison film was also shown in diverse locations around the country—in contrast to McKinley, who stayed in his Canton abode while *McKinley at Home* was only shown in a single New York City venue at any given time.

The vitascope first exhibited *Bryan Train Scene at Orange* in Proctor's New York City theaters on October 19, one week after *McKinley at Home* was first shown at the Olympia. As the *Mail and Express* reported, "Edison's vitascope has new wonders to reveal in the way of motion pictures, including a graphic view of Bryan making a campaign speech at Orange. Every movement and gesture of the boy orator is reproduced with startling accuracy."[75] The film was offered as a news-related item, as it provided a chance for people to see Bryan in a representative pose. The screening had none of the orchestrated enthusiasm provided for *McKinley at Home,* but was simply part of a program that offered variety—a series of discrete, unrelated attractions in which "other new animated views [were] washday at home, the feeding of chickens, a love scene, a spirited fire rescue, the landing of a Rockaway excursion, and some humorous subjects."[76] However, if there was no montage of attractions, there may well have been some associational editing. At least one should not dismiss the possibility that Bryan orating to an enthusiastic crowd was preceded by a woman doing the wash and followed by a girl feeding the chickens. (We should remember that Norman C. Raff and Frank Gammon were Ohio businessmen, and Raff was from McKinley's hometown of Canton.) The very mundane nature of these scenes discreetly deflated Bryan. Indeed, a clever ordering of films could have turned *Bryan Train Scene at Orange* into just another "humorous subject." Moreover, a long and probably unnecessary delay between the initial filming and the Proctor screening reeks of subtle sabotage, which enabled McKinley to become the first US presidential candidate to appear on the screen, with all the associated benefits.

When the *New York Sun* learned about the filming of *Bryan Train Scene at Orange,* the newspaper offered a highly satirical item in which motion pictures (including synchronous sound recordings with the phonograph) would ensure that "his speech is to fill the land, and every man, woman and child is to see and hear him."[77] Motion pictures provided an absurdist extension of Bryan's whistle-stop tour (itself dependent on the preeminently modern form of transportation—the train), for these hypothetical legions of Americans would see it in the out-of-date peep-hole kinetoscope. (See document 10 in the appendix.) Synchronizing sound and image was still a distant, fanciful dream—not unlike Bryan's hope for presidential success, the *New York Sun* seemed to

FIGURE 20. William Jennings Bryan's long-winded oratory and whistle-stop tour were constantly mocked by the pro-McKinley press. "Blowing Himself Around the Country," *Puck*, September 16, 1896. Courtesy the Library of Congress.

suggest. Bryan's candidacy thus offered a mixture of the outmoded past and the fanciful future. When the actual film was shown at Proctor's, the *Sun* used this occasion to lampoon both Bryan and the film, suggesting that the boy orator's speechifying before the motion picture camera had created a destructive windstorm of extraordinary force: "Immediately the ballast of the roadbed was laid bare, trees beside the tracks shed their foliage, and all this mass of sand, leaves and loose rails was lifted to go hurling ahead of the express train straight at the recording apparatus."[78] In this dreamlike burlesque, a rail landed on the neck of the photographer, knocking him out. Temporarily revived, he restarted his machine and shot the film then being shown at Proctor's. (See document 11 in the appendix.) Although *Bryan Train Scene at Orange* was an appropriate counterpart to *McKinley at Home*, exhibition companies and Republican newspapers treated them very differently.

PHONOGRAPH/TELEPHONE/BICYCLE

Cinema was one of many novelties mobilized for the 1896 presidential election. McKinley's campaign embraced them with a passion, providing a crucial subtext of his campaign. The way out of economic depression, his campaign implied, was through the mobilization of new technologies, particularly new forms of communication and transportation. This spirit of innovation became linked to Republican assertions that Sound Money and a protective tariff would benefit all Americans. Bryan, an advocate for the farmer and the workingman, took limited advantage of these emergent forms. Not only was he more eager to discuss income disparity, but the mobilization of new technologies already assumed a degree of financial affluence that was beyond the reach of most Bryan supporters as well as the available funds for his campaign. It is hard to imagine his backers having either the vision or the resources to fund a media start-up—with the notable exception of William Randolph Hearst, who was busy building his newspaper empire and becoming interested in motion pictures. Given the candidate's fame as an orator, it was not so much that Bryan embraced the phonograph as that the phonograph business embraced Bryan—if only as a source of potential revenue.[79]

Given that McKinley and Bryan were both renowned orators, it is hardly surprising that the nascent recording industry took advantage of the 1896 presidential campaign. Newspaper items are fragmentary and only hint at these activities. According to one report in early August,

Republicans were already using the phonograph in large cities to supply "campaign songs for the amusement and edification of enthusiastic Republicans."[80] This certainly touches on one characteristic of the 1896 election: song was a frequent component of Republican campaign rallies. There had been campaign songs for Cleveland and Harrison in 1892, but they did not enjoy the same prominence. The American Protective Tariff League, which had lost interest in the illustrated lecture and never mentioned motion pictures, filled the pages of the *American Economist* with lyrics and sheet music for campaign songs.[81] It also underscores another Republican campaign strategy—to align its candidate with the entertainment industry.

Bryan's unanticipated nomination put a new focus on oratory and its suitability for audio reproducibility. In early August it was suggested to Arkansas Senator James K. Jones, chair of the Democratic National Committee, that "Candidate Bryan and other noted silver speakers make ten or fifteen minute speeches for enrollment on cylinders of the graphophone."[82] Recordings of Bryan's speeches, it was suggested, would provide the core elements for phonograph concerts, which had been a moderately popular form of entertainment for the previous five or six years. This proposal was novel only to the extent that it was applied to political campaigning. Phonograph concerts often took place in lecture halls or even church meeting rooms and could be presented to reasonably large audiences. Baptists, Methodists, and other conservative Protestant groups generally saw this kind of clean entertainment as an effective way to counter the seductive and salacious attractions of the amusement world. They were much more respectable than the nickel-in-the slot phonographs that relied on private listening (with earphones) and were often located in barrooms and other places of doubtful repute. Phonograph concerts, which presumably would be free and open to the public (though admission fees could be charged if necessary), would provide a novel kind of campaign rally.

The phonograph angle may well have been explored when Bryan came to New York City to deliver his August 12 notification speech in Madison Square Garden (an event that Bryan Democrats hoped might be as successful at unifying the party as was Cleveland's visit to Madison Square Garden on a similar occasion four years earlier). Although the principle of recording Bryan's best-known speeches had a superficial logic, the available recording technology was still quite crude, as was the ability to make multiple copies, and it was impractical for Bryan to make actual recordings. Why should Bryan speak forcefully and repeatedly into a phonograph horn when he could use that voice to reach large crowds of people? Hiring skilled phonograph exhibitors might also have proved difficult. The issue was only partially one of expense. The number of qualified individuals was probably quite small, and finding such persons who were sufficiently loyal to Bryan would not have been easy. Even a professional phonograph exhibitor who favored Bryan would have been reluctant to alienate his Republican patrons. Perhaps there were a few grassroots efforts by semiprofessionals or even amateurs, but nothing that reached the major daily papers. The phonograph concert idea went nowhere. Instead Democrats gave wide circulation to Bryan's speeches in printed form. It was cheaper.

Independent entrepreneurs in the phonograph industry were the ones to exploit Bryan's political oratory. Companies could generate phonograph cylinders of the candidate's speeches and then sell them for use, primarily in nickel-in-the-slot machines located in phonograph parlors, saloons, or other public spaces. As Richard Bauman and Patrick Feaster have pointed out, such recordings may have offered speeches by Bryan but someone else recited them—presumably a vocalist familiar with the techniques of phonograph recording.[83] An 1896 catalogue from the United States Phonograph Company lists four speeches "as delivered by" Bryan:

HON. W. J. BRYAN'S CROWN OF THORNS AND CROSS OF GOLD SPEECH. The Peroration of the famous Address that won him the Presidential Nomination at Chicago. Very loud and distinct. Applause. No Announcement.

HON. W. J. BRYAN'S SPEECH AT THE NOTIFICATION MEETING IN NEW YORK. A part of his Address at the great Demonstration in Madison Square Garden, New York, on August 12th. Very loud. Applause. No Announcement.

HON. W. J. BRYAN'S REPLY TO THE CHARGE OF ANARCHY. From the Candidate's great Speech in Hornellsville, before 15,000 people in the open air. Very loud and distinct. Applause. No Announcement.

HON. W. J. BRYAN'S OPINION OF THE WALL STREET GOLD-BUGS AND SYNDICATES. As delivered at the Buffalo Ratification Meeting, where he declared that the Creator did not make Financiers of better mud than he used for other people. Very loud and distinct. Applause. No Announcement.[84]

Like *McKinley at Home* and *Bryan Train Scene at Orange*, these recordings offered an attenuated presence of the candidates, who remained absent. They acted as intermediaries, manifestations, and relays between the candidates and the voters.

FIGURE 21. The speeches of Bryan and McKinley were featured in phonograph arcades such as this one (circa 1895). Experienced phonograph orators, not the candidates, did the actual recordings. Courtesy Edison National Historic Site and Paul Spehr.

Records of Bryan's speeches were in circulation by late August, playing in a New York phonograph parlor and similar venues around the nation. They were among the many phonograph cylinders that patrons could pay to hear, and their inclusion would not have been considered an overt form of politicking on the part of phonograph entrepreneurs. Bryan, unlike McKinley, was himself a novelty, and his famed speeches aroused curiosity among people of all political stripes. However, they certainly became a topic of political commentary. A speaker at a Democratic rally in Los Angeles approvingly referenced one of the cylinders.[85] Not surprisingly, the loyally Republican *New York Tribune* mocked a "counterfeit" of Bryan's "Cross of Gold" speech and compared it to a Coney Island fakir: "It does not bear any resemblance to the Democratic candidate's oratorical efforts and the applause with which it is punctuated is so feeble that it could not possibly be mistaken for the storm of approval which swept the Chicago Convention off its feet."[86] These recordings were very popular, with customers lining up to listen. If patrons complained that it was not Bryan's voice, the manager pointed out that the sign did not say that it was: it promised his speech, not his voice. Thus, "there is no refunding slot, and no apparent redress."[87] In fact, the widespread practice of using intermediaries—including reenactments of boxing matches by expert pugilists in vaudeville houses and on film—was widespread, and these phonograph recordings functioned within that accepted practice.

The North American Phonograph Company also offered a McKinley speech:

> MAJOR McKINLEY'S SPEECH ON THE THREAT TO DEBASE THE NATIONAL CURRENCY. As delivered by the distinguished Republican Nominee at Canton, July 11th. Very loud and distinct. Applause. No Announcement.[88]

In phonograph parlors that offered a chance to listen to "comic songs, political speeches and other things of interest," this McKinley recording was often paired with a Bryan cylinder.[89] The two could readily be compared in a partisan fashion. "Never were two speeches more utterly dissimilar in every way," remarked the pro-Republican *Chicago Tribune*. "Maj. McKinley's was a thoughtful and dispassionate, though feeling, utterance on the occasion of receiving a greater honor. It was spoken without any great striving for oratorical effect, much in the manner that Lincoln delivered his addresses. Mr. Bryan's speech was almost wholly a striving for emotional awakening, looking more especially to stirring oratorical expression than to the ideas expressed."[90] The *Tribune* was constructing a binary in which McKinley was characterized as rational and Bryan as impulsive. By mid-October the novelty of these phonograph recordings was wearing out, as other cylinders received more patronage, at least if one Los Angeles emporium is any indication.[91]

There were various reasons why the phonograph companies favored Bryan: his reputation as a speaker, which roused curiosity across party lines; the interest of rural populations in the Populist message; and the well-publicized desire of the Bryan campaign to reach voters directly, bypassing the press, which, as previous citations underscore, represented Bryan and his speeches in a highly mediated and generally unsympathetic manner. There was also a shortage of surrogate speakers to spread Bryan's message. The phonograph became a new type of surrogate. Despite persistent suggestions that the Democrats should sponsor specialized phonograph concerts featuring speeches and campaign songs on Bryan's behalf, nothing along these lines was apparently done. This reflected the Democrats' limited funding, the thinness of their staffing, and also their relative lack of interest in directly employing emergent forms of technological reproducibility. Although audio reproduction was an impressive achievement, the recordings were of brief duration and the vocal quality far inferior to that of Bryan himself. Bryan and his campaign emphasized live oratory where his voice—augmented by his physical and thus visual presence—had maximum force. Talking directly to people also fostered notions of authenticity and truth telling.

The Democrats were content to have others take films or make phonograph cylinders and then let commercial showmen exploit them as they saw fit. In this respect the amusement impresarios who offered cylinders of both Bryan and McKinley echoed those who exhibited *Bryan Train Scene at Orange* and *Pat and the Populist* in a variety format. Cautiously introducing politics into the amusement realm, they were careful not to become too partisan lest they alienate patrons of different political persuasions. This approach was unlike the American Mutoscope Company's carefully structured pro-McKinley programs at Hammerstein's and Koster & Bial's music halls or the Democrats' unrealized campaign-sponsored phonograph concerts.

Long-Distance Telephone

The long-distance telephone was another emerging technology that Republicans mobilized for presidential campaigning. McKinley's front-porch campaign had serious limitations, which telephone aficionados nevertheless turned to the candidate's advantage. As the previous chapter showed, for the 1892 campaign the Democrats organized a huge parade of party loyalists who marched by the reviewing stand where they were greeted by their candidate, Grover Cleveland. The mobile Bryan could continue that tradition in 1896, but not McKinley. Republicans had to be content with organizing a succession of small parades in Canton, conducted by visiting delegations. These were an inadequate substitute for the massive displays of Sound Money loyalty that Republicans were eagerly organizing in many cities. How could the Republicans directly connect McKinley to his enthusiastic base? The telephone offered an unexpected solution.

It is not entirely surprising that this innovative use of the telephone took place in Chicago, given that the state of Illinois was critical to the 1896 election. The Chicago Business-Men's Sound Money Association was formed on September 9. Its president declared that Bryan threatened the very existence of the government by waging a communistic war against it. The organization's response was to plan a massive parade on Chicago Day, October 9, which commemorated the anniversary of the Great Chicago Fire.[92] Preparations took several forms. To ensure turnout, Republican operatives wanted Chicago Day to become a city-wide holiday. They asked City Hall to close its offices for the day and businesses to give "a full holiday on full pay to all employés who would turn out for the parade."[93] The organizers also wanted McKinley to attend as their guest so that he could witness this parade that they estimated would attract 100,000 marchers.[94] The Republican *Chicago Tribune* promoted the event with frequent updates. The Electrical Division of the Business-Men's Sound Money Association promised to introduce some appropriate novelties: for instance, having the marshals of each division ride in electric carriages (i.e., electric cars) rather than use horses, or holding the parade at night so they could use electrical illumination. Finally, when McKinley proved unwilling to leave his front porch in Canton, they proposed to install telephone transmitters at key points along the line of march and connect these by long-distance telephone lines to Sound Money men in the East so that marchers could demonstrate their enthusiasm.[95]

The telephone idea was quickly seized on, and it was decided that McKinley and Hobart would be "be present by telephone":

> The transmitters will be fitted with immense funnels, probably from three to six feet across, and signals will be given for each passing organization to shout its "battle cry" in unison or for any distinctive vocal demonstration it wishes to make.
>
> In this way it will be possible for marching clubs to pay their personal respects to McKinley and Hobart at long range, and for the candidates and their friends to imagine themselves settled on a grand stand in the midst of the demonstration.
>
> Banners will be stretched across the streets above the telephone transmitters calling attention to what they are there for. One line that has been suggested is: "Here's the Place to Tell McKinley What You Think of Him." Another one may bear these words: "Now Tell Hobart That Chicago Says Howdy."[96]

The telephone lines went not only to McKinley's home but to Republican headquarters in New York and possibly some other cities. The *Chicago Tribune* reported that "an army, 68,307 strong, marched through the heart of Chicago yesterday and won a victory for itself under the flag of Sound Money and Protection."[97] The *New York Sun* put the number of marchers at a slightly more modest 60,000.[98] The *New York Tribune* reduced it still further, to 50,000.[99] The novel deployment of the telephone was likewise declared a success despite some challenges. A float snapped one of the wires holding up the main funnel-shaped horn, requiring backups to be deployed. A nearby counter demonstration of Bryan men tried to have their voices reach McKinley but their chants were, not surprisingly, drowned out by the marchers.[100]

Many newspapers had reporters based in Canton, so the event was widely reported from that end as well. On the morning of the parade, the local manager of the Central Union telephone company installed two groups of six "telephone ear trumpets," one set in the candidate's library and another set in Mrs. McKinley's waiting room. But it was difficult to hear Chicago's cheering marchers due to the constant brouhaha of well-wishers outside the McKinley home (in particular the east Tennessee delegation). Nonetheless, the major was called to the phone at 10:52 a.m. and "showed great pleasure at the volume of enthusiastic sounds that reached him over the 400 miles of wire."[101] In New York, the sound from Chicago filled Republican headquarters:

> Mr. Hobart was one of the first to listen to the uproar over the wire. He sat down to talk with Mr. Hanna, and suddenly Mr. Hanna broke off and there could be heard the rattle and bang of a drum corps, and then a band crashed in with "Marching Through Georgia." Mr. Hobart spent almost a half-hour listening to the tumult in Chicago. Then Mr. Quay took a turn, and suddenly as some of the noise was borne faintly to him his face wreathed in a smile and he said: "Wonder how Altgeld likes that?"[102]

This telephonic spectacle brought the sounds of Chicago not only to Canton and New York but to small groups of avid Republican listeners in St. Louis, Milwaukee, and "a hundred places in the Central and Western States," if one pro-McKinley newspaper is to be believed. "It was a new idea thus to give distant sections an opportunity to share in a single celebration; but it was in every way a success," the *Chicago Tribune* affirmed.[103] Three days later the biograph debuted at Olympia Music Hall and transported McKinley and his Canton home to New York City. Each of these campaign novelties played with spatial and temporal disjunctions. For McKinley it was as if he was in Chicago reviewing his loyal Sound Money men. And for those in the music hall, it was as if they had been briefly transported to Canton. The biograph was arguably more successful in several respects: it was seen by a few thousand people on opening night and on a daily basis for the balance of the campaign. The press, however, generally gave greater attention to the Chicago telephone experiment not only in the key swing state of Illinois but also throughout the nation.

The use of the telephone as a campaign novelty did have noteworthy precedents in the form of "long distance telephone concerts."[104] A phonograph-telephone concert was held between New York and Philadelphia in February 1889.[105] Others brought Boston and New York into audio proximity. Soon after the American Telephone and Telegraph Company linked New York and Chicago in late 1892, a long-distance telephone concert—instrumental and vocal—was given. The music originated in New York and was received by avid listeners at the Chicago Long Distance Telephone Company's offices.[106] Once again a practice established for entertainment purposes was appropriated for presidential politicking. McKinley's first use of the long-distance telephone for such political purposes may have been more discreet: from his home, the contender quietly listened to various proceedings at the Republican National Convention, including the speech of Ohio Senator Joseph Foraker, who placed his name in nomination.[107]

Despite its flaws (which the Republicans were careful to minimize), the telephone campaign novelty set a new standard. Organizers in other cities were eager to imitate it. If a city's Sound Money parade was of the first order of importance, then McKinley needed to review its marchers telephonically. Pittsburgh held a "monster parade" with 30,000 Sound Money men in line on Sunday, November 1. "On Fifth avenue was placed an immense telephone receiver, which was connected by long distance telephone with Major McKinley's residence so that he could hear the cheers given as the marchers passed."[108] Only at the very end of the campaign was the long-distance telephone used so that people could hear McKinley as he had heard them. Perhaps the quality of the transmission needed improvement or different circumstances were required. In any case, on October 30 Major McKinley listened to the chants of the Commercial Travelers' Sound Money club of Buffalo, gathered together inside an auditorium. He then responded:

> I have heard distinctly from your distant hall your shouts of confidence in victory. I am glad to greet the Commercial Travelers' Sound Money club of the City of Buffalo and speak a word of congratulations to them. I appreciate most highly the splendid work they have done to preserve our currency from taint and the national honor from stain. They were never engaged in a better or nobler cause, and they have the thanks of every patriotic citizen. The contest is now nearing the end, and I join you in the hope and belief that on next Tuesday the overwhelming verdict of the American people will be registered against repudiation and dishonor. The devotion of the people of Buffalo and all New York to all that is good in government is an inspiration to the whole country.[109]

Was this the first "broadcast" by a presidential candidate? Did the force of novelty give greater weight to his declarations? Certainly this use of the long-distance telephone continued to energize McKinley's campaign in its final days. The Republican candidate used the telephone as a way to connect with his distant supporters both literally and symbolically. It was yet another way to demonstrate that he and his campaign were up to date and forward-looking. The telephone, like cinema, was the future, and McKinley embraced it.

The Bicycle

The Republicans' pursuit of innovative campaigning was not limited to their use of new modes of communication. The Republican National Committee had a Wheelmen Department, headquartered in the Boyce Building (owned by W. D. Boyce), devoted to the recruiting and mobilization of bicyclists.[110] The bicycle was an up-to-date form of transportation that was being adopted by the young and the middle class. It was transforming society, providing city dwellers with a new mobility, and loosening social constraints, notably for women (who began to wear bloomers so they could ride their bikes). The well-known patent lawyer Walter H. Chamberlin, who was serving as secretary of the National Wheelmen's McKinley and Hobart Club, was busy setting up local organizations across the country. Associating this popular phenomenon with McKinley was a way to suggest that the candidate was embracing the new and would be responsive to the needs of a modern society.

When the Republican campaign held its first big rally in Chicago, Governor Hastings of Pennsylvania was escorted from his hotel to the speakers' stand by hundreds of bicyclists from half a dozen wheelmen clubs.[111] Chicago Republicans were being organized along military lines, with the wheelmen forming its own division and its leaders given the appropriate military titles—generals, colonels, captains, and so forth. On October 1, 1,500 wheelmen paraded the streets of Chicago.[112] The next day some of them left for Canton to participate in a national wheelmen's delegation, which was greeted by McKinley. Their numbers were estimated at 3,000, with 400 or 500 from Chicago. (Incessant rain had forced many to take the train rather than bike to Canton.)[113] McKinley praised the delegation, noting,

> Political clubs on wheels are novel in political contests and are truly American. Their presence marks a new era in campaign work; and I congratulate you upon the inauguration of this mighty force in American politics. The bicycle is entirely a development of the nineteenth century, and in no age in the history of the world would its benefits and utility have been so quickly

FIGURE 22. McKinley speaks to Chicago bicyclists from his front porch in Canton, Ohio, October 3, 1896. Courtesy the Library of Congress.

and generally acknowledged. In the country of inventions I doubt if any vehicle or means of locomotion was ever so favorably received.[114]

Meanwhile the Republican National Committee declared October 17 to be Wheelmen's Day with parades and special meetings for cyclists to be held in every community in the United States.[115] In Chicago, inclement weather forced repeated postponements, and it was finally decided to hold a wheelmen's rally irrespective of weather on October 24.[116] That evening more than 3,000 cruised down Michigan Avenue. There would have been more except for the late hour (it did not start until 9:30). The long wait was caused by a Republican parade of railroad men, which had to disband before the cyclists could proceed.[117]

Similar efforts were made in New York City, where the McKinley and Hobart Wheelmen's League was particularly active. A recruiting corps cruised the boulevard one evening in early October and passed out membership forms, increasing its numbers. The *Mail and Express* then predicted that "the McKinley and Hobart wheelmen's parade on Thursday

FIGURE 23. An 1896 McKinley-Hobart campaign button features the Republican candidates bicycling their way to the White House. Courtesy the Museum of the City of New York, 96.184.238.

evening [October 8] will be one of the largest they have ever held as it is expected that fully 500 wheelmen will participate." Leaving the Wheelmen's headquarters at 19 West Twenty-Fourth Street, they proceeded by a circuitous route to Sixteenth Street and Broadway (still often referred to as "the Boulevard"), where the league participated in a banner-raising ceremony of the Nineteenth Assembly District.[118] The banner depicted McKinley and Hobart riding a tandem bicycle. Three weeks later, on October 30, the McKinley and Hobart's Wheelmen's League sponsored another bicycle parade, headed by a platoon of bicycle police. Approximately 1,500 bikers participated, starting at Sixty-First Street and Eighth Avenue and heading north to 123rd Street before crossing over to Fifth Avenue and heading down to Washington Square.[119]

The Republicans' organization of wheelmen's clubs for campaign purposes, like the use of the telephone and cinema, was consistent with the emphasis the RNC placed on mobilizing technologies that offered

Scene Off the Statue of Liberty in the Course of the Great Sound-Money Parade.

FIGURE 24. A pro-McKinley naval regatta or marine parade for Sound Money took place in New York Harbor on the evening of October 24, 1896. If Republican newspapers are to be believed, half a million people witnessed the spectacle. *New York Press*, October 25, 1896.

new forms of transportation and communication.[120] If cinema and the telephone could transport McKinley's voice and likeness across space and time, the bicycle metaphorically offered somewhat similar liberating opportunities—the pleasures of increased mobility—for his many supporters. The Bryan Democrats made little or no effort to organize bicyclists on their behalf. Bicycles were a middle-class luxury and beyond the financial means of the working classes and outside the practical needs of the farmers to whom Bryan was making his appeal. Efforts to compete would have only produced embarrassment.

A CELEBRATION OF NOVELTY AND TRADITION, SPECTACLE AND POWER

Although New York newspapers (except for Hearst's *Journal*) claimed that the state would go for McKinley by a comfortable margin, no one was taking any chances. Moreover, friendly competition between Republican organizations in different cities was a core aspect of the national campaign. The activities of a city's wheelmen's clubs or the size of its Sound Money parade became a form of civic boosterism. Likewise there was good-natured rivalry among McKinley and Hobart clubs within a given metropolitan area, each seeking to offer some distinctive twist to their demonstrations and win the most votes for their candidates. Local Republican organizations held numerous rallies on a daily basis. Some of these were in halls and auditoriums, but most took place on street corners to attract passersby and demonstrate the public support for their candidates.[121] If Chicago innovated McKinley's use of the telephone to review massive parades from afar, New York offered another type of novelty on October 24: a Sound Money naval parade.

> A mighty armada, every craft ablaze and spouting fire, moved down the North River last evening through a rain of many colored stars to the roar of rocket batteries and the chorus of harnessed steam.
> The citadel of commerce was speaking for an honest dollar, and speaking with no uncertain sound.
> Half the city was out in the crisp, moonlit air, watching and admiring.
> It was a great water pageant, this of the Shipping and Industrial Sound Money Association—altogether the most picturesque of political demonstrations in the city's history. There were more than two hundred steam vessels in Admiral Miller's fleet.[122]

This remarkable spectacle relied on fireworks and various forms of lighting to make its impression.

One week later, the Saturday before the election, New York Republicans reverted to a traditional campaign ritual and mounted a Sound Money parade or McKinley parade in Lower Manhattan, with so many participants that not all could march. The *Herald* characterized this "Pageant of Patriotism" as the "Greatest Demonstration in the Nation's History."[123] According to the *New York Times*, "100,000 Men March and Shout for Sound Money."[124] The *Brooklyn Eagle* considered that a severe undercount: "They Marched 150,000 Strong," it headlined.[125] Many of the men wore yellow chrysanthemums in their labels and pinned large "gold bugs" to their coats.[126] Although McKinley was anchored in Canton, Republicans once more employed that miracle of modern technology—the telephone—to bridge the spatial gulf. Again, "Major McKinley, at his home in Canton, will review the parade by telephone," as would Hanna from Chicago Republican headquarters.[127] It was announced that "one receiver will be at the reviewing stand, near Madison Square; another will be on Lower Broadway, and the third will probably be placed at the Washington Memorial Arch."[128] In 1892 Cleveland had reviewed a similar parade. This one was much bigger— and bigger than the pro-McKinley parade in Chicago earlier that month.

McKinley used the long-distance telephone to participate in campaign events on October 30 (Buffalo), October 31 (New York), and November 1 (Pittsburgh), but New York's Sound Money parade was the only one of these that was filmed. Although Biograph, Edison, and the International Film Company all shot scenes of the McKinley parade, they failed to show the films before the election. Biograph presented *Sound Money Parade* in the week following McKinley's victory, providing many with an occasion to savor and relive the success of this political demonstration.[129] These postelection screenings indicate ways in which the Republicans, despite their close alliance with the American Mutoscope Company, did not stage their spectacles with motion pictures in mind. If the naval parade had been conducted during daylight hours or the McKinley parade had been staged a week earlier, films of these events could have been used during the closing days of the campaign. These culminating events of the campaign season were designed with several publics in mind: first, those who would participate in the camaraderie of the parade itself; second, local citizens who would witness the actual events; and third, those who would read about them in the mass-circulation dailies, not only in New York but across the country. The Republican campaign was designed to project an unstoppable force, an army of voters who would defeat all who opposed it. In New York it succeeded: although Tammany Hall said New York City would go Democratic by 20,000 votes, McKinley conquered "Democracy's Gibraltar" by a 30,000-vote margin and won New York State by more than 268,000 votes.[130]

WATCHING THE ELECTION RETURNS

On the evening of Election Day 1896, across the nation eager citizens once again gathered outside newspaper office buildings to watch the returns. The crowd that gathered at Printing House Square near New York's City Hall Park "excelled its predecessors by long odds . . . in point of numbers, enthusiasm, and good nature."[131] Each of the five principal newspapers in that location—the *Times*, *Tribune*, *Journal*, *Sun*, and *World*—received returns by special wire in their offices and relayed the information to a nearby stereopticon stand, where it was transposed to slides and displayed. In this way, the newspapers offered returns that were "legible enough to be read 100 yards away."[132]

The *New York Times* reported the manner in which its evening began:

> Four minutes ahead of its contemporaries, THE NEW-YORK TIMES's stereopticon flashed the first message of the New-York City election boards to the canvas. It happened to be favorable to Bryan: "Twelve election districts of

the Thirty-third assembly District gave McKinley 51, Bryan 89, Palmer 2." A shrill yell arose from the rear of the crowd. In a moment every Bryan man in the crowd had joined the chorus, and silver enthusiasts here and there exchanged bon mots at the expense of McKinley. A moment later the flashlight threw a picture of the Republican candidate on the canvas. A thousand throats cheered the picture lustily. Before the tumult died away other bulletins began to come in, and the enthusiasts settled down to business. From that time until far into the night the cheering was continuous. But it came from sound-money throats.[133]

The *Times* also relayed returns to its familiar Madison Square site, where "bulletins will be displayed on the north wall of the building now bearing the electrical advertisement of The Times."[134] This was the front of a building on Twenty-Third Street facing north at the intersection of Fifth Avenue and Broadway—across from where the current Flatiron Building would be built in 1902. Bulletins were "printed on the lantern slides by typewriter, so that all the figures and text can be read with the greatest ease."[135]

The *New York Herald* showed returns on the stereopticon in many parts of the city. A large canvas was stretched across the south end of its new office building on Herald Square, which had opened in 1895. Here the stereopticon under the direction of Henry E. Northrup showed returns while a vitascope managed by the Vitascope Advertising Company, located just south of the Herald Building, screened films during the lulls.

> The white sheet was blank for a moment, and then the interior of a dentist's office with a patient under the torture appeared, life motion, laughter, grimaces, extraction and all.
>
> AMAZED AND AMUSED
>
> "It's Bryan," a leather lunged man yelled. "Pull his teeth now. We've pulled his leg." And the laugh was on the young man from Nebraska. Whirling dancers, breaking surf and melon eating darkies were all produced on the canvas whenever McKinley's march of triumph was not being reflected by the stereopticon. These were indeed living pictures. They lacked but voice, and the vast crowd had voice to spare. How it did roar with laughter over May Irwin's kiss.[136]

The stereopticon had become ubiquitous. Pulitzer's *New York World* had given up on its bulletin boards, and the painted figures of presidential candidates now climbed much smaller ladders than they had in 1892. Instead of climbing the world's tallest building, they merely ran up opposing sides of the main entrance. The *World* had covered the outside of its building with a canvas screen 170 feet high and 60 feet

FIGURE 25. Outside the offices of the *New York World* on election night, November 3, 1896. *New York World*, November 4, 1896.

wide, which was stretched from the second to the thirteenth floors. Images were then projected from at least six different lanterns. It was, the *New York World* claimed, "the largest magic-lantern screen ever made."[137] Pulitzer offered another innovation: at his paper's uptown office on Broadway and Thirty-Second Street, bulletins were projected onto two fifty-foot screens. It was for this location that Pulitzer's organization also employed the biograph to show films:

> So that the minds of the crowd may occasionally be diverted from the serious matter of reading and figuring on the election returns, a special entertainment has been arranged for them there. The wonderful biograph, the latest of the remarkable machines which have been invented to project animated scenes from real life on canvas, and which has been on exhibition at Koster & Bial's Music Hall for a short time, has been engaged for the night to give its exhibition on a screen in front of the uptown office of The World.
>
> WONDERFUL ANIMATED PICTURES
>
> These pictures, which are essentially living pictures, as they show every movement of the person or thing which they represent, are sure to arouse great enthusiasm, for among them are representations of Major McKinley receiving visitors in Canton, pictures of political parades, etc. There is also a wonderful picture of the Empire State Express traveling at the rate of sixty miles an hour.[138]

The suddenly pro-McKinley *New York World* used the services of the pro-Republican Biograph company. Motion pictures were added to the role played by lantern-slide photographs of the candidates and political cartoons for these election-night events. The lantern and screen functioned as a parallel, complementary platform to the newspaper. It offered the most direct and immediate means to learn the news as it arrived over the wire. Like the *World* itself, it incorporated words and a diverse array of images.

William Randolph Hearst's *New York Journal*, the only important pro-Bryan newspaper in New York City, was immersed in a bitter circulation battle with Joseph Pulitzer's *New York World*. That battle had intensified still further when Hearst hired cartoonist Richard F. Outcault away from Pulitzer's *World* in October 1896. This competition certainly extended to election-eve events. The *World* could boast that it snagged the biograph, but Hearst showed films and projected election returns in many more locations. At its downtown office, the *Journal* had a map of the United States that was ninety feet long and forty feet high. When a state went for Bryan a red light appeared by the name of the state, if for McKinley it was green. In addition,

On another canvas fifty feet square, the election returns will be thrown by a powerful stereopticon, and on the same canvas, between the reports from the various States and districts, a panoramagraph—that is the latest from Paris—will throw an entire variety show. It will project life-size pictures that run and walk and jump and move about in a way to make your eyes bulge. You will see a picture of McKinley walking up and down the lawn in front of his home as large and as natural as life. There will also be pictures of the train in which Bryan travels. It will make you stare and gasp.

And in order that there shall be nothing lacking to make the night joyous, the Seventh Regiment Band, of forty-four men, will play in front of the Journal office.[139]

This motion picture service was almost certainly "The Wonderful Panoramographe" provided by J. Whitney Beals Jr. of Boston, and it offered the only films shown in Printing House Square.[140]

The *Journal* was offering returns at seven additional locations: the set of attractions outside its offices in Madison Square was very similar to those at its main office in Printing House Square. Besides the electrified map, these included "a gigantic screen for election returns, shown by five stereopticons and . . . the same kind of life-size moving pictures that will be shown at the City Hall." Gilmore's band, under the direction of Victor Herbert, filled the square with music. The *Journal* also had stereopticons at City Hall in Brooklyn, which "will throw the returns upon a screen as fast as they come into the New York Office. Here, too, the panoramagraph will play upon a big screen, displaying moving pictures exactly like those shown in front of the Journal's main office."[141] Unlike the biograph, the panoramographe was said to offer films related to both candidates. The McKinley subject might have been a staged reenactment or faked picture—one that mimed the Biograph subject and was perhaps produced especially for this occasion—or more likely relied on creative associations.

The *New York Journal* also joined up with Oscar Hammerstein and showed election returns at his Olympia Auditorium using the stereopticon while a new motion picture machine, the cinographoscope (a recent arrival from France), was enlisted for its debut engagement.[142] Laurent Mannoni reports that the cinographoscope organization had its own system, which used "a 35mm film like Lumière, but not exactly the same size of holes and holes not exactly in the same place."[143] The cinographoscope could only screen films printed from its own original negatives—which was likely true for the panoramographe as well. The *Journal* was involved in the showing of motion pictures in four different locations while having simple stereopticon projections at its other election-night locales. This was William Randolph Hearst's first use of motion pictures, which he would employ much more extensively sixteen months later in conjunction with the Spanish-American War. Synergies between the press and motion pictures were already being forged with the 1896 election, building on the newspapers' previous deployment of lantern slide images.

In Brooklyn, the *Brooklyn Eagle* arranged an elaborate show with screens on different sides of its building. Returns were still given by blackboard, but the stereopticon on one side of the building projected returns and also employed two *Eagle* artists, who "entertained the great crowd during the night with cartoons and caricatures which vastly tickled those who looked on. As the results were flashed in upon them, the artists seized upon the ideas that they contained and deftly put these ideas into pictures."[144] On another side of the building, the stereopticon showed returns on one screen and the Lumière cinématographe showed films on another: "Over one hundred views were given during the night. It was the first time that the moving photographic pictures had ever been exhibited out of doors before, every view was new and their lively realistic character provoked the utmost enthusiasm and delight."[145] Not all newspapers went to such extremes. The *New York Sun* claimed that "it was not a favorable time for the exhibition of whirligigs and funny pictures in colors."[146] People wanted news, and that's what the *Sun* gave them, projected on the screen via the stereopticon.

Newspapers sponsored election returns outside New York City as well. On Newspaper Row in Boston, "a dozen or more stereopticons, some giving news, some guesses, some pictures and cartoons and some only advertisements, furnished entertainment for the gathering."[147] The crowd was estimated to be somewhere between 15,000 and 50,000. In San Francisco, the author Frank Norris visited the offices of the *San Francisco Chronicle* and provided a lengthy report of his election-night experiences in that city, in which a variety of communications technologies were brought together to provide crowds of eager citizens with updates of the election's unfolding drama. The telegraph, typewriter, artist sketches, stereopticon, and more, he said, were integrated into a complex system that enabled the newspaper to present election returns.[148] This was the nineteenth-century antecedent to the late-twentieth-century TV newsroom.

In Chicago, the *Chicago Tribune* projected its bulletins at four different locations: in front of its building at Madison and Dearborn Streets, at Haymarket Square, at Washington Square, and at the huge Coliseum, which was used for massive political rallies and political conventions. The gatherings were to be "of an entirely non-partisan character" and "include original sketches in illustration of the returns received during the evening."[149] Motion pictures joined the stereopticon at two of these locales as "John D. Hopkins of Hopkins' Theater . . . kindly surrendered to The Tribune for election night both of his vitascopes. One of these will be used at the coliseum and the other at the corner of Madison and Dearborn streets."[150] As many as 25,000 people reportedly filled the Coliseum, where the vitascope received considerable attention, showing films at three different times that evening. "The vitascope certainly was one of the big hits of the evening and fully shared with the band and the news itself the honors won," reported the *Chicago Tribune*.[151] The vitascope did not show *Bryan Train Scene at Orange*—nor a faked McKinley film, but this does not mean that the films were not read as political texts:

> As the vitascope scenes remained upon the screen comments of every conceivable character were made. In the wrestling match one of the contestants immediately was dubbed McKinley, and Bryan, of course, was his opponent. In the "Street Scenes in Paris" the crowd recognized "Grover [Cleveland]" and "Mary Ellen Lease," and even thought they had found "David Hill." In "The Burning of the Weeds" the old farmer with the big slouch hat and chin whiskers was heartily saluted as "Chairman Jones," and "Mark Hanna" most assuredly occupied a front seat in the boat that shot the chutes.[152]

The Imperial Quartet sang the campaign song "Illinois," accompanied by cartoons and other images prepared by W. D. Boyce for the stereopticon. This happened at a time when the illustrated song was just becoming popular in America's vaudeville theaters.

The stereopticon was the platform of choice for presenting election returns that were being delivered by telegraph and—more frequently than before—by telephone. (Indeed, there was an intensifying rivalry between these two means of communication, and many newspapers relied on both.) The telegraph, if casually mentioned, remained a crucial communication technology that enabled citizens to follow the national election as it unfolded in what was virtually real time. Newspaper publishing companies brought together minute-by-minute reports from around the country, gathering, shifting, and collating the material to present an unfolding picture of election results. In many respects the telephone and motion pictures shared affinities as emergent communication technologies. Although the lantern had almost universally replaced the old-fashioned posting of bulletins on boards in front of newspaper offices, this residual platform for communication could still be found in a handful of places. Of course the stereopticon was only one delivery mechanism in a larger media system that was used to provide election results—another being the newspapers with their various editions and extras.

AN ASSESSMENT

The 1896 presidential election can be characterized by a particular "structure of feeling"—to employ a term from Raymond Williams— that reflected significant changes taking place in daily life across much of the United States.[153] In many respects it began with the candidates. Bryan went to the people, and was the first presidential candidate to embrace the whistle-stop campaign. Although McKinley had the people come to him, both were far less removed from supporters and potential voters than their predecessors. Improved modes of transportation, notably the railway, helped make this possible. Nevertheless, a rapidly expanding mediascape was producing new forms and new layers of representation between the candidates and the citizen-voters in a country growing rapidly in population and size. Although McKinley's victory could be attributed to the Republicans' unexpected media hegemony via the press, the use of emergent media (motion pictures, the telephone) and the mobilization of political pageantry on an unprecedented, spectacular scale (bicycle parades, naval displays, Sound Money marches) set a new tone and provided a new outlook. Along with Sound Money and the tariff, the Republican Party effectively adopted the promise of the new and a technologically dynamic future as a third, largely unspoken element of its platform. Much of this was also related to an emergent consumer economy.

If this structure of feeling was significantly indebted to a radically new and dynamic media formation, bringing together politics and the expanding world of commercial amusements was an important component. Those who saw McKinley and his front porch in the music halls also read about him and the delegations that traveled considerable distances to express their homages. In one lengthy news report during the final weeks of the campaign, the *New York Sun* began,

> Canton, Oct. 24.—This has been a day of striking significance in the local campaign. It was not a record beaker in the number of speeches delivered by Major McKinley, for he managed to reach all of his visitors in an even dozen speeches. And probably the crowd was not the largest yet assembled here,

although there was an immense crowd about the McKinley home this afternoon and early in the day. The speechmaking had to be transferred from the front porch to the little stand from which the Major reviews parades. The striking feature was the long distance travelled by the visitors. The great majority left their homes on Friday, some of them as early as Thursday night, and travelled continuously. They came from New York, from Pennsylvania, from Kansas, from Iowa, and from Ohio.[154]

The text evokes a humble man who was nonetheless adored by citizens—secular worshipers who undertook an arduous pilgrimage to a politically sacred site. It was they who provided the dynamism, while McKinley offered stability and humility. In Canton he cared for his invalid wife, with whom he had lost his two children in childhood. He was a man who had fought throughout the Civil War, a man who knew suffering and courage. It is worth noting that the *New York Sun* headlined this news report with "M'Kinley Preaches Hope. He Says He Has No Part in the Doctrine of Hate." One of his 1896 campaign slogans was "The People Against the Bosses." News reports purposefully avoided specifics of policy and party. Predictably, he embraced patriotism: "Stand up for America, and America will stand up for you," he told the Republication Press Association of West Virginia on September 1, 1896.[155] The mute motion picture of McKinley, with its virtual but disembodied presence, had a vision-like quality that made him seem momentarily transcendent. Properly contextualized—which was Biograph's achievement—it provided a powerful icon that could be endowed with sincerity and power.

CHAPTER 4

Cinema as a Media Form

The extensive application of cinema to politicking within months of its successful commercial introduction raises intriguing questions about the conjunction of moving pictures and politics in subsequent elections. As cinema became an increasingly influential cultural presence and its systems of production, exhibition, and representation were transformed, its relationship to political campaigning inevitably changed as well. Its immediate appropriation for campaign purposes contrasts with that of the stereopticon, which was quickly used to perform significant ideological and political work but was seemingly disassociated from politicking for more than a decade. Part of this was circumstantial: the stereopticon appeared on the scene shortly after the 1860 presidential election, while the cinema appeared on the scene shortly before the 1896 election. Nevertheless the stereopticon and cinema were closely related media forms. We need to consider their relationship in a practical sense—in the sense of actual practice. Perhaps not surprisingly, the first part of this chapter on the early, transformative years of cinema parallels the first part of chapter 2, which explored the early, formative history of the photographic lantern slide and asked when and how it became constructed as part of a new media form that was known in the United States as "the stereopticon." The state of the questions, however, is quite different. With knowledge of the beginnings of cinema relatively well established at least in its broad outlines, the historiographical issues tend to be more analytical and theoretical, concerned with periodization and shifts in the *dispositif* rather than names and dates.[1] Certainly, an understanding of cinema's trajectory is extremely useful for placing it within the larger media formation of the 1900 election.

WHEN DID CINEMA BECOME CINEMA?

"When did cinema become cinema?" asks André Gaudreault.[2] This is arguably another way of asking: When did cinema become a media form—a stable, coherent media practice? That is, when did cinema possess a recognizable set of protocols along the lines laid out by Lisa Gitelman in the introduction (page 12)? Certainly we are faced with terminological issues that need to be engaged if not resolved. The term "cinema" has been used in many different contexts and has a variety of potential meanings. When people say, as they often do, that the Lumières invented cinema, they mean (I think) projected modern motion pictures in a theatrical setting of some kind. This would seem to be the first meaning of cinema in Gaudreault's equation: let's call it Cinema[1]. And it provides a starting point for my usage of the term as well.

One possible answer to Gaudreault's question is obviously tautological. Cinema[1] and Cinema[2] are one and the same. That is, cinema began when the Lumières showed their cinématographe in the basement of the Salon Indien du Grand Café in Paris on December 28, 1895. Although this answer might seem to reflect narrow technological determinations—the invention of the cinématographe apparatus—this event is already technology plus several other additional factors; it is not just a technology, it is already a *dispositif*. It might be possible to posit some "eureka moment" when the Lumières first "perfected" their new invention (perhaps on a dark and stormy night)—a technology for which there were not yet protocols, but such a moment, if it ever existed, seems to have little traction in relevant historiographies. Moreover, although the Lumières did have public, scientific screenings before December 28, these occupied, at best, an inchoate position. It was the screening at the Grand Café, when an admission fee was first charged, that many associate with cinema's true "beginning." Cinema is, at least implicitly, then, understood to involve something more than a technology—not just a new technological system of projected motion pictures but one that from the outset involved the projection of a *selected and arranged sequence* of *carefully shot motion picture films* onto a screen in a theatrical setting of some kind for an audience who paid to see it. This required a set of protocols, some structures of communication, which, however tentative, were nonetheless real. And not only real, but also part of a long history.

Such beginnings of cinema are the ones I have tended to emphasize in my own scholarship, but as Gaudreault implies by his question, there are other ways of thinking of Cinema[2]. In *Film and Attraction* he argues that "the fundamental rupture in film history was not the invention of the moving picture cameras in the 1890s . . . but the constitution in the 1910s of the institution 'cinema,' whose primary principle could be seen as a systematic rejection of the ways and customs of early cinema."[3] This idea of a decisive moment in film history, which occurred around 1910, is something Gaudreault shares with other film scholars. My colleague Dudley Andrew states that "the cinema came into its own around 1910 and it began to doubt its constitution sometime in the late 1980s."[4] They are both consciously echoing Edgar Morin, whose book *The Cinema, or the Imaginary Man* (1956) has a chapter entitled "Metamorphosis of the Cinematographe into Cinema."[5] Morin seems to think that those in the industry made films without worrying about its role as an art until roughly fifteen years after the cinema started—thus 1910.[6] To the extent that we treat *The Cinema, or the Imaginary Man* as a text of history, it is worth asking if it escapes the problems of other histories from that period. (I would suggest that it sometimes fails.) Moreover, although becoming an art and becoming an institution may be (or may not be) related, they are hardly the same thing.

As Lee Grieveson reminded me during the conference "The Impact of Technological Innovations on the Historiography and Theory of Cinema" in November 2011, according to the *Oxford English Dictionary*, the term "cinema" became popular in the United Kingdom over the course of 1910. Recall Virginia Woolf's famous pronouncement: "On or about December 1910 human character changed. . . . All human relations have shifted—those between masters and servants, husbands and wives, parents and children. And when human relations change there is at the same time a change in religion, conduct, politics and literature."[7] Did this change occur most of all in the cinema itself? Not everyone sees 1910 as the magical year. Jacques Deslandes and Jacques Richard suggest that the "cinématographe" had become "cinema" by 1906—not 1910 or 1915.[8] Their chosen year is loosely linked to Gaumont's incorporation on December 1, 1906, and somewhat related phenomena such as the rise of storefront or specialized motion picture theaters known as nickelodeons in the United States, penny gaffs in England, *kintopps* in Germany, *cinemagrafos* in the Philippines—and *cinemas* in France. It is a moment when "cinema" gains a certain weight and its own infrastructure.

All this perhaps signals a larger historiographic problem of periodization. For instance, Gaudreault's so-called "birth of Cinema[1]" or (the cinématographe), which he increasingly considers a minor event in its history, produced the cinema of attractions era, or that of kine-attractography, which lasted until 1903 (or perhaps 1906 or 1908), followed by the birth of Cinema[2] or its institutionalization, occurring around 1910 (or perhaps from 1910 to 1915).[9] According to David Bordwell, Janet Staiger, and Kristin Thompson, this eventually culminated with the establishment of the Classical Hollywood Cinema (its further institutionalization?) somewhere around 1917 with the establishment of Hollywood system of representation.[10] Another important watershed was the emergence of Hollywood's vertically integrated studio system around 1920, which roughly coincided with Hollywood's new global dominance. These various and sometimes fluctuating dates are one sign that periodization is floating between several different levels and need to be assessed more carefully. That is, we need to reground this historiography in a stronger understanding of motion picture practices (broadly conceived) as they went through a series of interconnected transformations.

In the spirit of this persistent idea that cinema proper was subsequently constituted at some critical moment in the history of cinema—what Gaudreault is calling "the birth of Cinema[2]" and in a more contemporary fashion might be called Cinema 2.0—I want to return to the when-did-cinema-become-cinema question and be particularly sensitive to the many changing elements of motion picture practice. Of course, one problem here is this: there have been more than a few transformational moments over the course of cinema's history. For instance, some (perhaps including André Bazin and certainly Rudolf Arnheim) might want to associate Cinema 2.0 with the coming of sound, while contemporary media scholars might identify digital cinema as Cinema 3.0.[11] These debates involve questions of 1) naming—I prefer to avoid applying birth metaphors to historical transformations;[12] 2) periodization—determining important moments of transformation or development and ultimately naming the most decisive or salient ones—or in the case of Gaudreault's second birth, *the* salient one; and 3) the kind of a history we are writing.

Assuming we look for a later and decisive formation, a hypothetical Cinema 2.0, there are quite a few possible answers. Although the

history of cinema as an art and the larger social and cultural ramifica-
tions that result from these changing formulations (that is, institutionalization) are interesting and important, I find it difficult to imagine
privileging a moment either in 1910 or even a longer period of "constitution" in 1910–14.[13] The process of institutionalization can be difficult
to define precisely, and identifying a decisive moment of institutional
emergence seems fraught. Certainly there would be compelling reasons
to argue for a new Cinema 2.0 in the wake of World War I, when American cinema asserted its global dominance and the vertically integrated
Hollywood studio system began to emerge. However, if we look at cinema practices at the end of the nineteenth century and in the first decade
of the twentieth, a period of rapid and far-reaching changes, there are at
least five important moments of transformation, and in three of these
instances one might say that Cinema 1.0 became Cinema 2.0—or, to
drop computer-age terminologies, that cinema became "Cinema."

5. When Cinema Became a Form of Mass Communication and a Mass Media

In 1908 cinema became a mass media, a form of mass communication
and mass entertainment. A key element of this was the introduction
of the regular release schedule as motion picture companies issued
their films on a systematic basis in which a given picture became available on the same day throughout the United States. Almost simultaneously a new mode of representation began to emerge, which was more
accessible and consistent in meaning to a broad range of spectators (by
relying heavily on intertitles and a newly asserted linear sequencing of
shots).[14] The result was a more self-sufficient form of storytelling. Filmmakers had been able to oscillate between already-known stories on
one hand or very simple, easy to understand stories (for instance chase
films) on the other, or complex narratives that usually required a lecturer. These strategies simply broke down in the need for many more
films that were also sufficiently original and complex. These developments also coincided with efforts to organize the film business in all its
aspects through the Association of Edison Licensees and then the
Motion Picture Patents Company—with related efforts in Europe. It
was also at this moment that film production, or what was called "negative production," moved away from a horizontal, partnership model
of filmmaking toward a hierarchical, military style or corporate chain
of command and responsibility.[15] The director emerged, with D. W.

Griffith an early and notable example. And it was at this moment that key motion picture companies began to build their stock companies of actors. The motion picture actor as such began to appear, for instance the "Biograph Girl," Florence Lawrence, or G. M. "Broncho Billy" Anderson. In addition, again in the United States, the *New York Dramatic Mirror* started reviewing films, suggesting that from an outside albeit closely affiliated perspective, films were being regularly judged on the basis of their artistic merit.

When I started to use the term "early cinema," it was meant to refer to the period up to this moment of transformation—an alternative to the term "pre-Griffith cinema." Indeed, this moment is the moment of emergence for what Tom Gunning calls the "narrator system."[16] Likewise Gaudreault refers to this as a new post-monstration era of narrative integration. This remarkable set of far-reaching transformations, which occurred more or less simultaneously on a number of levels in 1908, certainly seems to have produced a cinema that was thoroughly institutionalized. Moreover, as a newly formed mass media, cinema had come to share some of the same protocols as newspapers, magazines, and perhaps even book publishing. This, then, is one of the moments when we might locate a Cinema^2 if we were so inclined. Indeed, my 1908 might be seen as a more precise variant of ca. 1910 (a purposefully round number, one assumes).

4. When Cinema Gained Its Own Autonomous Exhibition Venues

The new cinema formation described above happened as a more or less direct result of another, earlier moment when one might argue that Cinema^1 became Cinema^2. Elsewhere I have remarked that "it is not too much to say that modern cinema began with the nickelodeons."[17] Here my term "modern cinema" might be seen as Cinema^2. It was in 1906 that the nickelodeons provided the motion picture industry with its own specially designated exhibition sites. To have specialized motion picture houses or cinemas but no "cinema" seems odd. This is the Deslandes-Richard date. Of course, any date always involves a certain amount of wiggle room: for instance the nickelodeon boom was getting under way in places such as Pittsburgh and Chicago in the second half of 1905 but not in Denver until mid-1907. The United States is, of course, just one instance in a global system, but even then its market was the preeminent one.

The extremely rapid proliferation of movie houses in the United States (and to some degree elsewhere) put the film industry on an entirely new basis—economically but also as a self-sufficient, self-sustaining cultural practice. These movie houses created tremendous demand for new films, which resulted in an increased rate of production both in the United States and internationally. The rental system accelerated with semiweekly and soon daily changes of film programs. The first trade journal devoted primarily to motion pictures, *Views and Film Index*, began publication in April 1906. Nevertheless, this large-scale revolution in exhibition, important as it is, may be too singular for us to designate this moment as marking a new kind of cinema. In key respects it set in motion the multifaceted transformations of 1908, but it took roughly two years for its impact to produce a new, more modern cinema.

3. When Cinema Became Pure Cinema

The nickelodeon boom was made possible and greatly facilitated by another, still earlier moment of reorganization in the year 1903. A new configuration of the *dispositif* that was sufficiently radical to be characterized as a second birth must be quite momentous, involving a wholesale reorganization of cinematic practices—a convergence of multiple changes that put motion picture practices on a new footing. Is there such a moment when cinema in a real sense becomes "cinema"—one that would at least rival 1908 or 1920? Certainly the year 1903 involved a multifaceted, far-reaching reorganization of the cinema's protocols that demands particular attention.[18] This includes an important though often overlooked technological component: the introduction of the three-blade shutter on motion picture machines/projectors, which sharply reduced the flicker effect and made spectatorship much more pleasurable. Its use was frequently advertised by traveling US exhibitors in the second half of 1903 and was simultaneously adopted by those motion picture companies competing for outlets in the nation's leading vaudeville houses. The three-blade shutter was part of a larger reorganization of cinema practices, which arguably produced a transformational moment with no equivalent in its far-reaching nature.

Before 1903, film programs were not, strictly speaking, *film* programs. Exhibitors were largely in control of postproduction, and almost all so-called film exhibitions involved moving back and forth between slides and short films. This was not only common, but desirable and in some sense necessary. Already with the McKinley program of October 1896, Biograph was alternating between title slides and motion picture films.[19] Title slides reduced the costs of materials, since motion picture film stock was expensive, but it also provided the spectators' eyes with a rest from the heavy flicker of projected films. By late 1896 and with increasing frequency thereafter, purveyors of illustrated lectures began to give evening presentations in which they incorporated short motion pictures and alternated between slides and film with something like a four-to-one or six-to-one ratio.[20] By 1897 or 1898, apparatuses for projecting films were generally combination stereopticon–moving picture machines: operators could alternate between the two mediums by either swiveling the image carrier back and forth or, more rarely, moving the light source between slide carrier and motion picture carriage. This meant that postproduction was not merely under the ultimate control of the exhibitor, but that the process of sequencing material into a coherent program was physically occurring in the course of the actual exhibition. That is, what we now call editing—the juxtaposition of shots to create meaningful connections—was performed by the moving picture operator (projectionist), who might or might not be the showman him- or herself. (Of course the exhibitor was also responsible for the sound—music, effects, narration, and so forth.) Shots or scenes were sold as individual films, and exhibitors of all kinds acquired them as building blocks for larger programs. Having assembled groups of short films and slides, exhibitors might combine them into a program that offered a miscellaneous collection of views *or* a program that possessed thematic and/or narrative coherence—of which the illustrated lecture presented one possible model. It was not unusual for programs to be somewhere in between.

The year 1903 was the pivotal moment when editing and other elements of what is commonly called "postproduction" moved decisively from the responsibility of the exhibitor to the production company in key areas (though not in the area of sound accompaniment). Even as the three-blade shutter was introduced in the United States, the Edison Manufacturing Company began to sell its longer films—*Uncle Tom's Cabin* (July 1903) was the first—with head titles and intertitles. Because the three-blade shutter reduced flicker, it became more viable to show filmed titles rather than title slides. Likewise film stock was becoming less costly, while other, more modest technological innovations reduced the time for perforating film as well as for the printing of film positives. The cost differential and potential savings were greatly reduced. Key elements of postproduction were rapidly centralized inside the production company—a process that had begun somewhat earlier but had been impeded by well-established exhibition protocols.

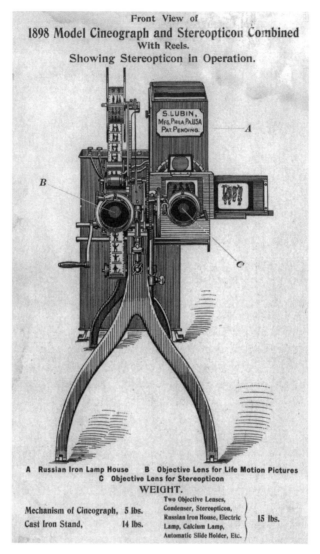

Front View of
1898 Model Cineograph and Stereopticon Combined
With Reels.
Showing Stereopticon in Operation.

S. LUBIN,
Mfg. Phila. Pa. USA
Pat. Pending.

A

B

C

A Russian Iron Lamp House   B Objective Lens for Life Motion Pictures
C Objective Lens for Stereopticon
WEIGHT.

Mechanism of Cineograph,	5 lbs.	Two Objective Lenses, Condenser, Stereopticon, Russian Iron House, Electric Lamp, Calcium Lamp, Automatic Slide Holder, Etc.	15 lbs.
Cast Iron Stand,	14 lbs.		

FIGURE 26. Exhibitors used projectors such as Lubin's Cineograph and Stereopticon Combined at the turn of the century so that they could alternate between showing slides and films. Courtesy Jack Judson and the Magic Lantern Castle Museum.

This centralization of postproduction had a profound impact on exhibition. Until 1903 exhibitors provided venues such as vaudeville houses with a full service that included films, title slides (and potentially other kinds of lantern slides as well), an operator, and a projector. Once titles were put on film and incorporated within the motion picture program itself, projectionists were simply showing a reel of film—a noticeable reduction in their responsibilities and required skill levels. Old-line exhibition services such as Percival Waters's Kinetograph Company became distributors who rented a reel of film to the vaudeville houses (and probably sold them a projector in the process). In many cases, the vaudeville houses gave the role of projectionist to the house electrician. Again this occurred in the later part of 1903, producing a new pattern of distribution—the rental system—in which the reel of film became a commodity.

It was also at this moment that narrative fiction began to dominate in vaudeville and elsewhere. In *The Emergence of Cinema*, I trace the kinds of film subjects that were being featured in Chicago vaudeville houses in 1903 using newspaper advertisements. The shift in subject matter was quite dramatic: although roughly 20 percent of the headline attractions were fiction or acted films early in the year, this percentage had increased to roughly 80 percent by the fall.[21] There were multiple reasons for this shift to story films, but certainly reduced flicker facilitated the kinds of pleasures one associates with fantasy and fiction. The moving picture houses that began to appear two or three years later reflected this shift, as they were given names such as Bijou Dream and Dreamland. This reorganization also meant that projectors were soon redesigned just to show films: they became motion picture machines. Only after mid-1903 was cinema constituted as a pure film program—as pure cinema. Although there were lots of old films without head titles, this transition happened surprisingly quickly. Exhibition-services-turned-distributors often had their own motion picture cameras and could easily shoot head titles and cut them into their film reels. (In fact, even into the nickelodeon era distributors sometimes replaced head titles supplied by production companies with their own as a way of asserting ownership of the film print, if not authorship of the film.) Production companies could also go back and shoot film titles for earlier films that displayed continuing demand (as Edison did for *Life of an American Fireman*).

Finally, there is the consideration of theory: of changing conceptions of cinema and its ontology. Not "when did cinema become cinema?" but "what is cinema?" As André Gaudreault and Philippe Marion suggest in "Measuring the 'Double Birth' Model Against the Digital Age," cinema was initially seen as a special kind of magic lantern.[22] Here we are certainly in agreement. In *Animated Pictures* (1898), C. Francis Jenkins remarked that "the moving picture machine is simply a modified stereopticon or lantern, i.e. a lantern equipped with a mechanical slide changer. All stereopticons will, sooner or later, as are several standard machines now, be arranged to project stationary pictures or pictures giving the appearance of objects in motion." Henry V. Hopwood echoed these observations in *Living Pictures* (1899), noting: "A film for projecting a living picture is nothing more, after all, than a multiple lantern slide."[23]

During the year 1903, cinema was largely invisible in the press—at least there was little said about what was going on in vaudeville houses. If very little was said about the nature of cinema, it was perhaps also a moment of profound realignment and reconceptualization. When the discourse resumed—indeed as story films clearly became dominant within the industry—the cinema was increasingly conceptualized as a special kind of theatrical entertainment, like the stage, rather than as an extension of the lantern or a visual newspaper. The appearance of film reviews in the *New York Dramatic Mirror* in 1908 embodied this new conception. From this point forward, at least for many years to come, comparisons between stage and screen would do much to structure theories of film.

2. Cinema and Stereopticon Together

In order to explain the transformation of cinema that took place in 1903, the previous section has already sketched out the basic *dispositif* that characterized cinema for the six-year period from about 1897 to 1903. We might think of this period as one in which two weak media— the established stereopticon and new motion pictures—were integrated and coexisted in a variety of ways.[24] As suggested in chapter 2, when the stereopticon emerged after 1860, it was a weak media form in that the stereopticon itself was able to show a wide range of materials—not just photographic lantern slides. With "weakness" came flexibility and the ability to accommodate and incorporate. It was a syncretic media form. For this reason, lantern practitioners were able to quickly incorporate motion pictures into their repertoire while exhibitors interested in showing films found it easy to show slides.[25]

In what way can we think about the cinema functioning as a weak media in the period between 1897 and 1903? Modern motion pictures as instantiated in Edison's 1893–95 kinetograph-kinetoscope system functioned as a minor or proto-media form of some kind. It required special cameras, special viewing devices, special ways of printing and developing. It was an entirely new technological system with a set of accompanying protocols. The new media had many constraints, which produced quite specific practices. The filming of scenes could only happen in bright daylight. Films were limited to certain lengths. And only the peep-hole kinetoscope could show films. With the introduction and immediate dominance of projection, there appeared a number of motion picture systems in which technological differences produced variations in image quality and in the ways that films were shown. The vitascope, for instance, showed loops, which would be repeated several times at each screening. To replace a film on a vitascope projector took more than a minute. So exhibitors either had to alternate between two projectors (which Raff and Gammon did at the Koster & Bial's premiere), alternate between live acts and films, or use lantern-slide titles to cover the time needed to remove one film and thread the next. The projection of film loops was one distinctive feature of the novelty era.

The move from cinema as a novelty in 1896 and early 1897 to the post-novelty period can be characterized by the integration of motion pictures with the stereopticon into a new *dispositif*. In this *dispositif*, as before, negative production employed camera technology that was able to perform just one task: the making of a film from which positive prints could be made. But the situation on the exhibition side was different. The incorporation of motion pictures into the stereopticon paradigm was one indication that projected motion pictures, as distinct from motion pictures shown in peep-hole kinetoscopes and vitascopes, were more than just a novelty or passing fad. As a weak media, the stereopticon could incorporate motion pictures. And perhaps vice versa. In this sense, Gaudreault and I are noticing the same phenomenon: cinema between 1897 (post-novelty) and 1903 was immersed in the world of stereopticon practices as well as the world of vaudeville and other forms of live theater, which were eclectic and often syncretic.[26] In this respect it was what I am calling a weak media. But even in this period, the cinema could have a powerful impact.

1. Cinema¹ is Cinema²; or, There Are Many Cinemas

Cinema¹, even as a novelty form, had its own array of protocols and representational strategies. The distinction between the invention of the device that can produce cinema and the cinema itself can be tricky.

In theory a device could be invented and not develop an adequate set of protocols (possible example: Louis Le Prince, whose mysterious death left behind a motion picture camera of sorts but little else).[27] Then clearly there is no cinema (not even Cinema[1]). Or the technology could be developed but not used for a cultural experience that we would recognize as cinema. Étienne-Jules Marey used his apparatuses only for specific scientific purposes—in which case, again, no cinema. But this did not happen. Cinema entrepreneurs introduced it into theatrical settings almost immediately (even prematurely, from a technological viewpoint, if we consider the Lathams' eidoloscope). But then one might argue, and this seems to be Gaudreault's point, that even though it was put into theaters, this new media form was not transformative. It remained little more than an extension of previous "pre-cinematic" practices. Its impact on culture and social life was minimal. In effect, it was a curiosity little different than the pre-cinematic peep-hole kinetoscope. Here I must strongly disagree. Between late 1895 and 1897, cinema emerged as a new phenomenon, a new worldwide cultural force that had a transformative impact in the United States on sports, religion, politics, theatrical culture, the newspaper, and American courting rituals between April 1896 and the end of 1897.[28] Biograph's McKinley program is but one example. One thing is certain: cinema was only "new" for a brief moment and then it became something else.

. . .

Although I have outlined a number of crucial moments in the ongoing transformation of cinema before 1910—moments when one might argue that cinema became more recognizably "the cinema"—I am reluctant to privilege any one of them. In this respect I align myself with Yuri Tsivian, who remarked that "in the course of cinema's history what cinema is has changed enough times for a history of the cinema's identities to be written."[29] I have listed a number of them above, and it is useful to think of the manner in which they were distributed across presidential elections. As chapter 3 demonstrates, the 1896 election fell very much in cinema's initial novelty period. The 1900 US presidential election is interesting in light of the periodization described above because it is the only presidential campaign that occurred in the years between 1897 and 1903—what might be considered cinema's second period. It is a moment when, on one hand, the technology and protocols of slide-film integration were firmly established and, on the other, big-city vaudeville managers (particularly in

New York City) had generally made motion pictures a regular feature of their programs. The presidential election of 1904 came shortly after this period but before the nickelodeon boom. The 1908 election came while the nickelodeon boom was fully under way and just as cinema was becoming a mass media with a standard release schedule— though developments in the nonfiction mode increasingly lagged behind that of fiction. Newsreels such as Pathé News were not introduced until 1910. These US presidential campaigns encountered a substantially different motion picture *dispositif* with each election. So how were the stereopticon, the cinema, and other emergent media utilized in the 1900 election?

POLITICKING AND THE MEDIA AFTER THE 1896 PRESIDENTIAL CAMPAIGN

The 1900 presidential election once again pitted McKinley against Bryan, though each had a new vice presidential running mate. Vice president Hobart had died of heart failure in 1899 and the Republicans replaced him with war hero and New York Governor Theodore Roosevelt. Bryan and the Democrats gave the number two spot to former Vice President Adlai Stevenson of Illinois, whose presence had multiple virtues: experience, ties to the conservative wing of the party, the ability to woo the South, and a positive but nondogmatic view of the Free Silver issue. Although Free Silver remained a key issue of the campaign, its potency was reduced because the American economy had done well during McKinley's tenure. Indeed, technological innovation—the subtext of his 1896 campaign—was a significant factor in this new era of prosperity. The other issue, what many saw as the paramount one, was American imperialism, in particular the US government's efforts to annex the Philippines, which resulted in the brutal Filipino-American War (1899–1902) as US troops fought to replace the Spanish and defeat the First Philippine Republic under its leader, Emilio Aguinaldo. Although Bryan had been a staunch supporter of the Spanish-American War, his fervently anti-imperialist pronouncements during his 1900 presidential campaign sharply distinguished him from the expansionist and colonial policies of McKinley.

The candidates pursued the same basic campaign strategies despite the nation's changed circumstances. McKinley spent the summer and fall at his home in Canton, only making a few brief trips to Washington, DC, when he needed to deal with domestic and international crises. In

Canton, however, he acted presidential, generally avoiding the speeches and meetings with delegations that had characterized his previous campaign.[30] This continued his 1896 front porch campaign in appearance rather than substance. Bryan reprised his whistle-stop campaigning, giving numerous speeches as he traveled the country by train—though at a somewhat reduced pace.

Bryan, much more than McKinley, needed to find a way to alter the politicking mediascape. Everyone recognized that the press would continue to be heavily pro-McKinley—or anti-Bryan. Traditional Democratic newspapers such as the *New York Times*, the *Brooklyn Eagle*, and the *New York Sun* once again supported McKinley. After pointing out that the nation's prosperity was "the wonder of the world," a *Brooklyn Eagle* editorial explained its endorsement of McKinley by noting that "it would seem to be more advisable to let well enough alone."[31] Still one of the rare publishers to support Bryan, William Randolph Hearst launched the *Chicago American* with its debut issue on July 4, 1900. Although the pro-Democratic Chicago newspaper was vitally important, it hardly changed the overall dynamics so far as print media was concerned. Bryan and Democratic operatives also recognized that they needed to be more proactive in using emergent media, particularly motion pictures and the phonograph. They had some sense of what needed to be done but lacked the resources, sophistication, and ultimately the vision to use audiovisual media effectively.

Republicans simply needed to continue their dominance. In this respect, nominating the dynamic Governor Theodore Roosevelt as McKinley's vice presidential running mate was helpful. He executed his own version of the whistle-stop tour, traveling farther and speaking more often than Bryan: 21,209 miles, 24 states, 673 speeches.[32] Then, after returning to New York City, Roosevelt participated in another Sound Money parade on the Saturday before Election Day. Beginning at the southern tip of Manhattan, the governor led the way, his carriage heading uptown under the Dewey Arch and through the rain until he took his place on the reviewing stand at Twenty-Third Street and Broadway. The *Brooklyn Eagle* claimed that a record-breaking 110,000 businessmen trudged by him in the rain (the *New York Times* estimated a more modest 84,000 marchers).[33] If the marchers roughly equaled the 1896 Sound Money parade in numbers, Bryan did better in New York City than four years before. He still lost the state, but this time by "only" approximately 143,000 votes, almost halving his earlier margin of defeat.

FIGURE 27. A 1900 stereocard features Republican standard bearers William McKinley and Theodore Roosevelt. Courtesy the Library of Congress.

Motion Pictures

In her study of the presidential campaign film, Joanne Morreale has suggested that Theodore Roosevelt was the first president to understand film's propagandistic appeal, offering a fanciful account of the cavalry officer bringing two Vitagraph cameramen to Cuba to chronicle his march up San Juan Hill. Although Morreale points toward something worth noting, the specifics are all wrong.[34] Edison's *Battle of San Juan Hill* did enjoy modest prominence during the 1900 campaign, but it was a reenactment filmed near New York City in 1899. Moreover, no one in the picture can be readily identified as playing the role of Roosevelt.[35] Edison-licensed cameraman William Paley had filmed *Roosevelt Rough Riders Embarking for Santiago* on June 8, 1898, but Roosevelt does not appear in that film, either. *Terrible Teddy, the Grizzly King* (Edison, February 1901), a short film comedy in which Roosevelt is accompanied by a photographer (not a motion picture cameraman) who shoots everything done by the vice president–elect (while Roosevelt shoots animals), suggests that Roosevelt was at the center of a new relationship between political figures and the US media. Although this film, which was based on a political cartoon in Hearst's *New York Journal*, certainly mocked Roosevelt's relations with the media, motion pictures were not part of the equation.

Not surprisingly, the American Mutoscope & Biograph Company took several films of the future president in 1898 and 1899. These included *Theodore Roosevelt Leaving the White House* (circa April 1898), in which the assistant secretary of the navy (soon to be the former assistant secretary) was filmed. *Roosevelt's Rough Riders* (July 1898) and *Col. Theodore Roosevelt and Officers of His Staff* (September 1898) gave him some added visibility. *Governor Roosevelt and Staff* (September 1899) was taken during the Dewey celebrations in New York City. By comparison, Biograph took fifteen or more films of McKinley during his first term in office. These films were screened in vaudeville houses, and while they lent an implicit Republican bias to the programs, they also were short news films of the nation's chief executive or (in the case of Roosevelt) a political celebrity.

Although Biograph's 1896 McKinley program provided a model for the kind of politically powerful presentation that could be generated using motion pictures, vaudeville and other amusement venues appeared unwilling to repeat such a *coup de theatre*. Theatergoers had diverse political allegiances, and undue partisanship would alienate patrons and reduce box office. (New York City voters would not skew pro-Republican in 1900 as they had in 1896.)[36] Film programs used in conjunction with regular campaigning was something else. When a series of Republican mass meetings and nighttime parades were scheduled to converge on Durland Riding Academy on Manhattan's Upper West Side near Central Park, party organizers arranged for "a mutoscope and biograph display" in addition to speeches.[37]

In Chicago, Congressman William Lorimer (R-Ill) who had become well known for his "circus tent scheme" in which he interlaced political speeches with amusements, wanted to offer a "Festival of Republican Prosperity" featuring motion pictures that would emphasize the economic success of the previous four years. The subject matter included "wheat fields in harvest time, busy factories in operation, ships carrying the products of the country across the oceans, and divers other illustrations of prosperity." The films were to be "sandwiched between the orations, and the whole show is expected to wind up with a grand display of fireworks."[38] Lorimer's proposal was also promoted by Colonel E. C. Culp of Salina, Kansas. He was set to present a "Prosperity Show" of moving pictures in Topeka, Kansas, on October 9, following a speech by Senator Albert J. Beveridge of Indiana. Whether or not this actually happened is unclear. Culp claimed that his proposal had the written approval of the Republican National Committee, but it may not have come with funding, nor been accepted (and funded) by the Republican State Committee of Kansas.[39] Since reviews of the actual show have yet to be found, this may have been promoted in the press and elsewhere but never successfully launched.

William Jennings Bryan was essentially assured of the Democratic Party's nomination for president by May 1900. The following month the Democratic National Committee arranged for the taking of motion pictures of the candidate for use in the upcoming election, specifically to be used in illustrated lectures as part of the campaign. They almost certainly engaged William Selig, whose Chicago-based Selig Polyscope Company was providing an exhibition service to vaudeville theaters and other venues in the West and South, where Bryan was popular. Democrats were trying to plan ahead and effectively exploit this vibrant new media form. Once again the *New York Sun* quickly reported on the shooting of such pictures in pseudo-heroic terms.[40] As Stephen Bottomore has pointed out, newspapers—particularly those of a Republican persuasion—ridiculed this filming of Bryan.[41] The *Lincoln Nebraska State Journal* derided the whole idea as "Napoleonic," while the *Baltimore American* and other newspapers offered a mock poem on the topic.[42] It began:

FARMER BRYAN'S PHOTOGRAPHS

They're taking Farmer Bryan with the biograph machine—
The moving-picture man says it's the best he's ever seen;
They show him in his overalls, with boots up to his knees,
A-picking luscious melons from the watermelon trees,
They have a splendid view of him behind the old pig pen
Presenting moving arguments to his old setting hen.

And, best of all the films they've got, is one of William J
A-driving his self-binder in a waving field of hay.
Another view depicts him with a heavy-handed hoe—
He's hilling up the growing wheat in a well-planted row,
And then they have him in a tree, where earnestly he tries
To find enough dried apples to concoct some tasteful pies.[43]

But then, as the *Washington Post* noted, "The Republicans are trying to release Mr. Bryan's hold upon the agricultural masses by intimating that his farm is nothing more than a nine-hole golf course."[44] Did such mockery deter Democratic efforts in this area? The possibility of touring an illustrated lecture that was devoted to Bryan, one that combined these films with some slides, was not unlike the idea of giving phonograph concerts that was ballyhooed in 1896. Like that idea, it seems to have gone nowhere.

Although the poem's reference to Biograph was a false lead, Biograph did send a cameraman to Lincoln, Nebraska, and on September 4 he took two films of Bryan, including *William J. Bryan in the Biograph*. Biograph had established a national reach for its exhibition service and whatever the politics of its investors, its reputation as a visual newspaper and the sensibilities of vaudeville managers and their patrons needed to be kept in mind. Of course, if the occasion were to arise, some creative editing and sound accompaniment could turn a Bryan film into something effectively pro-Republican. In contrast, the Edison Manufacturing Company showed little interest in the election. *Bryan Train Scene at Orange* was no longer even for sale in its 1900 catalog.[45]

Once presidential politicking had entered the theater world, it would not leave. Screening films of the candidates was one way for amusement entrepreneurs to bring politically active citizens into their venues during the election. The policy that the Vitascope Company pursued at Proctor's vaudeville houses in 1896—that of showing a miscellaneous selection of political films—evolved into a more formal bipartisan format in which exhibition services screened films of candidates from both major parties. Two weeks after filming Bryan, Selig went to considerable effort to add Roosevelt to his repertoire. According to one news report:

> The picture man had importuned Governor Roosevelt in vain to pose before his machine, but the governor froze him. When Roosevelt went to St. Paul the agent preceded him and learned who was to drive the carriage that carried him through the streets. He paid the driver to stop the carriage before his camera machine.
> When "Teddy" and his escort came up the street from the depot the man with the machine stepped out from the crowd and waved his cane. The driver slowed up and then came to a stop in front of the picture machine. The nominee rose in his usual manner, bowed and smiled to the crowd and all the time the picture machine was getting in its deadly work.[46]

By mid-August Selig was offering "Bryan and Roosevelt in the Polyscope" at Chicago's Hopkins Theater.[47] Two weeks later, Hopkins vaudeville house announced, "The Polyscope motion pictures will include . . . President McKinley laying the federal building cornerstone. William Jennings Bryan at his Lincoln home, and Governor Roosevelt in the parade at St. Paul."[48] Such focused programs could attract patrons and gain desirable comments in newspapers.

Biograph also featured pictures of President McKinley and William J. Bryan at Detroit's Wonderland vaudeville theater in September: "That of Bryan was taken at his little home in Lincoln, NEB. And shows him standing in front of the house with his hat off and appearing as it does in every-day life."[49] It is quite possible that this film was paired with *McKinley at Home*, producing a pleasing symmetry. Likewise one week before the election, Manhattan's Huber's Museum showed films of McKinley and Bryan as each arrived in New York City.[50] Cinema's role as a visual news-paper was in full force; however, unlike most newspapers these exhibition services were generally careful to offer a more neutral, balanced, and seemingly objective view of both candidates and the contest.

Balance was the goal that the rapidly expanding entertainment indus-try seemed determined to pursue when it came to presidential elections. Such an approach was also evident at Boston's Music Hall, where life-like wax figures of McKinley and Bryan graced the foyer.[51] And it was evident in vaudeville, as impersonators carefully caricatured candidates from both parties. This was turning into a formula that would continue into the nickelodeon era and beyond. For the 1908 election, which pit-ted William Jennings Bryan against Republican Howard Taft, the Kalem Company was selling 350 feet of *Taft Pictures* (about five minutes). One of its advertisements noted, "This film, run in conjunction with the Vit-agraph film of Bryan, is now being heavily featured in New York."[52] But not just New York: "The small theaters throughout the country are at present making a bid for popularity by exhibiting the Taft and Bryan films."[53] Bryan's motion picture situation in 1900 was an improvement over the way vaudeville had treated him in 1896, but it hardly solved the problem of his media deficit.

The Phonograph

Of the various emerging media, William Jennings Bryan and the Demo-crats were most invested in the phonograph. On August 13 at Demo-cratic national headquarters in Chicago, Bryan recorded two excerpts from his acceptance speech, which he had given five days earlier in Indi-anapolis. He reprised portions of his strongly worded, anti-imperialist statement on the Philippines, which included the right of Filipinos to resist Americans efforts at recolonization. "Those who would have this Nation enter upon a career of empire must consider not only the effect of imperialism on the Filipinos, but they must also calculate its effect upon our own Nation. We cannot repudiate the principle of self-govern-ment in the Philippines without weakening that principle here," he asserted.[54] "So far as is known this is the first instance on record of a Presidential candidate in the United States addressing audiences by phonograph," reported the *New York Times.* "Democratic politicians say the idea is an excellent one, and that it will prove popular in the country: furthermore, that it will serve as an excellent substitute for the 'front porch' used so successfully by McKinley four years ago."[55] It was widely "expected that the Bryan Speech as ground out by the phonograph will play an important part in the campaign."[56]

The phonograph, however, did not live up to Democratic expectations. Three weeks after Bryan's recording session, the Democrats sued the M. A. Winter Company for failing to deliver graphophone records in accordance with the terms of their contract. The *Washington Post* reported that the plaintiffs entered into a contract "by the terms of which they were to secure records of campaign speeches by prominent Democrats to the number of ten, and that the defendant company was to furnish 250 duplicates of each record." These were to be used for campaign purposes. "The plaintiff says that in pursuance to the contract they induced William Jennings Bryan, Adlai E. Stevenson, Charles A. Towne, James D. Richardson, chairman of the Democratic congressional committee Representative John J. Lentz, William Sulzer and Attorney A. A. Lipscomb to orate into the machines, and placed an order with the defendant for duplicates of the records. The order, they claim, the defendant refuses to fill."[57] The M. A. Winter Company, which was in the process of making its owner's fortune by selling proprietary medicines, asserted that it had provided the complainants with mastered records but that they refused to accept them. Perhaps there was a problem with quality. One week later Justice Bradley ruled against the Democrats and for the defendants.[58] Not surprisingly there is no evidence that these recordings were used for campaign purposes. Nor do they seem to have survived. The loss of the phonograph proved a serious disappointment for the Bryan campaign.

As Election Day approached, consumers could purchase a substantial number of campaign records, which catered more or less equally to supporters of both candidates. As New Haven, Connecticut, prepared for Bryan's visit in late October, the local MacGowan Cycle Company advertised eleven different cylinders for sale. "Bryan's Speech of Acceptance" and "Bryan's Speech to Labor" were matched by "Roosevelt's Speech to Labor" and "McKinley's Letter of Acceptance." It seems unlikely that any of the actual candidates lent their voices to these recordings. In addition there were three pro-McKinley campaign songs ("We Stand By McKinley," "You Can't Keep McKinley from the Chair," and "Republican Campaign Shout") and one that was pro-Bryan ("Democratic Campaign Song").[59] Once again it was left to the recording industry to provide product on a commercial basis in which balance remained an important factor. However, unlike the 1896 campaign, these phonograph recordings seemed to be geared more for the home market than for phonograph parlors or penny arcades. More often than not consumers with disposable income were Republicans eager to purchase pro-McKinley cylinders. Any edge that the Democrats hoped to gain with the phonograph was lost.

Telephone, Bicycle, and Stereopticon

The telephone and the bicycle both faded in importance relative to their 1896 appearance as campaign novelties. The idea of sending cheers via long-distance telephone had originated in Chicago and was reprised for the city's "Parade of Sound Money Men" on October 27, 1900. It was not McKinley, however, who would be on the other end of the line. Rather, according to the *Chicago Tribune*, "the mingled music of the bands and cheers will create a din that will be heard in other cities. This will be literally true, for the Chicago Telephone company has arranged to hold open some of its long-distance lines for the benefit of the people in Cincinnati, St. Louis, Cleveland and Detroit."[60] The extent to which people actually listened remains an open question.

Instead of Republicans organizing the wheelmen as in 1896, it was the wheelmen who were organizing the politicians. The League of American Wheelmen was determined to get a "good roads plank" in both the Republican and Democratic platforms, and succeeded. In a campaign stunt, bicyclists delivered a message from President McKinley to the citizens of Wheeling, West Virginia, congratulating them on a festival that was promoting the protective tariff. Starting from Canton, Ohio, successive teams of bicyclists traversed the seventy-five miles that separated the two municipalities and delivered his letter through a series of relays in less than eight hours.[61] (Was Wheeling just a convenient distance from Canton, or did Republican wheelmen select the city due to its appealing name?) Republicans devoted more attention to the newest mode of transportation and often incorporated automobiles into their parades. In addition, McKinley and Roosevelt were both honorary members of the Automobile Club of America, while Bryan and Stevenson were not.[62]

By the late 1890s the stereopticon was hardly a "new media"; rather it had a wide-ranging and well-established presence in American political culture, which continued and even increased in 1900. Across New York State, Democratic campaign managers believed "many votes will be made for their candidates by the use of epigrams and cartoons flashed by the stereopticon."[63] In Gotham, the *New York Times* reported, "the Democratic stereopticon plasters everything in sight," hurling "precepts, apothegms and pictures against the bulwarks of the enemy." Expressions included "Smash the Trusts. The Young Man's Enemy" as well as "Tammany and True Democracy."[64] According to one newspaper, the stereopticon had never been so active on Chicago's streets. The Republican Hamilton Club had a veteran operator to project cartoons along with numerous "mottoes and expressions, assertions, declaration and statements" onto a canvas at 114 Madison Street in the middle of downtown:

> "When peace and order are restored in the Philippines, then the people shall have that government which is best suited to their needs." —President McKinley.
> "Wherever our flag goes, liberty accompanies it."
> "What's the matter with Teddy? He's all right."

The show, which was started "for purely educational purposes"(!), had reached 100,000 people according to stereopticon operator Coyne.[65] The nighttime use of the stereopticon on the city streets had become part of the cityscape, a familiar and even reassuring ritual.

Like the 1892 presidential election, the 1900 contest was a rematch. Novelty in this context must have seemed somewhat silly and out of place. Indeed, the men who were plugging songs and various odd devices at Democratic and Republican headquarters had become a source of mild ridicule. "Beginning weeks ago the campaign song man and the man with 'freak' devices for sale, have overrun the headquarters with more kinds of inventions, more volubility of description and more persistence than can be conceived of," a bemused *New York Times* reported.[66] Bryan's failed phonograph efforts and the absence of serious motion picture endeavors by either party were consistent with this tone. McKinley's two campaign slogans, "Four more years of the full dinner pail" and "Let well enough alone," likewise suggested a very different tone. Prosperity made a difference. In the end it was largely left to amusement entrepreneurs to deploy new media as a moneymaking scheme, keeping in mind the diverse political allegiances of their patrons.

THE ILLUSTRATED LECTURE, IMPERIALISM, AND THE ELECTIONS OF 1898 AND 1900

There was, however, one easily overlooked media phenomenon that played a significant role in the 1900 presidential election: the illustrated lecture. These documentary-like programs were delivered by people who had no formal ties to the Republican Party. Unlike Judge Wheeler and his epigones, they had no prior history of political oratory, nor did their schedule narrowly conform to the campaign season; rather, they operated according to another kind of calendar. Because many of these platform orators offered personal accounts of their experiences during the Spanish-American or Filipino-American wars, or after having visited America's new overseas empire, they did not generally seem to be particularly political. Nevertheless, if America as an imperial power was the paramount issue of the 1900 election; former and current soldiers, ministers advocating for a muscular Christianity, and stereopticon lecturers such as E. Burton Holmes became effective propagandists for annexation, expansion, the new American empire—and so for the Republican ticket. Their impact was immediately evident, as two key figures, Mason Mitchell and Dwight Elmendorf, promoted Theodore Roosevelt as a war hero.

Promoting Teddy Roosevelt

Within days of the July 1, 1898, Battle of San Juan Hill, newspapers were reporting on efforts to draft Teddy Roosevelt as the Republican candidate for governor of New York State.[67] There was one serious impediment to this drive: Republican Frank S. Black, the current governor, was eager to run again. By the end of the month, Mason Mitchell, a veteran actor and Roosevelt Rough Rider who had been wounded at the Battle of San Juan Hill, was preparing his return to the vaudeville stage with a twenty-five-minute illustrated lecture, *How We Placed "Old Glory" on San Juan Hill*.[68] The future of the draft Roosevelt bandwagon remained uncertain when Mitchell opened at Proctor's Pleasure Palace on September 5 as a headline attraction.[69] As the *New York Clipper* reported, "Hispano-American interest was centered in Mason Mitchell, rough rider actor, in illustrated recitals descriptive of the battle of La Guisamas and San Juan, his effective word pictures being not only interesting but instructive, made so by the fact of the actor's personal experience in Cuba."[70] *Vogue* magazine called it "a tremendous sensation," while the *New York Sun* gave the routine an extensive review, concluding, "The eighteen-minute narrative's dramatic height was its praise of Roosevelt at the climax."[71] Of the various heroic soldiers whom Mitchell mentioned, Colonel Roosevelt was the only one to survive the battles. (See document 12 in the appendix.)

On September 27, after Mitchell had completed the third and final week of his run at Proctor's Pleasure Palace, New York Republicans nominated Roosevelt for governor on the first ballot. Mitchell had been his crucial propagandist. Two days later the grateful candidate wrote him, "About the only request I have made of the State Committee is that they shall surely have you do that piece of work you suggested." Roosevelt was requesting a meeting at the Fifth Avenue Hotel for the following evening: "You are the only Rough Rider with dramatic and literary capacity and I am very sincerely obliged to you if you can meet me at the hour named."[72] After their consultation, Mitchell went to Albany, the state capital, to perform his Roosevelt routine at Leland's Opera House. With Roosevelt's nomination secured, Mitchell took his headline attraction to Chicago and St. Louis. The actor then left the vaudeville stage for a few weeks and joined his former commander on October 22 in Gloversville, New York, where, according to the *New York Times*, "The Kasson Opera House was packed and an overflow meeting was held. It is estimated that Col. Roosevelt spoke to nearly 7,000 people." For the many who could not gain admittance, "overflow meetings were being held in Bleecker Square and several thousand people were addressed by Mason Mitchell, the actor and Rough Rider, who described the battles at Santiago. Col Roosevelt appeared later."[73] Roosevelt and Mitchell then traveled together to Syracuse, Utica, Schenectady, and other cities. In 1896, politics had moved into vaudeville with Biograph's program of McKinley; two years later, an actor temporarily left vaudeville to take a prominent role in the performance of politics.

Following Roosevelt's victory, the veteran Rough Rider continued to proselytize on Roosevelt's behalf in key cities across the country. Mitchell played Keith's vaudeville houses in Boston, Providence, and New York City; he then went on to Washington, DC, Cleveland, Cincinnati, Des Moines, Indianapolis, and St. Louis (again). Afterward he played summer parks and venues of lesser prominence, helping to make Roosevelt a war hero with a national reputation and so strengthening his attractiveness as a vice presidential candidate for 1900. Nor was Mitchell the only Rough Rider to deliver illustrated talks on Roosevelt's behalf. On the West Coast, Roosevelt Rough Rider George C. King delivered illustrated lectures on the Battle of Santiago.[74]

Roosevelt's other prominent marketeer with a stereopticon was Dwight Elmendorf, a highly regarded amateur photographer. Elmendorf had been a teacher of the deaf until he lost his job in April 1896 after vigorously defending his students from an accusation of murder.[75] Like Roosevelt, he was from an old, prominent Dutch family, and his

FOR **GOVERNOR·**   FOR LIEUT·**GOVERNOR**

OL·THEODORE ROOSEVELT·   TIMOTHY L·WOODRUFF·

FIGURE 28. Theodore Roosevelt ran for governor of New York State as a war hero and wore his military uniform in this 1898 campaign poster. Courtesy the Library of Congress.

plight received sympathy as he began a new career. By April 1897 he was giving an illustrated lecture on the Windward Islands (the Lesser Antilles in the Caribbean) for the Baptist Social Union.[76] He then took photographs for the well-known travel lecturer Albert Bickmore to use in his stereopticon lectures for the 1897–98 season.[77] Based on Elmendorf's experience, reputation, and connections (his father was a prominent Republican), *Scribner's Magazine* hired him to photograph US troops at their base in Tampa, then follow them to Cuba and finally to Montauk Point, where they recovered from illnesses and were discharged. He spent a significant amount of this time with Roosevelt's Rough Riders.

In mid-October Elmendorf presented his war views to a large audience at the University Club in New York.[78] By November he was presenting *The Santiago Campaign and the Destruction of Cervera's Fleet* in small, nontheatrical venues such as the Harlem YMCA and the Chapel of Hope:

> Dwight L. Elmendorf, who was with the army when it entered Cuba and remained with it during its stay there, took a large number of photographs. From them he has made several hundred slides, which give a graphic picture of the Hundred Days' War. . . . The charge of the Rough Riders up San Juan Hill with a view of the blockhouse seems far more real, when the eye as well as the ear, can receive the impressions.[79]

His largest and most prestigious venue was the Carnegie Lyceum in January 1899: "There were numerous pictures taken among the 'Rough Riders,' and a very impressive one of these showed the regiment kneeling and sitting on the grass in camp with uncovered heads on a Sunday listening to a sermon by their Chaplain, 'Fighting Parson' Brown. Another view showed the three mascots of the regiment—the eagle 'Teddy,' the little dog 'Cuba,' and the wildcat 'Josephine.'"[80] Eventually Elmendorf added motion pictures to the mix with publicity suggesting (incorrectly) that he had shot them (the actual cameraman was Edison-licensed William Paley, who was not embedded with the Rough Riders in Cuba).[81] Perhaps this is how the myth got started that Roosevelt had a filmmaker at the Battle of San Juan Hill.

While consistently playing nontheatrical venues, Elmendorf also traveled the Northeast—Boston, New Jersey, and Baltimore. Certainly this is one high-profile instance where an independent media maker promoted Roosevelt as a war hero. Yet Elmendorf's impact was broader than his individual stereopticon lectures: he and William Dinwiddie, another photographer attached to the Rough Riders, provided lantern slides to other stereopticon lecturers such as Mason Mitchell.[82] Their photographs were published in *Scribner's Magazine*, *Harper's Weekly*, and other outlets. These materials were eventually deposited with the Theodore Roosevelt Association and now reside in a special collection at Harvard Library. Lantern slides and the stereopticon, rather than motion pictures, were integral to promoting a Roosevelt persona that complemented the muscular self-confidence of a nation exercising its military strength overseas. These then were deeply political expressions that cast McKinley's vice presidential candidate in heroic terms. And per Morreale, it was an unusually prominent profile.

Illustrated Lectures on the Cuban War

Illustrated lectures on Cuba and the Spanish-American War were successors to the Civil War lantern shows that had been immensely popular since the 1860s. Many speakers delivered their word pictures based on

FIGURE 29. Dwight Elmendorf took this photograph and used it for his stereopticon lectures on the Cuban War. Entitled "Varsity Rough Riders," this hand-tinted slide features "Teddy" Roosevelt. Courtesy the Houghton Library, Harvard University, Roosevelt R560.3.EL64–110.

their own experiences in the war zone: Elmendorf's closest counterpart was the well-regarded photographer William H. Rau, who photographed the war and presented his illustrated lecture *The Cuban War Crisis* under the auspices of the Photographic Society of Philadelphia (he was on its board of directors).[83] Even before the Spanish-American war, Harry F. Lincoln, who worked in the electrical field and spent two years on the island, offered *The War in Cuba* at the YMCA in Worcester.[84]

A number of military men, like Mitchell and King, gave accounts of their experiences in Cuba. Reverend W. G. Cassard, a chaplain in the US Navy, presented *Through the War on the "Indiana,"* "illustrated by more than seventy stereopticon views taken by him in the West Indies."[85] Charles Mason Fuller, also affiliated with the US Navy, presented *Cuba and Her Struggle for Independence* to the Belton Art Club.[86] Lieutenant Godfrey L. Carden, who had seen active service during the blockade of Havana and Santiago, showed his own pictures on the stereopticon for

The Men Behind the Guns.[87] Lieutenant J. P. O'Neil spoke of his personal experiences during the Cuban campaign at the Unitarian church in Portland, Oregon.[88] A few others who spent time in Cuba also spoke from personal experience.

Ministers and church officials constituted a second large category of illustrated lecturers: lacking direct personal experience, they used their expertise as public speakers to assert a moral stance on the war, enhance their reputations, and perhaps make additional income. They were frequent advocates of a muscular Christianity that linked manliness with the expansionist impulses set loose by the Spanish-American War.[89] Reverend H. C. Scotford of Chicago was often traveling with his presentation. On May 10, as the war was still in its early stages, he "gave his interesting and popular stereopticon lecture on Cuba, the Maine and the American Navy at the First Church . . . to a large and appreciative congregation, eliciting hearty applause."[90] His illustrated lecture included moving pictures projected via the optigraph marketed by Sears, Roebuck & Co.; they were considered to be of great interest. Ten days later he gave the same lecture at Pilgrim's Church in Chicago.[91] Other Chicago-area presentations followed. Scotford's relationship with Sears and Roebuck was such that the mail-order business began to sell a published version of Scotford's lecture, *America's War with Spain for the Freedom of Cuba*, along with a set of fifty-two lantern slides.[92]

Although Scotford provided Sears, Roebuck & Co. with a way to reach out to the religious community, he was not a particularly prominent figure in evangelical circles. Of the many ministers who lectured on the war, a few may have acquired his show, though which ones is impossible to ascertain. Reverend J. H. Adams delivered an illustrated lecture entitled *Cuba* at the Congregational Church in South Hadley, Massachusetts;[93] Reverend George C. Bliss gave a similar lecture illustrated by stereopticon views at the Baptist Church in Savoy, Massachusetts;[94] Reverend Clarence R. Gale traveled across the country presenting *Cuba and the Cuban War* with eighty superb views;[95] Reverend Hanns of Wilmington, Delaware, delivered *Cuba and the War with Spain* at a camp meeting ground for the Epworth Methodist Episcopal Church;[96] Reverend Arthur C. Ludlow gave an evening sermon (likely illustrated) on *Picturesque Cuba: Manners and Customs of the People* at the Bolton Avenue Church in Cleveland;[97] and Doctor E. Homer Wellman, rector of the Church of Atonement in Brooklyn, "delivered his finely illustrated lecture *Cuba and the Philippines* before an appreciative audience" at the Lenox Road Baptist Church in Flatbush, Brooklyn.[98]

Educators and doctors less frequently served as platform orators. Thomas O. Baker, principal of Yonkers High School, presented *Cuba and the West Indies*,[99] while Charles G. Frowert MD presented *Cuba and the Cuban War*, illustrated with lantern views, for the Woman's Club of the Knights Templar.[100] Many men lecturing on the Cuban War seemed to have had no established profession. Some may have lost their jobs or were otherwise looking for a fresh start (not unlike Elmendorf). J. Frank Davis, who would become a successful writer of fiction in the late 1910s, delivered *The Five-Barred Flag of Yara, or Cuba and Its Struggle*, a "patriotic lecture" with nearly one hundred stereopticon views at various Pawtucket, Rhode Island, venues.[101] Others never seemingly found stability or success: A. C. Colt gave an illustrated lecture on Cuba in Cleveland;[102] E. A. Haven presented *Under the Cuban Star* to the YWCA on Fifteenth Street in Manhattan;[103] E. P. Fitch, a sometime insurance salesman and occasional stereopticon lecturer, presented *Cuba* with "over 100 Views of Cuba and pictures of the vessels of the U.S. navy . . . as well as many pictures of the Maine, before and after the explosion in Havana harbor" at White's Opera House in Plattsmouth, Nebraska;[104] Henry L. Bailey, who billed himself as formerly a newspaperman in Cuba, presented *The Cuban War* at Ford's Opera House;[105] W. E. Youngquist, who would later become a phrenologist, gave two illustrated lectures on the *Maine* disaster and Cuba in West Duluth, Minnesota.[106]

Cuba was also a topic for professional travel lecturers. Professor Albert S. Bickmore delivered a lecture at the American Museum of Natural History in New York on *Cuba-Havana and Santiago* in which "the listeners and watchers were enchanted by views illustrating the wonderful fertility of the island."[107] John C. Bowker, who was in the early stages of his career delivering travel lectures, gave a presentation on Cuba and Spain that explored differences in national character.[108] These speakers thus offered a counterpart to the accounts of heroic US military actions, hinting at the peoples and resources that had come under America's colonial umbrella.

Two illustrated lectures stand out as somewhat unusual. The first was widely covered in the US press: Count Avon Goetzen, a former German military attaché who accompanied the US Army to Cuba, presented his illustrated assessment to military men in Berlin. Remarking that "the only good volunteers were the 'Rough Riders,'" he praised the United States by declaring that "the Americans are prime colonists."[109] The other, *Cuba and the Spanish War*, was given by the Guatemalan

Don Jose de Herrera and combined moving pictures with lantern slides. He was far more cautious about American military omnipotence, suggesting that the war "might continue for another five years."[110]

These illustrated lectures were complemented by motion picture programs. Biograph and the Edison Manufacturing Company had sent cameramen to Florida and Cuba, where they shot a variety of war-related film subjects. Many exhibition services showed war films in vaudeville under the brand name of Wargraph. Traveling exhibitors also screened these films in smaller cities and towns in late 1898, 1899, and beyond. The programs were generally jingoistic in orientation. The screen remained Republican. While these audiovisual genres were only part of a larger media formation that was activated by the war, they provided occasions for citizens to come together in public spaces—a crucial complement to the mass-circulation daily newspapers that were read privately and thus engendered individual responses. The theater, auditorium, and church provided a space for group participation and expression. In such venues a community could recognize itself, its beliefs and political commitments.

The war in Cuba was America's first major conflict after the Civil War and did much to heal the psychic wounds that remained from that bloody ordeal. As aging Confederate and Union soldiers fought together for the first time, the nation was made whole (or, more accurately, the white nation was reunited, as blacks and other people of color were largely excluded from this calculus). The Spanish-American War in the Caribbean was certainly about the United States' emerging role as a world power and its ability to project that power overseas. The Caribbean had been a sea chock-full of European colonial possessions. Suddenly the United States had assumed a preeminent role in the area. The illustrated lectures on Cuba told of these achievements, engineered by the McKinley administration, again and again.

Presentations on the Philippines

Illustrated talks on Cuba did not address the nation's role as a colonizing and imperial power as forcefully as presentations on the Philippines. Few if any lantern shows focused on the Philippines before the Spanish-American War, but that quickly changed. In his presentation a few days after Admiral Dewey's victory at the Battle of Manila Bay on May 1, 1898, Reverend Dan F. Bradley told a large audience that the Philippines was a prize that the United States should keep—and use. "I have a dream that the stars and stripes may float permanently over Manila," he declared.[111] J.E. Stevens presented *Manila and the Philippines*, and explained the many reasons Filipinos had to revolt against the brutal Spanish.[112] Annie S. Edwards presented *Manila and the Philippines* at the Central Congregational Church, Brooklyn, "showing the Manila girls and women and their mode of dress."[113]

World traveler Frank R. Roberson, who had lived in the Philippines, quickly returned to the islands with a photographer.[114] By early December 1898 he was on the Lyceum circuit with *Manila and the Philippines*, with 275 lantern slides, giving "his audience a new view of the Filipino and a clearer conception of the situation in the islands."[115] "The people were not all savages . . . fully nine-tenths are cultured, many of them graduates from European colleges," he remarked.[116] Roberson was "strongly opposed to the annexation of the Islands by the United States" and feared "that the United States will have trouble with the Filipinos in the near future."[117] Was the Philippines to be a new colony, a resumption of America's westward expansion, or were Americans there to help liberate the Filipinos, who had all but defeated the Spanish before the Spanish-American War? Roberson's concerns proved prescient. Although Filipinos and Americans were initially allies, tensions escalated and the two sides fought the Second Battle of Manila on February 4, 1899, with US troops victorious.

As the Filipino-American War continued, returning soldiers presented illustrated lectures on the Philippines. These were almost always stories of good Americans pacifying a country that they had taken from the Spanish, one in which the local populace was primitive, uneducated, and not yet ready for self-government. Douglas White, war correspondent for the *San Francisco Examiner-Journal*, discussed the activities of the California soldiers in the Philippines, "illustrated by over a hundred original views most of which were made by Mr. White."[118] Captain P.J.H. Farrell of the Medical Corps delivered *The War in the Philippines*.[119] Two recently returned members of the US Signal Corps presented an illustrated lecture on the Philippines at the People's Club in New York City.[120] They were almost certainly Sergeant Fritz Andreae and Private William H. Reeves, who subsequently took their lecture *Stirring Scenes in the Philippines* on the road. They had taken many of the photographs themselves and offered a grunt's view of the war.[121] Captain H.L. Wells traveled the far west, giving his illustrated lecture, *War in the Philippines*, using more than 150 stereopticon views, "the large number taken by the captain, and these will be used to illustrate the many scenes of camp life and battle-field which are graphically depicted."[122] Lieutenant Clarence I. Boardman gave two lectures on the Philippines using "60 excellent stereopticon views taken from Kodak pictures, comprising scenes about the cities, in the trenches and on the battlefield."[123] Charles Lisle, a journalist who had joined the First Montana Volunteers, lectured with views he had taken while in the Philippines.[124]

Recently developed camera technology—particularly the Kodak camera—enabled ordinary soldiers (or at least ordinary officers) to document their wartime experiences, resulting in quite personal programs. Colonel Campbell gave particular attention "to the Island of Luzon, the seat of the rebellion against American authority, and the views with which the descriptions were accompanied were clear and lifelike." He "advised young men with capital to go to the Philippines feeling that for every $1,000 invested five times the amount will be made in a few years."[125] Reverend Father William D. McKinnon, who was chaplain for the First California Volunteers, lectured across the country, often using the stereopticon. He minimized the strength and moral merit of Filipino freedom fighters: "What we need here in America is more patriotism and less criticism," he declared. "This war would long since have ceased were it not for the criticism which has reached the camp of Aguinaldo and his followers and revived their drooping spirits and encouraged them to persevere in their madness. The natives are not capable of self government, nor does any large proportion of them wish it."[126] Many Americans saw the struggle to put down native resistance in the Philippines as a continuation of the Indian wars, which had ended with the Wounded Knee massacre on December 29, 1890. This was certainly true for General Elwell Otis, military governor of the Philippines during this period, who had fought Native Americans in the decades following the Civil War. These illustrated lectures were facilitated if not actually sponsored by the Department of War—in short, the McKinley administration. At a time when US military involvement in the Philippines was highly controversial, having ordinary solders provide personal, stirring accounts of their wartime experience was effective propaganda for its continuation.

Very few lantern lectures took an anti-imperialist perspective. Ramon Reyes Lala, a native of the Philippines, presented one possible exception. At various New York venues he discussed "the problems of the islands from an inside point of view of particular interest at this juncture."[127] Lala also published a book, *The Philippine Islands* (1899), which was

FIGURE 30. Sears, Roebuck & Co. produced this poster for semiprofessional and amateur showmen giving illustrated lectures on Cuba and the Philippines, circa 1900. Courtesy Terry and Deborah Borton.

praised in *The Dial* as fairly impartial, well written, and instructive, and "leaving a more favorable impression of the Filipinos than found in other writers."[128] Like some other lecturers, Lala also emphasized the mineral wealth of the Philippines. Dr. David T. Day of the United States Geological Survey, for instance, delivered an illustrated lecture on *The Mineral Resources of Cuba, Porto Rico, Hawaii and the Philippines* at the American Museum of Natural History.[129] While Lala may have seen these natural resources as a boom for the islanders, his counterparts generally saw them as one more reason for annexation.

The preeminent lecturer to present on the Philippines was Burton Holmes, who had "won unusual popularity not only on account of the beauty of the lantern views, which he showed, but also because his subjects were far from hackneyed and treated in a fresh and attractive manner."[130] During the 1898–99 season he delivered a travel lecture on Hawaii. Holmes had arrived in Honolulu on the ship that brought news that the United States had annexed the Hawaiian Islands, and was thus able to present a first-person account of America's newest possession. "The life in the islands, the customs of the Islanders, their most productive industries, coffee and sugar-raising, picturesque bits of Hawaiian scenery, the abundant and varied vegetation of the country were entertainingly described by the lecturer and illustrated by his pictures," noted the *Baltimore Sun*. "The possibilities of Pearl harbor as a future naval station were suggested and views along the shores were shown."[131] Holmes offered a convincing case for US acquisition of the Hawaiian Islands even as he reassured his audience that Honolulu was already heavily Americanized.

For Burton Holmes, a lecture on another one of America's newest possessions in the Pacific—the Philippines—was an obvious follow-up for his next season of programming. He had arrived in Manila by the beginning of June 1899 in the midst of fighting and was confined to Manila and the small amount of territory that the US Army controlled beyond it. The world traveler claimed to have brought the first motion picture camera to the Philippines, and so covered his trip with both still and moving picture cameras.[132] Much of his time was spent in Manila, where the US Army had assumed the role of an occupying force. Curfew was necessary to prevent Filipino sabotage at night. Holmes met with many of the top officials of the occupation and was ultimately embedded with the Third Infantry based in Baliuag, where soldiers used the local church as a barrack and waited for Emilio Aguinaldo and his troops to attack at night. Premiering his program entitled *Manila* in late

October at Chicago's Central Music Hall, Holmes praised the American soldiers as "brave fellows and honorable," sketching out their difficult situation as they fought an enemy who remained essentially invisible.[133]

Holmes's lecture was considered "matters of news": an up-to-the-minute report from the front when first presented.[134] In the opinion of one reviewer, it offered "some hints of the task which the Nation has before it in the solution of the Philippine problem," but "if the audience learned anything they were never allowed to lose sight of the fact that they were entertained."[135] Although Holmes told his story from the American side, he was ready to criticize General Otis for his cultural insensitivity when he banned the Filipino pastime of cockfighting. Importantly, it was not just what was being said, but how. As the *New York Tribune* noted, "The motion pictures which were shown were an important part of the programme and formed a most pleasant innovation in the illustrated lecture field. Mr. Holmes has long used motion pictures, but they have usually been placed at the end of the lecture. Now they are placed within it, in the series of regular illustrations."[136] Holmes was delivering an evening-length program, which combined his own slides and his own films: that he was one of the first platform orators to do so also contributed to his success. In the process he was offering McKinleyism lite. He offered his experiences as a traveler, carefully balancing his criticisms with praise as a way to avoid any strong ideological pronouncements that might separate him from a significant portion of his audience. It was only at the end, almost in passing, that he confirmed what was implicit throughout—that the United States' expansion was inevitable.

Reviews suggest that Holmes refashioned his lecture as he presented it around the country during the 1899–1900 theatrical season. (See document 13 in the appendix.) A final version of his lecture was soon published in book form. It concluded:

> We are far from satisfied with the results of our war-time visit to the Philippines. In fact, we have not seen the Philippines, we have seen only the city of Manila and the narrow strip of Luzon territory held by our forces. Of the wonderful Philippine Archipelago we have seen virtually nothing. We depart, therefore, with the firm resolve to return on the conclusion of the war to study the Americanized Luzon of the near future and to explore the other islands of the archipelago when peace shall have made them accessible to the traveler.
>
> Yet it is something to have been witnesses to the transformation of Manila, to have seen the sleepy haunt of Spanish inactivity suddenly become the busy center of American enterprise in the Far East.[137]

Although the main body of his lecture was respectful of Filipinos and their traditions, Holmes saw annexation and the Americanization of the Philippines as an essential part of the unfinished story.

These documentary-like programs cannot be seen in isolation. They were part of a larger media formation in which Americans engaged the issues associated with the United States' new role as an imperial power on the world stage. Although this "paramount issue" of the 1900 election was extensively addressed in audiovisual formats, these programs were not sponsored by the Republican National Committee nor by associated political action committees. The pervasive presence of military personnel recounting their experiences in Cuba and the Philippines must make us look to the Department of War and the Department of the Navy as governmental agencies that could function as effective political propagandists. The military's self-promotion, which Peter Davis would expose in his television documentary *The Selling of the Pentagon* (CBS, 1970), was already operative some seventy years earlier.

There was, to be sure, a strong anti-imperialist movement in the United States. The American Anti-Imperialist League took shape in the second half of 1898 and had among its members Andrew Carnegie, John Dewey, Mark Twain, William James, Henry James, and Grover Cleveland.[138] At a mass meeting at New York's Cooper Union in May 1900, Carl Schurz, former secretary of the interior under President Rutherford Hayes (1877–81), was among the several speakers. Closely associated with the reform wing of the Republican Party, he "urged his hearers to put an end to the war in the Philippines by the overthrow of the Republican Party at the next election and declared that the United States had broken its faith in its dealings with the Filipinos."[139] As the presidential campaign intensified, a meeting under the auspices of the Greater New York Association of Anti-Imperialist Clubs took place at the Murray Hill Lyceum of the East Side. There John Vernon Bouvier, whose granddaughter would later marry John F. Kennedy, declared that "the early traditions of our country are being overturned; it means that we have gone 12,000 miles out of our way to knock out the Monroe doctrine. It is in this frenzy of conquest instituted by the Republican Administration that it is going against every tradition of our land."[140]

These rival perspectives on the Filipino war occasionally collided, for instance at a meeting sponsored by the Brooklyn Philosophical Society in which a speech by Murat Halstead turned into tumultuous debate.[141] Halstead, a newspaperman who was serving as a flack for the McKinley administration and the US Army, asserted that Emilio Aguinaldo, president of the Philippine Republic, did not represent the Filipino people and "there never was such a thing as a Filipino Republic." He also argued that "peace could only come by the establishment by American arms in the Philippine Islands of a stable form of government and one upon which the people could rely."[142] Mr. Leverson then spoke, attacked Halstead's McKinleyism, and called the speaker a liar. According to the *Brooklyn Eagle*, "Clinton Furbish then took the platform and declared, 'No man has a right to govern another man without that man's consent,' he said amid applause. 'It is a pity that what President Lincoln said cannot be repeated by Mark Hanna and McKinley.'"[143]

The 1900 election saw the revival of the illustrated lecture as an effective political weapon. As had been true throughout the 1890s, Democrats—and the anti-imperialist clubs—avoided the illustrated lecture even though they did not lack for speakers and printed pamphlets. Their speeches and rallies usually presented more explicit arguments against expansionism, and they sometimes complained that the Republicans avoided the topic of imperialism and focused on the issue of Free Silver.[144] But Republicans were making arguments through the personal stories of military personnel and the moral persuasion of preachers. These illustrated lectures were particularly effective because they provided many different versions of a story that supported McKinleyism but did so, or appeared to do so, outside the framework of party politics and argument. It was politicking by other means—and for that reason perhaps all the more effective. As Bryan campaigned across the country, his political operatives discovered that "the people . . . were deaf to a prophet proclaiming the error of their ways and their transgression of the faith of their fathers."[145]

These lantern lectures established an essential narrative of courageous Americans in ways that helped to ensure McKinley's electoral victory even before the traditional campaign season had begun. Generally mixed with a healthy dose of racism and American exceptionalism, it was a narrative of the good Americans risking their lives to bring freedom, resource development, and lessons of responsible government to third-world peoples—an ideological predisposition that would be mobilized again and again during the twentieth century and beyond, whether in Panama, Haiti, Guatemala, Korea, Vietnam, or Iraq.

CHAPTER 5

Coda

The previous chapters have examined four presidential campaigns that reveal the shifting concerns of Americans as the United States prepared to enter the twentieth century. From debates about the tariff and protectionism (1888, 1892) to concerns that focused on the nation's money supply (1896), and finally America's role as a world power (1900), these elections raised issues that remain very much with us, from the Trans-Pacific Trade Partnership to the role of the Federal Reserve Board or the US military's role in the Middle East. Although this study takes these debates seriously, its chief purpose has been to investigate the successive media formations of these quadrennial contests, paying particular attention to emergent media: the stereopticon, phonograph, telephone, and cinema. Before this period the newspapers were not only the dominant but the sole modern media form that directly impacted US presidential elections, aided to be sure by the telegraph and the railroads. After the Democrat-leaning press broke twenty-eight years of Republican hegemony in 1884, the next four presidential campaigns witnessed the deployment of new forms of audiovisual reproducibility—forerunners of the complex mediascape of the present day.

From my first encounters with the 1892 stereopticon lecture *The Tariff Illustrated* to the final rewrites, this book has taken shape through a series of surprising encounters with the historical record. As I grappled with this new research as well as fresh analytical and theoretical perspectives, my investigation became Janus-like, looking in two opposing directions. One has faced toward a series of intellectual engagements around such terms as "early cinema," "media archaeology," and "new media." The other gazes into the world of presidential politicking, looking for commonalities, disjunctions, and longer-term trends even while recognizing that every election is unique, differing from others in the issues, the state of the nation, available finances, the candidates' personalities, and their own political histories as well as the specific media formations in which each campaign unfolds.

ELECTORAL POLITICS AND THE MEDIA

Media has proved a productive starting point for exploring the dynamics of electoral politics. They came together geographically in New York City, which was both the media capital of the United States and also, so far as political calculations were concerned, the key swing state for achieving electoral victory. The daily press was the dominant media form throughout this period and played a critical role in presidential politicking. New York City's mass-circulation dailies leaned Democratic in the 1880s and early 1890s. They were key to Democratic victory in two of those three elections: 1884 and 1892. When these newspapers shifted their allegiances to William McKinley in 1896 and 1900, the Republican candidate emerged victorious. New York's leading newspaper publishers saw themselves as power brokers and defenders of American values, eager to construct ethical binaries in which their favored candidates embodied the virtues of civil society while their opponents violated the social contract. They were larger-than-life personalities. Joseph Pulitzer built the (arguably) tallest building in the world on Park Row, then filled its lower floors with commercial tenants. He was a businessman who embraced Grover Cleveland's conservative politics but, like most other capitalists, shared a deep antipathy toward William Jennings Bryan. William Randolph Hearst and his father, George Hearst, were also long-standing Democrats who supported Cleveland. The family fortune was made in silver mining, however, which meant that Bryan's advocacy for Free Silver appealed to Hearst's economic roots if not his strict economic self-interest.[1] His enthusiastic support for Bryan in 1896 and 1900 also paid dividends in the newspaper world, placing him in a unique position as principal media champion of the new Democratic Party.

A slightly different book, one focusing on the intersection of the mass media and politics, could easily study political intrigues among New

York City's newspaper publishers in much greater detail. It wasn't only Whitelaw Reid of the *New York Tribune* who ended up personally involved in party politics and running for political office. Pulitzer stumped for Democratic presidential candidate Samuel Tilden in 1876 and was a delegate to the Democratic National Convention in 1880. After acquiring the *New York World* in 1883, he championed New York Governor Grover Cleveland, advocating for his nomination in 1884 and contributing mightily to his electoral victory.[2] That same year he was also nominated and then elected as a Democratic congressman for the Ninth District of New York. After missing almost 90 percent of the roll call votes in Congress during his first year, he resigned due to journalistic responsibilities. Hearst served as a Democratic congressman for the Eleventh District of New York between 1903 and 1907—with an equally bad voting record. All three newspaper publishers continued in the tradition of Horace Greeley, editor of the *New York Tribune* before, during, and after the Civil War. Greeley, who also served briefly in Congress, went on to be the Liberal Republican and Democratic nominee for president, losing to Ulysses S. Grant in 1872.

Although the leading newspapers of the 1890s were strongly aligned with either the Democrats or the Republicans, they were considered independent—and they were in the sense that their publishers were free to choose the candidates and even the party that they championed. For better or worse, both parties lacked their own official newspapers, perhaps accounting for their eagerness to pursue other media possibilities. Abner McKinley and Benjamin Harrison could own pieces of a media start-up (the American Mutoscope Company), which could then be used to promote the Republican nominee (whoever that might be). The Republican National Committee could arrange for a long-distance telephone to connect their candidate with thousands of cheering supporters. Bryan and the Democratic Party could try to create a novel Speakers Bureau using phonograph recordings that featured their chief standard bearers. Such efforts potentially had a widespread impact, as they provided evidence that a candidate was active, creative, and up to date. These new media landmarks held great promise, which was not always realized. When successful they provided important stylistic flourishes: they were necessary parts of a quadrennial ritual, crucial to the candidates' performance of politics.

The media played a critical role in electoral politics, as it did in almost all aspects of American life, but it was not necessarily determinative. Among other things, Americans tend to vote their pocketbooks. As

Bill Clinton's campaign was wont to emphasize: "It's the economy, stupid." Economists have estimated the gross national product of the United States in the 1880s and 1890s.[3] From this they approximate its annual growth rate. A brief, mild recession in 1888 was serious enough to have hurt incumbent Cleveland at the ballot box. Infighting among New York Democrats as well as Judge John L. Wheeler's lantern lecture further ensured Harrison's victory. The next presidential campaign occurred during a boom year, but by November 1892, the early stages of the Financial Panic of 1893 may have already been under way. Certainly the West was alienated enough from politics as usual to empower the Populists. With the economy not favoring incumbent Harrison, a united Democratic Party and a sympathetic press were enough for Cleveland to succeed in New York and elsewhere. Four years of full-blown economic crisis followed. The situation in 1896 was volatile given the Free Silver politics of the Democrats (and their fusion with the Populists), but financial disarray typically helps the party out of power: a press that deserted Bryan effectively ensured McKinley's victory. Finally, 1900 was a year of remarkable economic prosperity, which certainly contributed to President McKinley's reelection. For many voters, prosperity and America's overseas expansion were arguably linked. The state of the nation—particularly its economic circumstances—and the mass media were crucial factors in the outcome of these elections.

Stereopticon lectures such as *The Tariff Illustrated* or *The War in the Philippines* occupied an intermediate position between the powerful daily press and the tentative first steps of a media future, mobilizing audio and visual reproductions of performance. In ways that I did not anticipate when this project began, they became a central feature of this undertaking, threading their way through all four presidential elections of the long 1890s. Here politicking intersected with the documentary tradition to produce a loosely constructed genre that has persisted for more than 130 years even as it has been repeatedly reshaped by technological innovation. The political documentary began with Judge Wheeler's *The Tariff Illustrated*, which operated in the expository mode as Wheeler provided the "voice-over" narration that accompanied the images.[4] Of course, Wheeler's program lacked an impersonal "voice of god" narration given that its author was at the podium offering a personalized version of familiar Republican rhetoric. (As Lisa Gitelman has pointed out, sound traditionally had a visual component, which audio recording often eliminated. The disembodied voice or "voice of god" came only later—first through intertitles and then with recorded voice-over after 1930.)[5]

The following election, Wheeler was joined by five other lecturers offering their own versions of his popular program celebrating the protective tariff. None of these men were full-time lanternists. Rather, they used the illustrated lecture as a form of political oratory, to distinguish themselves from other speakers on the stump. They had other careers and might be described as semiprofessionals, with the speaker's platform offering social and political capital more than significant supplementary income. The latter was particularly true for W. D. Boyce, who delivered a final variant in this cycle of tariff programs in 1896. Although such shows were not inexpensive to produce in themselves, most of the speakers had previously given illustrated lectures, so they owned or had access to equipment; acquiring the necessary lantern slides for such a program was only a modest additional cost. They provided Republican organizations and their political action committees with distinctive, personalized programs that resonated with other media components of their campaigns.

The illustrated lectures that flourished at the end of the 1890s were different in kind: they did not function as innovative extensions of political oratory but as timely offerings within one of the illustrated lecture's preeminent genres, focused on war. This is one reason why they worked so effectively on Roosevelt's and McKinley's behalf. If analyzed within a documentary studies framework, they clearly functioned within a variety of modes. Some—like the Cuban War programs presented by preachers—might be seen as operating within a "voice of god" expository mode (the obvious pun is worth taking seriously given the status of these ministers within their communities). Others offered a personal account of the Spanish-American and Filipino-American wars, in which the speakers at the podium had themselves taken many of the photographic lantern slides—often snapshots from their Kodak cameras. These individuals appeared inside the program's narrative as well, not only by showing what they witnessed through the photographs they shot but by appearing on screen in other photographs. Such programs offered a sophisticated mix of expository, observational, and self-reflexive elements.

The prevalence of these many stereopticon presentations during political campaigns of the long 1890s marked this period, giving it a particular character or structure of feeling. Although these illustrated lectures were secondary to the press, political oratory, and pageantry, the Republicans used them effectively, and this would provide a foundation for their continued mastery of the screen throughout most of the twentieth century. Writing in 1926, Terry Ramsaye remarked that "the motion picture screen was . . . born Republican, which it has remained ever since in striking consistency."[6] He honored *McKinley at Home* as the foundational moment, but the screen was already firmly Republican in 1888 and remained so throughout the next decade. These illustrated lectures are of particular interest for us today given that their many descendants—from Robert Greenwald's *Uncovered: The Whole Truth About the Iraq War* (2003) to Citizens United's *The Obama Effect* (2008) and Dinesh D'Souza's *2016: Obama's America*—have been significant and recurring factors in recent presidential campaigns. While the documentary tradition in its stereopticon, motion picture, and digital media articulations has played a significant but uneven role in presidential politicking, it has perhaps never quite rivaled the mass media of the press, radio, television, or the Internet. Moreover, when the specifics of this long history are examined, the genre does not necessarily align with the introduction of new media technologies.

The media stories behind democratic struggles for presidential power are always fascinating. Given the recurrent nature of these political campaigns, possible parallels between the 1890s and our more contemporary moment can be tantalizing. Similarities between William McKinley's successful 1896 campaign and that of Barack Obama in 2008 are particularly compelling. Both took full advantage of the new media of their day as active and passive beneficiaries. McKinley was an active beneficiary of his brother's motion picture start-up while the Republican National Committee developed fresh variants of political pageantry with bicycle parades, a nighttime spectacular of light on the North River, and the substitution of telephone transmitters for the candidate himself. The McKinley campaign also benefited from the efforts of independent media entrepreneurs such as the Edison Manufacturing Company. Obama's campaign produced a compelling Internet strategy even as he benefited from the short videos generated by formally unaffiliated digital media producers: many were amateurs or semiprofessionals while others, notably Robert Greenwald and the Brave New Films team of filmmakers, were veteran professionals.

If McKinley represented an urban future ready to exploit the possibilities of technological innovation, Obama possessed a cosmopolitan sophistication that had new media fluency as an essential component. Correspondingly, William Jennings Bryan was necessarily suspicious of modern media, seeing it as an intermediary that would distort and diminish his message, while Obama's opponent, Republican candidate

John McCain, was stuck in old-media paradigms of the past—relatively clueless as to the Internet's possibilities. If Bryan was fighting battles on behalf of the yeoman farmer who was part of a fading agrarian past, McCain was a hero from an earlier war and an earlier time (the Cold War era) and did his best to appeal to the conservative religious values of rural evangelical voters. Of course, there were many aspects of these campaigns for which such party-switching correspondences do not apply or are not so neat. Obama and Bryan were both fighting against corporate money and income inequality. Irrespective of his reliance on drone warfare, Obama was the candidate—like Bryan—who wanted to impose constraints on the projection of US military power overseas. In this respect Republicans and Democrats have retained many of their core values across more than a century.

If political operatives know one thing, it is that campaigning is unpredictable. As the 2016 presidential contest has already demonstrated, it is impossible to know for sure what elements of a campaign will resonate with voters and have an important impact on an election's outcome. The Republicans gave considerable credit to *The Tariff Illustrated* in 1888—more than it perhaps deserved. Expecting a great deal from its various 1892 reiterations, they were disappointed. Although six political orators had blanketed New York, Connecticut, and New Jersey with lantern presentations, Harrison lost all three states to Cleveland. Their presentations may have remained rhetorically effective in themselves, but they had lost some of their potency and certainly their ability to surprise. Prepared for this latest incarnation, the Democrats made sure to aggressively challenge their rhetoric and accuracy. This was, of course, what Republicans did with *Fahrenheit 9/11* in 2004. They were aided by the fact that Michael Moore already had a controversial reputation based on his previous documentaries; he had been active in the 2002 midterm elections on behalf of the Democrats, piggybacking off his Academy Award–winning *Bowling for Columbine* (2002). Two years later, Republican operatives quickly remobilized an array of critics with their previously established websites and largely nullified the threat that his documentary posed to George W. Bush's reelection.[7]

When the 1890s began, politicking and entertainment operated in two opposing cultural spheres. Then, as politics entered the realm of theaters and arcades, entrepreneurs were generally careful to offer fair and balanced programming. Phonograph parlors offered dueling cylinders for McKinley and Bryan in 1896 and 1900. Exhibitors employed such calculated neutrality or "objectivity" for their film programs in vaudeville houses and other venues with surprising regularity by 1900. Exceptions, such as Biograph's 1896 McKinley program or Mason Mitchell's vaudeville salute to Teddy Roosevelt in 1898, could be highly effective but difficult to engineer. Mitchell's Roosevelt routine not only hid behind a stirring account of battlefield heroics by the Rough Riders, but he delivered his spiel before Roosevelt had become the official Republican candidate for governor of New York. Once Roosevelt was the nominee, Mitchell entertained people in other parts of the country, only returning to New York State as an official Roosevelt campaigner where he did much of his talking *outside* the theater. Because Michael Moore's *Fahrenheit 9/11* enjoyed unprecedented theatrical access with no apparent Republican counterpart, its appearance was deemed particularly clever and made him a Democratic celebrity—and the Republican's archenemy—for much of the campaign.

Repeated comparisons between the new media moment of the 1890s and that of the new millennium may be intriguing, but they can also produce a deceptive—and reductive—binarism. The intervening century witnessed a number of technological breakthroughs that transformed politicking. Radio expanded and changed the role of political oratory, which had been of the utmost importance to presidential politicking. Douglas G. Craig has eloquently illuminated its impact on political campaigning in the 1920s and 1930s. Given the Democrats' hesitant and somewhat inept embrace of new audiovisual technologies in the 1890s, it is not entirely surprising that the party remained true to form in the 1920s. "The Democratic Party was less successful with early radio," Craig tells us. "Defeat came early to the Democrats in 1924 and it came through radio."[8] That changed famously when Franklin D. Roosevelt became president. But radio's place in the broader mediascape of electioneering still needs further investigation. In the 1948 campaign, where radio played as prominent a role as the press, a campaign film—*The Truman Story* (1948)—ended up being the decisive media event. Republican presidential candidate Thomas Dewey had planned to put his campaign film biography *The Dewey Story* into movie theaters as paid advertising, following widely accepted practices in broadcasting. Truman could not afford even to make such a film, never mind pay theater owners to show it. Instead, the Truman campaign successfully protested based on the principle of political symmetry that was established in the early 1900s. Universal Pictures ended up producing *The Truman Story*, which followed *The Dewey Story* into theaters, appearing the week before the election. At the time movie attendance was 96 million per week, while the number of actual voters was roughly half of that (48,793,535). It was "the most important and most successful publicity break of the entire campaign," according to Jack Redding, publicity director for the Democratic National Committee, while the motion picture industry was ruefully convinced that the film had elected Harry S. Truman as president.[9] Even though the screen was Republican, some well-laid plans backfired.

Dewey may have been too media savvy for his own good, but this did not deter Republicans in the next presidential contest. Dwight Eisenhower's embrace of the new media of television in 1952 gave him a decisive edge in that campaign, though he likely would have won without it. His new media advantage was not unlike McKinley's with the biograph in 1896. One obvious difference: McKinley's efforts were confined to a single theater, while Eisenhower's reached private homes across America. Eisenhower's use of television was an effective embrace of a new technology, and it was new technologies such as radar that had won World War II and would assure continued American economic and military dominance. By relying on Madison Avenue to sell his candidacy, Eisenhower also aligned himself with a postwar consumer culture. Affinities among the first presidential campaigns of McKinley, Eisenhower, and Obama are worthy of serious reflection.

Consider, too, the role of government-fostered media in presidential politicking. By permitting and most likely encouraging illustrated lectures celebrating the US interventions in Cuba and the Philippines, the McKinley administration mobilized government resources and personnel to promote its foreign policy agenda and, in effect, the platform on which McKinley and the Republicans would run in the impending presidential election. Certainly there have been many subsequent instances of this maneuver. With considerable justice Republicans saw two New Deal classic documentaries—*The Plow That Broke the Plains*, released in May 1936, and *The River*, released in February 1938—as campaign films for Franklin D. Roosevelt and the Democrats, paid for by the US government.[10] Various documentaries made by the Department of War during World War II undoubtedly fostered Roosevelt's candidacy for an unprecedented fourth term despite the fact that Republicans and Democrats were in fundamental agreement about the aims of the war. In 2003, making use of newly developed technologies of communication, the Bush administration and Department of Defense embedded journalists with American troops; the results certainly helped candidate George

W. Bush as he ran for reelection in 2004. From 1900 onward, government-sponsored and -fostered media often benefited the occupant of the White House as they sought an electoral mandate. Not only are government-promoted public information and public education never ideologically neutral, they typically profit the incumbent administration and its president.

Incumbency can make presidential campaigning more difficult for political opponents in other ways as well. Consider Emile de Antonio's *Millhouse: A White Comedy* (1971), a satirical look at President Richard Nixon and arguably a counter to the standard hagiographic documentaries produced by a candidate's campaign committees and party organizations. The filmmaker, who made it with the 1972 election in mind, ended up on Nixon's enemies list, and had his FBI file leaked to journalists and his tax returns audited by the IRS.[11] *Millhouse* was shown during the 1972 presidential election, but screenings were limited to revival houses and nontheatrical venues, with its distributor, New Yorker Films, targeting college campuses.[12] Television was obviously impossible. The most likely outlet—PBS—consistently refused to play de Antonio's films.[13] In some respects the 1896 counterpart was the Vitascope Company's slow response in getting *Bryan Train Scene at Orange* into New York vaudeville houses so that it would not upstage *McKinley at Home*.

This investigation has certainly been concerned with the strategies of political operatives, the dynamics of a particular media formation, the decisive moments of individual campaigns, and the convergence of factors that lead to particular electoral outcomes. It has also, however, attended to the ritualistic nature of these contests as well as the eccentric, the superfluous, and the everyday. Ritual was important in the 1890s: the determined effort to generate another bigger, better Sound Money parade in New York City during the 1900 campaign (and the *Brooklyn Eagle*'s determination to have more marchers despite the rainy day) only makes sense as a necessary reprise of something performed four years before. Nothing was more incidental and ineffective than the act of an audacious Bryan supporter who booed *McKinley at Home* and was forced to leave the theater. Nevertheless, it perversely mirrors the pragmatic affection between McKinley and his brother Abner, which was evident in their shared making of that film.[14] The structure of feeling of these campaigns is found not only in the formal rituals of citizenship but also in what exceeds any rational political calculation. Electioneering mixed elements of the carnivalesque with the gravitas of selecting a national leader. This may be particularly evident in elections with a fresh slate of candidates—such as the elections of 1896, 1952, 2008, and (at least on the Republican side) 2016. If campaign songs generally contained both comic and utopic components, they were unusually prominent in 1896 with the illustrated song and phonograph recordings, in 1952 with the television jingle, and in 2008 with the online music video. Such deployments of song often evaded the sponsorship and constraints of political operatives.

Mixing the carnivalesque of the barroom and local political clubs with the responsibilities of citizenship, 1890s politicking generally reaffirmed male camaraderie and hegemony. It fostered various forms of male sociality along the lines of ethnic and workplace identities. Even so, assumptions of masculine preeminence in the public sphere were being challenged at the edges. Women marched on behalf of candidates and spoke on their own behalf at political rallies. They attended election-night celebrations sponsored by newspapers, cheered McKinley at Hammerstein's and Koster & Bial's music halls, and cast votes in presidential elections from 1892 onward. Journalistic responses suggest that some of these developments were unexpected and seemingly spontaneous. Like the bicycle, which gave some women new and unprecedented mobility, they seemingly just happened.[15] Late nineteenth-century politicking evolved as popular commercial amusement was on the rise—part of an emergent consumer culture. Perhaps not surprisingly, the dozen years covered by this investigation trace the moment when commercial amusement and political performance began to merge after a long antagonism. These four campaigns reveal much more than the official political concerns of the nation as it prepared to enter the twentieth century: they reveal a nation at a turning point.[16]

FROM EARLY CINEMA TO MEDIA ARCHAEOLOGY?

As a work of scholarship, *Politicking and Emergent Media* operates within a discipline that has been undergoing significant changes in its self-conception over the last fifteen to twenty years. Generally identified as film studies or cinema studies prior to the new millennium, the discipline has expanded its areas of scholarly interest and now operates under the rubric of film and media studies.[17] This book consciously explores a period (the 1890s) to which I had already devoted considerable research and writing vis-à-vis motion picture history and undertakes an associated project within a media studies framework. In this respect it reflects a shift from the study of "early cinema" to "media archaeology." Although media archaeology has emerged as a dynamic new subfield, the extent to which this current endeavor fits comfortably under its umbrella remains an open-ended question. In any case this undertaking continues my own intellectual journey that began in the mid-1970s.

As the discipline of film studies solidified in the 1970s, film theory dominated the field—whether informed by structuralist, psychoanalytic, phenomenological, feminist, or Marxist models. As scholars pursued alternative areas of inquiry with new vigor, one of these was "early cinema." The study of early cinema as a subfield began to coalesce with the 1978 Brighton Conference, which focused on cinema from 1900 to 1906 and brought together a critical mass of scholars interested in this period before Film D'art in France and D. W. Griffith in the United States. At this gathering, sponsored by the Federation of International Film Archives (FIAF), scholars screened more than a hundred fiction films made in this seven-year period and presented an array of papers, which were subsequently published. My own contribution, entitled "The Early Cinema of Edwin S. Porter," was one of three presentations that engaged *Life of an American Fireman* (1903); the other two were by Noël Burch and André Gaudreault.[18] There were two conflicting versions of the film in circulation at that time: a copyrighted version with extensive narrative/temporal repetitions and a modernized version at the Museum of Modern Art, which involved crosscutting and was widely accepted as the true or historically accurate version. Much film history had been written using the MoMA print: the widely read Gerald Mast was one of many who favored this version even though he declared it impossible to determine definitively which variant was historically correct.[19]

Given that the copyrighted version of *Life of an American Fireman* was particularly radical in its temporal constructions, such unresolved issues challenged a still-emerging discipline in the process of its legitimization. Could we establish the integrity of a seminal film "text"? A successful resolution to this issue was needed in order to sketch out cinema's changing mode(s) of representation. This certainly included pre-Griffith cinema (cinema before Griffith started to direct at Biograph in 1908 and, according to general historical consensus, began to turn cinema into an art form).[20] In this respect we were following in the footsteps of André Bazin and his call for a history of "film language."[21] Tom Gunning was also a central participant in this Brighton event with his essay "The Non-Continuous Style of Early Film (1900–1906)."[22] A few years later he would rework these ideas into his famous formulation of pre-1906/07 cinema as preeminently a "cinema of attractions."[23] Yet it was Noël Burch, not with his Brighton essay but with his influential book *Theory of Film Practice* (1973), who provided us with a way to analyze and think about the pre-Griffith cinema.[24] The Brighton Conference was thus indicative of two developments. The first was a new, active collaboration between film scholars and archivists. The second was an interrogation of cinema's changing systems of representation in the pre-classical period as well as the nature and extent of narrative in early/pre-Griffith cinema.

In coming to grips with the historical record, many in the Brighton Group rejected two tropes.[25] The first was a biological model of film history that relied on the pathetic fallacy that cinema went through a process of development similar to that of human beings. Cinema, in short, was often said to be born; and as it grew up, it learned to talk and was eventually capable of great artistic expression. As I have argued here and elsewhere, cinema always already had a set of protocols and methods of communication and representation, which were much more complex and sophisticated than is generally acknowledged. Such an anti-natal outlook was accompanied by a de-emphasis of the category of "Art": we were much more interested in films as cultural artifacts. Whether they were art or not was either a question to be explored as a historical construction or a highly subjective characterization and largely immaterial. Second, we rejected the notion that early cinema was "primitive" and that writing its history was a project of archaeology. In particular we were distancing ourselves from Terry Ramsaye's *A Million and One Nights* (1926), in which he repeatedly characterizes cinema of the 1890s and early 1900s as primitive, and C.W. Ceram's *Archaeology of the Cinema* (1965).[26] Given that the cinema had existed for little more than seventy-five years and was a cutting-edge, modern technology, the proper approach to our subject was not that of archaeology but of cultural history. Cinema was not like the buried city of Pompeii.

We were scholars of the relatively recent past, which made the strangeness of early cinema all the more fascinating. Yet our methods were not unlike those working on late nineteenth-century and early twentieth-century painting, literature, and material culture. Films, correspondence, and other primary-source materials had been lost but much was waiting to be rediscovered. Archives needed to be visited, films needed to be located and preserved, reels of microfilm needed to be perused. To accept the analogy with archaeology seemed to affirm Mast's acceptance of the unknowability of basic fundamentals lost in the mists of distant time. Laurent Mannoni's remarkable *The Great Art of Light and Shadow*, with its subtitle *Archaeology of the Cinema*, was a rare exception that far exceeded its conceptual template but did not, at least in some respects, escape it.[27] These and other books, such as the first volume of Georges Sadoul's *Histoire générale du cinéma*, focused on technological precursors—the so-called "pre-cinema, which were originally informed by patent disputes in the courts of law."[28] Here again there were disagreements, since everything from before 1895–96 was, at least from my point of view, before cinema and therefore "pre-cinema." Pre-cinema then became a field of inquiry that was so immense that it was unmanageable, which is why a narrower focus on specific cultural practices was needed if we were to grasp meaningful continuities across the pre-cinema/cinema divide (this current book is an obvious example of such an application).

If the Brighton group began by analyzing early cinema's mode of representation, we more or less quickly expanded our interests to include other aspects of motion picture practices. We needed to understand the dynamic relationship between cinema's mode of representation and its mode of production. My own interests in this area were shared with David Bordwell, Janet Staiger, and Kristin Thompson and their groundbreaking book *The Classical Hollywood Cinema: Film Style and Mode of Production to 1960* (1985).[29] Although the difference between their investigations of a changing film style/mode of representation in relationship to the mode of *film* production versus my interest in its relationship to the mode of *cinema* production may seem a matter of nomenclature, it proves to be quite significant when investigating the pre-1920 era. For me, the mode of *cinema* production included exhibition practices and distribution as well as the actual manufacturing of film prints (that is, not just what was known as "negative production" in the early 1900s)—from preproduction to showing and seeing a motion picture in a theater. Postproduction was in the hands of the exhibitor in the 1890s, while key elements of both production and postproduction were subsequently centralized within the production company in the early 1900s, allowing for a whole new basis for filmmaking: this is a fundamental development in the history of cinema practices. The rapid proliferation of storefront theaters also generated fundamental pressures on how motion pictures were used to tell stories, as well as the kinds of stories they told. Without this framework, developments in representation are more difficult to explain. They become more self-generative—closer to the birth metaphor that we were seeking to avoid. Undue explanatory pressure is then put on significant but finally secondary features such as the accommodation of cinematic style to middle-class tastes.

The term "early cinema" quickly became a common reference point among those studying pre-classical Hollywood cinema. When was the term "early cinema" first used? Anthony Slide had published his first book, *Early American Cinema*, in 1970. For him early American cinema constituted the period up through 1915. Occasionally Slide refers to the "early years of American cinema" or the "early history of American cinema" but he does not use the term "early cinema" in those pages.[30] In the pre-Internet age, when historical research was more dispersed and disconnected, Slide's book was not on my radar.[31] Nor did Slide attend the 1978 Brighton Conference. I began using the term "early cinema" with my work on Porter in 1977, but not unlike Slide and many of my colleagues I sometimes used the term "early American cinema" or "early French cinema" as readily as "early cinema"—until Nancy Klebold, a local New Jersey historian (and my aunt), mocked this labeling by remarking that "early American" (as in "early American furniture") referred to the last half of the seventeenth century when, so far as she knew, there was no cinema. After her tongue-lashing I became more careful and wrote about American early cinema or French early cinema. My deployment of the term "early cinema" was also an attempt to reframe John Fell's references to "early film." I was interested in cinema practices, not just film practices: to me the difference was crucial.

The term "early cinema" as I was using it served as a replacement for the term "pre-Griffith cinema"—a way to get away from the great-man approach to history. Early cinema did not come to an end because of Griffith's appearance as a director per se but because cinema went through a series of interconnected changes and became a form of mass entertainment in 1908 at the very moment that Griffith assumed that role (a moment of transformation discussed in chapter 4). It was for this reason that the system of representation being used by Edwin S. Porter in the early 1900s was breaking down and being replaced by one that Griffith was particularly adept at exploiting. Film academics were quick to adopt the term. In the first book to contain "early cinema" in its title, Thomas Elsaesser emphasized the pre-1908 period but also included essays such as John Fullerton's "Spatial and Temporal Articulations in Pre-Classical Swedish Films" and Leon Hunt's essay on *The Student of*

Prague (1913).[32] When did cinema cease to be early cinema? That was apparently up for grabs. Some scholars seemed to be using the terms "silent cinema" and "early cinema" interchangeably.[33] After one graduate student proudly told me that he was studying early cinema—meaning films like *King Kong* (1933)—it seemed time to retrench and accept the inclusion of 1910s cinema under the early cinema rubric, a way to designate either cinema before *Birth of a Nation* (1915) or else pre-classical Hollywood cinema, prior to the vertically integrated studio system that fell into place around 1920. In this respect the timeframe designated by Anthony Slide has prevailed. (Moreover, various scholars still evoke the term "early American cinema.") Nevertheless, I continue to regret that we do not have a specific name for the pre-1908/pre-Griffith cinema.[34]

As the Brighton group of scholars moved forward, our interests often expanded along similar lines. More or less quickly, we began to more vigorously explore early cinema's relationship to other cultural practices, to popular entertainment forms, and to other media. Although these concerns were evident in John Fell's influential pre-Brighton study *Film and the Narrative Tradition* (1974), they were reformulated in terms of intermediality by André Gaudreault, who was instrumental in establishing the Centre de recherche sur l'intermédialité (CRI) at the Université de Montréal and served as its first director from 1997 to 2005.[35] Truth be told, we have always been interested in genealogies and cinema's relation to other cultural forms, but there was a necessary oscillation between investigating cinema as a dynamic media practice with its own trajectory and looking at its relationship to other cultural forms of expression. The move from Fell to Gaudreault involved two significant modifications. Fell looked at film's relationship to the *popular arts*—song slides (lantern slides used for illustrated songs), cartoons, and the stage—while Gaudreault was interested in its relationship to *media forms*. Fell also focused on what the cinema took from these other arts, while Gaudreault championed a broader variety of possible interactions. The pursuits of intermediality and media archaeology are closely linked.

Erkki Huhtamo and Jussi Parikka have suggested that the "new film history" often pursued under the rubric of "early cinema" was a parallel enterprise to scholarship investigating the history of other media forms as conducted in Germany, the United States, and elsewhere.[36] As early as 1990 Thomas Elsaesser saw the study of early cinema as participating in a move "from linear history to mass media archaeology." He was advocating for a "cultural archeology of the new medium" in conjunction with a "new film history" as represented in a collection of essays that he edited as *Early Cinema: Space, Frame, Narrative* (1990).[37] This transition to a new historical paradigm was reinforced in his influential essay "The New Film History as Media Archaeology" (2004), which offered media archaeology "as a way to analyze the turn-of-the-century media conjuncture."[38] He rejected conventional notions of pre-cinema, pointing out that sound (the phonograph, the telephone) and much more needed to be considered: "Given the cinema's opportunistic adaptation to all manner of adjacent or related media, it has always been fully 'grown up' and complete in itself. At the same time, it has yet to be 'invented.'"[39] Elsaesser often put biological metaphors in quotes as a way to problematize or ironize them.

In his references to archaeology and the cinema, Elsaesser was taking his cue from Walter Benjamin, but also from Michel Foucault's *The Archaeology of Knowledge* (1969; English translation 1972), in which systems of knowledge "are governed by rules, beyond those of grammar and logic, that operate beneath the consciousness of individual subjects and define a system of conceptual possibilities that determines the boundaries of thought in a given domain and period."[40] This finds resonance in Elsaesser's declaration that "the field of audio-visual experience needs to be re-mapped, clarifying what is meant by embodiment, interface, narrative, diegesis, and providing new impulses also for the study of non-entertainment uses of the audio-visual *dispositif.*"[41] Readers will necessarily judge for themselves the extent to which my current historical investigation has successfully met such a mandate, but my own sense of surprise and discovery leads me to believe that my engagement with the historical record has remapped significant elements of what we thought we knew about cinema and other media in this period. Film scholars have investigated the nature of embodiment in films such as *McKinley at Home*, but similar articulations in other media add a new context and complexity. On the other hand, the common practice of relying on intermediaries in politics was loosely related to the use of stand-ins in various reenactments or reproductions of events on the stage and in motion pictures. The tension between these two forms of embodiment is a topic that merits further exploration. Related inquiries might involve several of Elsaesser's other key terms.

Whether media archaeology as it is generally practiced is necessarily Foucauldian might be disputed. Certainly the association of media archaeology with one of the most prominent and inspiring intellectuals of the late twentieth century can only enhance the term and what it is said to represent, but, as Simone Natale notes, "different authors who have been working under this have developed substantially different versions of it."[42] For Jussi Parikka, "archaeology here means digging into the background reasons why a media apparatus or use habit is able to be born and be picked up and sustained in a cultural situation."[43] Such an approach can fit comfortably within an intersection of the history of technology with media studies.

Politicking and Emergent Media shares many of the concerns of media archaeology even as it may not fit fully within its somewhat amorphous orientation. Like much media archaeology, it has been engaged in excavating nineteenth-century media technologies with the present moment of digital media and the Internet fully in mind.[44] Of course, one could argue that this relationship between past and present is evident in most historical writing. Nevertheless, while the interplay of media with nineteenth-century politicking is interesting in its own right and for its own particularities, its role as a foil for the contemporary moment is evidenced by this book's publication in an election year.

Those embracing a media archaeology approach generally resist simple notions of linear development and progress. As Parikka has remarked, "Through media archeology, the contexts, objects and processes of media studies have increased explosively thereby troubling notions of the temporality of media culture; instead of a linear, progressive time of media, do media follow cycles or other modes of repetition?"[45] Certainly the study of emergent media in the second half of the nineteenth century can reveal patterns that are cyclical—as when the first years of the stereopticon and the first years of cinema are compared. In both instances, audiences felt transported to a different time and place. But there are others as well. For instance, the four elections examined in this study essentially involved only two sets of presidential candidates: that is, two of the four contests were effectively rematches, and if these repeats are any indication, rematches have tended to closely reprise many elements of the prior media formation. The general mediascape changed little from 1888 to 1892. The major innovation of 1888—*The Tariff Illustrated*—was simply reprised and expanded in 1892. Once again, although the 1896 election precipitated a very different mediascape, the change from 1896 to 1900 was less dramatic as motion pictures, the long-distance telephone, and the phonograph were no longer politicking novelties. Indeed, by looking at the 2012 campaign as an unofficial rematch (with Romney replacing McCain as the Republicans battled Obama), a similar media formation seems to have been carried over. This pattern also seems to hold for the Eisenhower-Stevenson rematch of

1956. Whether these are the kinds of repetitions Parikka has in mind is unclear, but they at least seem worth noting.

Media investigations uncover complex histories that do not always follow a straightforward path. There are many instances of gaps, unexplained (for the moment, at least) delays, and setbacks. The emergence of the stereopticon as a recognized media form involving the projection of photographic slides was delayed for a decade until subtle improvements in technology could be instituted and, perhaps more importantly, related cultural advances could occur. Why was the illustrated lecture not used for campaign purposes in the decades prior to 1888? What accounts for this retardation? And no sooner did the campaign lantern lecture emerge than it was virtually set aside, only to reappear in a new generic articulation for the 1900 contest. Indeed, the campaign documentary would continue to fade and then explode onto the electoral scene throughout the twentieth century and into the twenty-first. Likewise, the phonograph was available for campaign politicking in 1892 but was not employed for such purposes until 1896, and even then in surprisingly limited ways. As historians we constantly encounter unexpected gaps between what we assume and what actually happened. Yet the remarkable rapidity with which cinema was mobilized for purposes of politicking—the lack of any delay—might be considered just as surprising. This lack of a simple linear history with consistent correspondences between technology and its deployment is strongly connected to the forgotten, marginal, and unexpected uses of successful ones—in this study, the cinema and the telephone.

Despite its affinities with media archaeology, *Politicking and Emergent Media* retains important differences, as it investigates areas that have been of little concern to media archaeologists. The first is live performance in the form of political oratory and public pageantry; the second is the role of print culture, particularly the newspaper. The dynamic between these two fields of political expression was such that they dominated presidential politicking. A third area may be this book's sustained encounter with the documentary tradition. Here again, the extent to which the illustrated lecture emerged as a central expressive form in all four chapters of this book was unanticipated. Nor did I expect to come to a deeper understanding of the origins of the documentary as a vibrant mode of expression. Even now, more work needs to be done to understand the virtually simultaneous and co-joined emergence of the terms "stereopticon" and "illustrated lecture." This is particularly true because this conjunction was a specifically American phenomenon. Britain, in many ways the home of the lantern lecture, adopted different nomenclature, which leaves open the likelihood that it possessed a different cultural valence. My sense then is that this historical investigation falls less under the rubric of media archaeology and more at the intersections of film and media studies with cultural, social, and political history.

This encounter with the formation and early articulations of the documentary tradition has been cause for some self-reflection, given my lifelong association with documentary filmmaking. Has my work in nonfiction audiovisual media put me somewhat at odds with scholars interested in cinema and other media forms that mimetically express the shocks and disorientation of modernity through representations that marginalize or eschew narrative? As Laura Poitras, the director of *Citizenfour* (2014) and other documentaries that engage the Kafkaesque world of contemporary communications, has remarked: "Documentary filmmaking is . . . storytelling that reveals something more about the human condition."[46] Whether it was the history of the tariff, an account of Rough Riders in the Spanish-American War, or the experiences of American soldiers in the Philippines, storytelling was an essential element of the screen throughout the 1890s. The documentary tradition generally constrained and contained cinematic attractions by its reliance on argument, discourses of sobriety, and rhetoric as well as narrative. That does not mean that lantern lecturers did not incorporate nonnarrative elements in the service of a larger cause. In various illustrated lectures from 1899 and 1900, a platform orator such as Burton Holmes would stop his spiel when showing a film. The audience would view and enjoy the film for itself, for instance a Filipino cockfight or fire run. These offered temporary relief from the gravitas of the lecture. In the realm of long-form nonfiction of the 1890s, attractions might interrupt the narrative flow, but they nonetheless functioned within a coherent storyline.

In ways that might please aficionados of media archaeology, there are unexpected if not uncanny affinities between the illustrated lectures of the 1880s and 1890s and the documentaries of today. The soldiers and sailors giving illustrated lectures on Cuba and the Philippines were typically projecting photographs that they had personally taken with their Kodak cameras. The low cost of photography had reached a point where many ordinary Americans could afford to employ that technology. In a subsequent era, when motion picture film (nitrate and then acetate raw stock) was used in the making of illustrated lectures and documentaries, equipment was more elaborate and costs were much higher. From World War I to the Vietnam War, primarily professionals made documentaries.

In contrast, in the twenty-first century the costs of digital cinematography and postproduction have been reduced to such an extent that similar kinds of low-budget documentary production have again become possible. For *The War Tapes* (2006), Deborah Scranton gave cameras to New Hampshire National Guardsmen who fought in Iraq, then used that material to make a feature documentary on their experiences. Other low-cost, low-tech programs that brought personal insights to the war include Bassam Haddad's *About Baghdad* (2004) and Paper Tiger's *Shocking and Awful* (2004–5).

One important difference between 1899–1900 and 2003–4: the US military was generally reluctant to have American soldiers use cameras to tell their own stories of surviving the Iraq War. The government preferred to embed reporters in military units. Given the kinds of photographs taken by enlisted men and women at Abu Ghraib, the wisdom of such a decision from the government's point of view cannot be denied. The role of reaching some deeper understanding of the war was taken up by young, audacious men and women often working in a cinema verité or observational style: Matthew O'Neill (*Baghdad ER*, 2006, made with the veteran filmmaker Jon Alpert), Michael Tucker (*Gunner Palace*, 2004), Garrett Scott and Ian Olds (*Occupation: Dreamland*, 2005), Andrew Berends (*Blood of My Brother: A Story of Death in Iraq*, 2005), and Laura Poitras (*My Country, My Country*, 2006). Other filmmakers, such as Alex Gibney (*Taxi to the Dark Side*, 2007), Robert Greenwald (*Iraq for Sale: The War Profiteers*, 2006), and Errol Morris (*Standard Operating Procedure*, 2008), took a more directly critical and investigative approach. The anti-imperialist audiovisual programming that was surprisingly absent in 1900 had found an array of articulate practitioners. All of this returns me to Danny Schechter, whose documentary video *WMD: Weapons of Mass Deception* (2004) so brilliantly analyzed the cinematic attractions offered by the George W. Bush administration's "Shock and Awe" tactics. Likewise his writings, including *Embedded: Weapons of Mass Deception: How Media Failed to Cover the War on Iraq* (2003) and *The Death of Media: And the Fight to Save Democracy* (2005) brilliantly unveiled the disturbing story of media complacency and accommodation with the Bush administration. These, too, were linked to presidential politicking for an upcoming election. The distance between the late nineteenth century and the early twenty-first can seem small, indeed.

Appendix

Referenced Documents for *Politicking and Emergent Media*

The Tariff Illustrated

AN OBJECT LESSON IN PROTECTION
GIVEN BY EX-JUDGE WHEELER

"The Tariff Illustrated" was the title of what was appropriately termed a "unique" lecture by ex-Judge John L. Wheeler of New Jersey, at Everett Hall, Brooklyn, last night. It was in point of fact, an object lesson on protection. Judge Wheeler addresses his arguments to the eye as well as to the ear, appealing to the former by means of stereopticon views. He gave a history of the tariff policy of the various Administrations from Washington to Cleveland, accompanying it by portraits of the Presidents and eminent men who played a conspicuous part on one side or the other.

The speaker was once a Democrat, but the free-trade tendencies of the party have driven him into the Republican fold. He showed how by the protective policy the young Republic was freed from pecuniary embarrassment and soon made a paying concern, so that Jefferson found himself confronted with a surplus. But instead of ridding himself of the policy which had brought about that happy state of affairs, he continued it and expended the surplus on improvements. Coming down to the present time Judge Wheeler showed how much cheaper woolen goods were under the high tariff of 1888 than under the revenue tariff in existence in 1860. "But how about the wages?" yelled some obstreperous and sceptical Democrats. That was Judge Wheeler's opportunity. He had thrown on the screen a table showing that the wages of the workmen were just as much higher in 1888 as compared with 1860, as the goods were cheaper. His triumph was complete. "I deal in facts," said Judge Wheeler, "and the Democrats in theories. The theories are very nice theories, but they don't square with the facts. I propose to fight this campaign with facts." Judge Wheeler intends that his facts illustrated shall be extensively seen before the election comes off, and he wants Democratic audiences. ("The Tariff Illustrated," *New York Tribune*, 3 July 1888, 2)

DOCUMENT NO. 2

Pictured Politics

Judge Wheeler Delights a Big Audience with an Illustrated Protection Talk

MR. BLAINE IN BUFFALO

Democrats Skirmishing Around to Raise Money
to Pay for the Jefferson's Cruise.

POLITICAL NEWS AND GOSSIP.

The most unique and pleasing campaign talk in this city as well as one of the most instructive was delivered in Liedertafel Hall last night. The speaker was Hon. Joel [sic] L. Wheeler of New Jersey, and the hall was far too small to hold the crowd that flocked to hear him. His talk was illustrated by means of a stereopticon and Judge Wheeler made a decided hit with his magic lantern, though it wasn't very pleasant for the newspaper men to report the speech in the necessary twilight.

On a large canvas filling the proscenium arch, the pictures were thrown from the rear of the hall.

"We find the Democrats denying," said Judge Wheeler, "that they are for free trade." He spoke of the St. Louis platform as a free trade platform and said that Henry Watterson went into the convention with that platform in his pocket. "Take away the tariff," he said, "and you have free trade."

Then a picture of Washington was thrown upon the canvass, and there was a great cheer. Then followed the sub-treasury building in New York, where Washington delivered his inaugural address in the exact spot where his statue stands. The speaker quoted Washington's words in which he advised protection to native industries. "Then was passed the first tariff law. The country began with the protective policy. Now here is Alexander Hamilton, the first Secretary of the Treasury, the man who brought into life the great American system of protection. (Cheers.) This system has lasted until the present day. It has fought back all the assaults of free trade."

The next picture was that of President Adams. "The country," said the speaker, "was now enjoying the fruits of the protection policy. The balance of trade with the old world was in our favor. The first effect of the protection system was to make us creditors, not debtors."

The picture of Thomas Jefferson, the father of Democracy followed. Jefferson was a protectionist. He was not afraid of a surplus but devised that it be expended on roads, bridges, canals and education.

Then came the picture of James Madison. "President Madison," said the speaker, "was the father of the first tariff law and he was a strong protectionist. He had for his Secretary George Clinton (showing his picture), one of that illustrious family that confer so much honor on the state of New York. [Cheers.] At the close of the war of 1812, at the battle of New Orleans," and a picture of the battle burst into view, "there was not a free trader of consequence in the whole union. Now here you see James Monroe, a President who was a strong protectionist. Monroe was more than a protectionist, he was a lover of America."

Judge Wheeler then spoke of the dark days that came with free trade legislation. "We had free trade and we had free rum," he said. "Here is Lord Brougham, who made that famous speech, advising that English goods shipped to America be sold so low that American manufacturers be driven out of the field."

As an illustration he showed a waterfall hurling American manufacturers into an abyss while John Bull looked on.

"This," said Judge Wheeler, "was actually done from 1842 to 1853, particularly in iron. Then England sold us iron for $40 a ton, putting it up to $75 in '54. In the latter year 800,000 tons were imported and our gold went to England. If we had had protection then we could have kept our gold and sold our iron at $50 a ton. Monroe urged Congress to protect American industry and this was done. He was succeeded by John Quincy Adams, whose picture you see here, and during his time there was no active free trade party in this country, only a few in the South. Mr. Adams did not defend protection, so when Gen. Jackson, "Old Hickory," whose picture you see here [Cheers] and who was a protectionist, came up in opposition to Adams, Jackson's friends said Adams was a free trade, and it was strenuously denied. Both sides claimed they were protectionists."

John C. Calhoun, Jackson's vice-president, was pictured on the canvas and spoken of as a man who led a strong party in the South who said cotton was king and wanted free trade.

The face of Eli Whitney, the perfecter of the cotton gin, was also displayed. "The South was now seduced by England," said the speaker, "and here is Paul R. Hayne, the Southern Senator who said South Carolina would pass a nullification ordinance if a tariff law was passed."

Then came the picture of Webster, whose famous reply to Hayne is familiar with everybody. The tariff bill became a law, being signed by Jackson and he was triumphantly re-elected. South Carolina passed a nullification ordinance and then Henry Clay introduced his compromise tariff.

"It was now," said the speaker, "that we first left the protection system. Then the government began to run behind. The nation stood on the brink of a precipice and when Van Buren (his picture appearing at this moment) came we plunged over the precipice. In some parts of the country the people were starving. There was no work, there was no money. Hear the words of Horace Greeley—"

The noble face of Horace Greeley looked down from the canvas and the audience broke out into uproarious applause.

"Greeley said that the tariff law of 1833 brought ruin to the country. In 1840 the people took hold of affairs and actually sang into the Presidency old Tippecanoe Harrison."

"Hip! Hip! Hip! Hurrah!" came with a wild cheer from the audience, and for several minutes there was a scene of indescribable enthusiasm. The picture of Old Tippecanoe flashed upon the canvas and the cheers came with increased volume.

"The protection principle," said the Judge when order was restored, "lies very near to the heart of the American people. When they are convinced it is in danger they rouse themselves and defend it." President Tyler's picture was received in dead silence. "In 1841 a new tariff bill was passed and once more prosperity began to shine on the land." The pictures of Polk and Dallas were shown. "Cotton was king. In 1846 we had the Walker tariff bill passed, which passed by the casting vote of George M. Dallas.[1] Once more we departed from the protection policy, but Dallas was never heard of again. Yes, he was, though. He was remembered for one thing. In a year the iron mills of Pennsylvania were nearly all shut down and barrels were placed on the smoke stacks all through Pennsylvania. They were called Dallas night caps. Now the country began to run in debt."

The picture of President Fillmore, Buffalonian, was loudly applauded. Then came the pictures of President Pierce, Secretary Guthrie and Jefferson Davis, all free traders, and the history was brought to the time of the war and the Battle of Gettysburg. Abraham Lincoln's picture provoked prolonged applause. He was a pronounced protectionist. His cabinet were also shown. "They restored the protection policy, and from that day to this we have been prosperous and happy."

The Republican League Glee Club sang some campaign songs after which Mr. Wheeler devoted himself to the Mills Bill, incidentally showing some very clever cartoons. One was Cleveland unsuccessfully trying to fit Uncle Sam with free trade clothes. He showed that under a protective tariff clothes are cheaper than they were in England, throwing on the canvas advertisements taken from New York papers to prove his statements.

"You can buy more clothes with less money in the United States than in England," he said, and proved it by comparative tables. Same with blankets and all goods. "One man in this country saves as much on an average as 13 Englishmen. It isn't a question of raw materials, but a question of wages."

He also spoke of the lumber, salt and other interests, showing in the clearest way what disaster free trade would bring. He said salt and lumber didn't have a Democratic vote, but rice and sugar did.

Blaine's picture was received with mighty cheers, the red bandana was hissed. "Do not hiss it," said the speaker; "It is the red flag, the signal of danger. Here is our own flag," and at once appeared the stars and stripes. The audience went wild again, which culminated in a tremendous burst of enthusiasm when the pictures of Harrison, Morton and Miller followed in quick succession. (*Buffalo Sunday Morning News*, 21 October 1888, 1)

---

1. George Mifflin Dallas (1792–1864) was vice president under President James Polk (1845–49).

DOCUMENT NO. 3

Protection Illustrated
The Stereopticon in Politics

E. R. KENNEDY PICTURES FREE-TRADE AND
RED-DOG MONEY EVILS TO SOUTH ORANGE

One of the most brilliant engagements of the brilliant campaign, which is being fought to restore New Jersey to Republican rule took place at South Orange last night. Major Elijah R. Kennedy, of New York, was in command of the Republican forces, which were entrenched behind breastworks of American tinware. It was in the nature of an artillery duel, and Major Kennedy fired solid shot from a double-barreled stereopticon into the ranks of the Democracy, and followed that up with a rattling volley of statistics and arguments. Illustrations showing the condition of the working classes of free-trade Europe were thrown upon the screen from photographs taken by the speaker in Europe.

Empire Hall was crowded when Robert Ward, vice-president of the local club, called the meeting to order, and made a neat little opening address. He said that the Democrats of the Oranges had talked so much about the apocryphal nature of American tin that the South Orange Republican Club had resolved to give them an object lesson. The club had received from Hahne & Company, of Newark, the 500 samples of their tinware product for display that evening, and turned the meeting hall into a tin museum. One pile of 3,207 pieces cost on an average only 10 cents apiece, and many of the groups were marked "3 cents for any of these articles." He thought the outcry about the high price of tin under the McKinley law would have to go down before these brutal facts. Among those present were Charles H. Taylor, president of the club, Henry Lilly, secretary; George A. Halsley, Jr., corresponding secretary; W. F. Allen, John Meeker, Charles Pearson, E. R. Vanderveer, E. V. Connett, Jr., H. W. Jessup, Ira C. Kilburn, L. V. Taylor, John E. Alexander and Robert Warren.

Mr. Kennedy reminded his audience that the Government had to be supported. It was a question as to whether it should be done by direct taxes or by the indirect form of making foreign made goods pay toll for their admission to the markets of the United States. He threw upon the screen a copy of a tax bill of a traveller's guide or courier in the city of Berlin. The man, whose income was less than $500 a year, paid a direct tax of over $7.50 for three months—that is to say over $30 a year. This tax was partly, as shown by the receipts, on his income. The Republican party favors instead of this direct tax a tariff for revenue, said Mr. Kennedy, and it favors distinctly making that tariff also protection of American industries.

Such protection is not rendered necessary by a lack of raw materials. The Creator made iron ore, coal and the great primary raw materials as cheaply for this country as for any other. The only absolute necessity for a protective tariff arose out of the higher wages paid to this country than are paid by competing manufacturers in other countries. Mr. Kennedy's illustration of this point was well chosen for the particular locality of his speech, as there are numerous and extensive hat factories in Orange. He supposed the case of a German coming to this country with his family and looking up a job in a local factory. When the employer mentioned wages, the German says: "Why that is the same amount I earned in the old country."

"Well how can you expect me to pay more?" replies the employer. I can't rent my factory for less than my German competitor can, I can't buy raw material for less than he can. If I pay higher wages I must charge more for hats, and then I can't sell them. If I tried to do business on any such plan as that, the result would be bankruptcy for me and no more work for you."

"Right here," said Mr. Kennedy, "the Republican party takes a hand in the discussion and says to the manufacturer, "We see a way for you to pay this man a great deal higher wages than they are paying in Germany, and still enable you to sell your hats. The Government needs some money to pay its soldiers, its sailors and its Congressmen; to buy new ships and other things. Now, when those German made hats arrive at New York, we will say: "Wait a minute! You can't come in till you have paid something to support the United States Government."

"Well," the German hats say: "We don't object to that if you draw it mild. We rather favor a tariff for revenue only. Make it a dollar a dozen and we'll continued [*sic*] to arrive in thousands."

"But," the Republican party says, "the tariff for revenue only people aren't doing business at this stand just at present. We want some revenue and we also want to enable a hat manufacturer over in Orange to pay his men better wages than are paid where you come from. So you'll have to pay about $2 a dozen—$1 for revenue and $1 for a judicious mixture of revenue and Protection."

To this the German hats reply: "Well if you say so, I suppose we must pay the $2, but you won't get as much money as you would if you charged us only $1; for there won't be a quarter as many of us come over." "As to that," says the Republican party, "give yourself no uneasiness. This government has never run short of funds since we took charge of it and it never will while we remain at the helm. And as to the other matter, the American people won't have to go bareheaded. They can make as good hats in Orange as are made in the world, and will continue to do so as long as they get good wages." (Loud cheers.)

Taking up another branch of his subject, the speaker said:

"No convincing test of a system can be obtained by picking away at times, but is to be observed in general results obtained by the application of that system. The United States has applied Protection more thoroughly than has any other nation, and has been more highly prospered."

At this point the hall was darkened and the pictorial illustrations of Mr. Kennedy's argument began. To show the less fortunate condition of people in other countries, views were given which had been taken by Mr. Kennedy with his own Kodak, showing women yoked in harness with cows and dogs, to do the work of horses and oxen; also women carrying enormous burdens through the streets of the most brilliant capitals of Europe, acting as load-carriers in Vienna, and doing all the street-cleaning in Munich. The picture of Parnell preceded another view, showing a quotation from that Irish patriot in favor of Protection. Then a portrait of Bismarck was shown, followed by a view of Bismarck's statement that "the prosperity of America is mainly due to its system of protective laws."

The tinplate industry was fully illustrated. The speaker said the Democrats had asserted that tinplate cannot be produced in this country. This was effectively proved untrue. A photograph was enlarged on the screen, showing the tinplate works at Demmler, Penn., as they were in 1889 and as they now are, much more than double in size. The views included the new tinplate works in Ellwood, Ind., and a letter from the proprietor, showing that the erection of these works was due entirely to the protective tariff. The new tinplate factory at Baltimore was shown with a letter from the owners, stating: "We turn out 1,500 boxes of tinplate per week." Another, of the new tinplate factory of Somers Brothers, in Brooklyn, was shown, with a letter from D.M. Somers, stating: "The works are pronounced by English experts to be the finest tinplate works in existence." Views were also given of a large number of factories, which have either been greatly enlarged or entirely built since the passage of the McKinley bill and in each case the view of the factory was followed by an enlarged facsimile of a letter from the proprietor, directly ascribing their prosperity to the protective tariff.

The success of the Harrison Administration in extending the foreign trade of the country was fully set forth. Pictures of some of the new American steamships were shown and facsimiles of letters from their owners or agents. Following a view of the steamer Althanea, which sails from this port, was a letter from her agent, stating that this was "the first American built merchant steamer that ever sailed from the United States to Uruguay and the Argentine Republic"; that she carried "a full cargo of American manufacturers," and that she goes "to ports where regular lines of merchant steamers arrive almost daily, not one of which has hitherto flown the American flag."

The probable results of the carrying out of the Democratic proposition to remove the 10 per cent tax on state bank circulation were shown by a full display of red dog currency, and of the literature rendered necessary by such banking methods—reports of hundreds of worthless banks, of hundreds of counterfeit notes, and page after page of bank reports showing that even the bills of the genuine banks passed at discounts ranging all the way from 1 to 80 per cent.

The speaker closed by asserting that the Republican party had furnished the country a currency which, in the language of Governor McKinley, is "as National as its flag." Then the grand old Stars and Stripes were flashed upon the screen, and the meeting broke up amid loud cheers for the flag and applause for Mr. Kennedy. (*New York Tribune*, 25 October 1892, 3)

DOCUMENT NO. 4

Kennedy's Great Speech
Illustrated with Pictures of Scenes in "Free-Trade" Europe

E. R. Kennedy, the insurance Republican, took a little kodak with him when he visited Europe last Summer and photographed horrible examples of pauper labor. Monday night he took his views, made ready for a stereopticon out to South Orange, and according to the *Tribune*, he regaled the Jerseymen with a lot of fol-de-rol on the subject of the "working-classes of free-trade Europe."

It was evidently Mr. Kennedy's idea that he had an audience from the backwoods, for the pictures with which he tried to horrify them were of "women yoked in harness, with cows and dogs to do the work of horses and oxen," a field scene in highly protected Germany; women acting as hod carriers in Vienna (behind protection bulwarks and the like).

The *Tribune* report, which was highly eulogistic, seemed to give Mr. Kennedy's speech all the space it would safely stand, but the best it could do for him was to make him ridiculous by citing illustrations of the evils of free trade, arguments based on scenes in countries so highly protected and taxed that, with the poor, the struggle for life is always a fierce one.

An attempt was made yesterday to draw out Mr. Kennedy on his speech and photographs. Not being then in Jersey, he refused to talk, declining even to stand by the eulogistic report of him in the *Tribune*. (*New York Times*, 26 October 1892, 8)

DOCUMENT NO. 5

LANGENHEIM'S PHYSIORAMA—Under the name of a Physiorama, Mr. Langenheim, whose reputation as a daguerreotypist was once unequalled in this city, has recently opened an exhibition, of a somewhat novel character, at the Polytechnic Lecture Rooms. His pictures are daguerreotypes of actual objects, transferred by some process to glass, and then magnified and thrown upon canvass by the magic lantern. These views possess the accuracy of detail, and exquisite finish of daguerreotypes, with the warm coloring of paintings. The finest are the representations of architecture, many of which were of familiar objects, and scenes in and around our city, or in neighboring cities. The pictures of Niagara Falls would have been passable, but for the attempt to exhibit the falling water and the rising mist by actual motion. This movement of the great cataract by crank power is a decided improvement upon the original, as in case of accident it can be checked, and reversed;

and beside, as its motions would not impede the inland migrations of shad and herring, it might be of essential service to fishermen above the falls; then if it appeals less to our sense of the sublime, it does more to the love of the ludicrous, which is some compensation for that loss. (*Pennsylvania Freeman*, 8 May 1851, 3)

DOCUMENT NO. 6

De Cordova's Lyceum
720 Broadway
Facing the New York Hotel

Mr. DE CORDOVA

Begs to announce that he will recite this evening, July 25, and every evening until further notice, at the above hall,

HIS NEW

Historical Poem,

"THE REBELLION AND THE WAR,"

Illustrated by

DISSOLVING VIEWS

of the

PRINCIPAL EVENTS OF THE CAMPAIGN

After designs by several of the most eminent American artists,

AND WITH APPROPRIATE MUSIC

———

PROGRAMME OF THE VIEWS:

"The Star Spangled Banner"—four designs by Darley.

Fort-Sumter during the Bombardment from Fort Moultrie.

The Fort on Fire.

Sumter after the Bombardment.

Anderson, the Hero of Sumter.

Attack on the Massachusetts Troops in the Streets of Baltimore.

The Seventh Regiment N. Y. S. M., on their way to embark for the Seat of War.

Portrait of Lieutenant General Winfield Scott, "The Old Man at the Capital."

Portrait of Colonel Ellsworth.

The Seventy-ninth Highlanders.

Departure of the Garibaldi Guard.

Duryee's Zouaves at Fortress Monroe.

Portrait of the late Colonel Vosburgh, of the Seventy-first, N. Y. S. M.

The Reinforcement of Fort Pickens.

The Sixty-ninth Regiment N. Y. S. M. in the Trenches at Arlington Heights.

Allegorical Tableaux, after a design by Nehlig.

The Alexander Organ used in this entertainment is from Messers.
　　Chickering & Sons, No 694 Broadway.
The music arranged and performed by Mr. Van Cocklen.
Every attention has been paid to the securing of
　　proper ventilation.
The entertainment under the direction of Mr. B Frodsham.
N.B.—THIS POEM IS COPYRIGHTED
Admission 25 cents. Reserved seats 50 cents.
Box office open from 9 A.M. till noon. Doors opened at
　　7 ¼ and the entertainment will commence at 8 precisely.

(*New York Herald*, 25 July 1861, 7)

DOCUMENT NO. 7

Our Bulletin

Scenes and Incidents at the Times Election
Returns, Corner of Twenty-Third-Street—
One Hundred and Seventy Dispatches Displayed

All Day on Tuesday the people in this City who had the election interest in Pennsylvania, Indiana and Ohio at heart, were eagerly watching for the first whisper of news from these States. Naturally the bulletins were scanned through the afternoon, and every letter indicating the chances devoured with avidity. But the center of attraction in this City was certainly at the Erie offices, corner of Twenty-third-street and Broadway, where it was announced the NEW YORK TIMES returns would be given to the public by the Stereopticon Advertising Company. Certainly their novel method of advertisement found general favor with the throngs of merchants, brokers and professional gentlemen packed on the sidewalks and crossings that evening. Nothing could exceed the efficiency of their operators and apparatus for the rapid transfer of communications from the telegraph wires to the illuminated canvas outside. People had heard of this new bulletin in the morning, and were ready to see it at night, if, thought they, the thing can be done. But they had grave doubts of its success, believing that the issue of the returns must be attended with delay consequent on the transmission of messages from Printing-house-square to Twenty-third-street. The facts proved them unfounded.

A wire was laid between the office down-town and Mr. Keeler's office, in which the stereopticon is fixed; telegraph operators were specially engaged for the occasion, and just as fast as the editors of the TIMES received their specials from the three States, they had them repeated to the Twenty-third-street office. There was an attaché of the paper in charge of matters in that place, and his duty was to see the messages properly transferred to the glass plates by Mr. Keeler's assistants and displayed as rapidly as possible. From the time that each dispatch was received at the up-town office until the crowds in the streets read it on the canvas, scarcely five minutes elapsed. From the moments of the first announcement at 7:25 P.M. until "good-night" was shown, the interest in the display and its purpose never once abated among the people.

This was not ordinary gathering of *quid nuncs*. Every man present had a lively sense of personal interest in the news for which he awaited. Moreover, the persons who came at the beginning and stayed until the end, at 1 ¼ o'clock yesterday morning, were of the best classes of society. No ribald jests or vulgar slang found countenance or toleration there. Indeed, scarcely any was heard. This was an assemblage of the wealthy, well-to-do and commercial citizens of New-York, who, having large pecuniary and life-long reasons for wishing this country a good Government, had worked and hoped for the continuance of Gen. Grant's Administration. There was no need of Police, except to look after pick-pockets, of whom it is only natural to suppose there would be a great many where well-filled wallets and costly watches were so numerous. Their presence for any other use was needless. Rowdies if any sauntered thither, were overawed by the weight of sterling respectability, and subsided for the nonce into orderly citizenship. Alas! poor Tammany and its Liberal friends, they were few and hid their diminished heads. In front of the Fifth-avenue Hotel, down Twenty-third street and Fifth-avenue, around the park opposite and in the windows of the houses near by, were thousands of people. Seen from the window of the stereopticon, the square and open space at the juncture of the streets presented the appearance of an immense arena filled with a highly-pleased audience, whose upturned faces formed a white surface running far up and down each thoroughfare, ever swaying, undulating and sending forth cheers of enthusiasm.

———

At last the first dispatch came from the Times office, and with almost incredible rapidity was written on the glass plate, and shown on the canvas by Mr. Keeler's operator. It read: "Philadelphia has given [John F.] Hartranft from 12,000 to 15,000 majority at least." Then such a cheer rent the air as had not been heard in this section of the city since the announcement of Lee's surrender at Appomattox Court-house. Another came, increasing the figures, and still another, until they reached 23,000. At this point, the shouts and hand-clapping must have frightened the horses and aroused the people on Sixth-avenue, who had not yet heard of the new enterprise. Pennsylvania news grew better and more decidedly victorious, until the gladness of the spectators knew no bounds, and they gave cheer after cheer for Grant, [Republican vice presidential candidate Henry] Wilson and the NEW YORK TIMES. But the supreme moment of rejoicing might be said to have been reached when the bulletin told, in splendid letters two feet long, that Ohio had gone Republican. Verbal description is faint here. Thunders of applause and jubilant shouts followed each other in quick succession, which broke or rather dissolved into peals of laughter as the face of the canvas grew dark for a moment and lit up anew a portrait of a delighted Southern colored man in an attitude of exuberant dance. But this moment of pleasant relaxation was quickly followed by the good news from Indiana, and this by that from several counties of Pennsylvania. And so the people were made the recipients of the best tidings they had heard for many a day. Immediately after the Indiana dispatch came the portrait of the extremely Liberal candidate [Greeley], blowing a trumpet, and in the next picture the well-known phrase, "Gen. Grant never has been defeated and he never will be.—H. G." Loud screams of laughter and re-echoes of this sentence greeted its presentation, and the good humor of the people could not have been greater. . . .

At 1 o'clock, after announcing that the Presidential election returns would be shown at the same place in November, and displaying Washington, Lincoln, patriotic mottoes and the Goddess of Liberty, the Times bid its audience good night in three languages—English, French and German. (*New York Times*, 10 October 1872, 1)

DOCUMENT NO. 8

Stereopticon Illustrates Politics

W. D. Boyce Arouses Great Enthusiasm at Baker's Hall with Vivid Picture Arguments for McKinley

W. D. Boyce has introduced a new factor into campaign work. This is the stereopticon, which was used by him last evening with telling effect in an address he gave at Baker's Hall, Thirty-eighth street and Archer avenue, before an audience which listened to his remarks and watched the apt illustrations with the closest attention.

The departure is one of Mr. Boyce's own invention. He has prepared a number of colored pictures that present in a vivid manner various phases of the campaign and the questions at issue. He has sixty of these, which deal with national, State and county affairs, and his remarks were confined to terse comment upon them.

Judging from the humor of the audience Mr. Boyce's best picture is one in which William McKinley is shown holding aloft the Stars and Stripes. When this was shown the applause was deafening. Others are striking, particularly his illustration of the birth of the Popocratic bird and the picture of Uncle Sam's hold-up by "the long and short men—Silver and Free Trade." Others that were especially timely were pictures of workingmen in silver countries, the foreclosed home, the Sheriff's sale, a map of the world showing the contrasts between nations which have the gold and the silver standards, the broken mill dam and dismantled factory of free trade days, and the busy mills of protection times. (*Chicago Tribune*, 16 September 1896, 3)

DOCUMENT NO. 9

The Biograph at the Olympia

A Notable Company of Spectators, Political and Otherwise

Gen. Powell Clayton[2] stood at "attention" in Olympia Music Hall at 9:45 o'clock. From that hour the gallant Arkansaw fighter never took his attention from the stage until the political part of the programme was ended with the "intermission."

It was McKinley night at the Olympia, although Bryan came in for individual representation and a few hisses. Sound money sentiment was in possession of every seat and box. And to spur it on, were many leaders of the Republican Party in conspicuous boxes, behind the Stars and Stripes, and in the company of smartly dressed women.

Cornelius N. Bliss[3] helped Matthew Stanley Quay[4] and [N.]B. Scott[5] to show their appreciation. Gen. William McKinley Osbourne[6] and Joseph H. Manley[7] tried to be a chorus to Melville E. Stone's[8] solos of approval, while

2. Powell Clayton (1833–1914) was a Union general who settled in Arkansas after the Civil War. He became Arkansas's first governor after the state was readmitted to the Union (1868–71) and then one of its senators (1871–77). An important figure in Republican national politics, he was appointed ambassador to Mexico by McKinley in 1897.

3. Cornelius Newton Bliss (1833–1911) was treasurer of the Republican National Committee from 1892 to 1904 and president of the American Protective Tariff League. A prominent merchant in New York City, he was secretary of the interior in President McKinley's administration from 1897 to 1899. See "Cornelius N. Bliss, Merchant, Is Dead," *NYTimes*, 10 October 1911, 1.

4. Matthew Stanley Quay (1833–1904), a former chairman of the Republican National Committee (1888–91) and Pennsylvania senator (1887–99, 1901–4), was considered "an immensely powerful political boss." http://en.wikipedia.org/wiki/Matthew_Quay.

5. Nathan Bay Scott (1842–1924) was the Republican national committeeman from West Virginia, whom McKinley appointed commissioner of internal revenue. "Mr. Scott's Coming Office," *NYTimes*, 24 March 1897. In 1899 he became a US senator from West Virginia.

6. William McKinley Osbourne (1842–1902), cousin and confidant of William McKinley, was secretary of the Republican National Committee in 1896 and later US consul general in London (1897–1902).

7. Joseph Homan Manley (1842–1905) was a prominent Maine politician and chairman of the executive committee of the Republican National Committee. He headed the campaign of Thomas Brackett Reed, McKinley's principal rival for the Republican nomination, but switched to McKinley on the eve of his nomination. "Joseph H. Manley, Dead," *NYTimes*, 8 February 1905, 9.

8. Melville Elijah Stone (1848–1929) was general manager of the Associated Press, president of the Globe National Bank of Chicago, and a friend of William McKinley. Melville Elijah Stone, *Fifty Years a Journalist* (Garden City, NY: Doubleday, Page and Company, 1921).

Mr. Perkins,[9] Mark Hanna's private secretary,[10] and the ladies in the party were successfully outvying the rival trio.

Gen. Charles H.T. Collis[11] and C.M. Meade[12] were conspicuous in a party. C.F. Weeks had a box in the centre of the first tier and Gen. Horace Porter,[13] Col. A.W. Soper[14] and a party of ladies were not far away.

Frederick S. Gibbs[15] was present and General Passenger Agent Daniels[16] of the New-York Central Railroad stuck to his post until he saw a

9. Samuel A. Perkins was Mark Hanna's private secretary and assistant secretary of the Republican National Committee. "Talk of the Day in Politics," *NYPress*, 29 October 1896, 1. After returning to Tacoma, Washington, in 1898 he became a newspaper publisher, purchasing the *Tacoma Daily News* and the *Tacoma Ledger*. He also remained an important figure in Republican politics, at one point serving as a national Republican committeeman.

10. Marcus (Mark) Alonzo Hanna (1837–1904) was a businessman from Cleveland who rose to fame as McKinley's campaign manager. He was chair of the Republican National Committee from 1896 to 1904.

11. Charles Henry Tucker Collis (1838–1902) was a Union general who became active in Republican Party politics. He was commissioner of public works in New York City under Mayor Strong from 1895 to 1898 and a director of the American Mutoscope & Biograph Company. "General C.H.T. Collis Dead," *NYTimes*, 12 May 1902, 2.

12. Clarence W. Meade, a former police justice in New York City and father-in-law of Frederick S. Gibbs, was at one time on the Republican State Committee. He ran as a Republican candidate for Congress, to represent the Tenth District of New York, in 1896—losing to Democrat Amos Jay Cumming by 3,000 votes. After McKinley's election he was mentioned as a possible postmaster of New York. "Charges Against Divver," *NYTimes*, 23 November 1894, 7; "Candidates for Postmaster," *NYTimes*, 19 November 1896, 8. In May 1897 New York Mayor Strong appointed him a city magistrate, which elicited an angry reaction from the *New York Times*, which called him "a politician of the lower order" and declared his appointment "disgraceful." "Meade Mystery," *NYTimes*, 10 May 1897, 6. He was also a delegate to the Republican State Convention in 1896.

13. Horace Porter (1837–1921), a Civil War general, had been President Ulysses S. Grant's personal secretary from 1869 to 1872. He subsequently became vice president of the Pullman Palace Car Company and president of the Union League Club of New York (1893–97). A prominent Republican and public speaker, from 1897 to 1905 he was US ambassador to France. http://en.wikipedia.org/wiki/Horace_Porter.

14. Arthur William Soper (1838–1901) was president of the Safety Car Heating and Lighting Company and a prominent railroad man.

15. Frederick Seymour Gibbs (1845–1903) was president of the Metropolitan Water Company and influential in Republican Party politics. In 1896 he was New York's Republican national committeeman.

16. George Henry Daniels (1842–1908) was the advertising guru for the New York Central Railroad, coining and applying the term "America's Greatest Railway" to the New York Central. He also published *Health and Pleasure on "America's Greatest Railroad." Descriptive of Summer Resorts and Excursion Routes, Embracing More Than One Thousand Tours by the New York Central & Hudson River Railroad* in 1890 with subsequent editions in 1893, 1894, 1895, and 1896. He was general passenger agent of the New York Central Railroad from 1889 to 1907 and enjoyed a certain amount of celebrity status in his day.

marvelously moving picture of one of the greatest achievements of the company with which he is connected.

Amann, the impersonator, prepared the way for enthusiastic outbursts by giving lifelike representations of McKinley and Palmer, but the triumph of the night was in the so-called "biograph." It is wonderful in its presentation, after the manner of the Vitascope and kindred inventions, of life and action.

McKinley stepped out of his house in Canton, and, strolling down his lawn, seemed to smile in appreciation of the roar that greeted his appearance. McKinley paraders tramped through Canton streets, and a New York assemblage applauded them to the echo. Niagara Falls made a realistic pouring picture, but their noise in the original could not be much louder than the cheers that greeted the picture of them.

The finest of all these pictures was one of the Empire State Express going at sixty miles speed. The train is seen coming out of a distant smoke cloud that marks the beginning of a curve. The smoke puffs grow denser on the vision, and soon coach after coach whirrs to the front and it seems as though the entire left-hand section of the house would soon be under the wheels that are racing for New-York. The cheers that greeted the picture and its repetition were as great as those for McKinley, and in taking part in them, Mr. Daniels found his opportunity.

The other pictures represent "A Stable on Fire," "Joseph Jefferson in the Drinking Scene of 'Rip Van Winkle,'" "Trilby and Little Billie," and "The Washing of a Pickaninny by His Mother."

The Poluski brothers, Sampson, the strong man, Kitty Mitchell, and the others in the long programme are good entertainers. ("The Biograph at the Olympia," *New York Times*, 13 October 1896, 5)

[Other prominent men said to be attending the event included Charles W. Hackett,[17] Rueben L. Fox,[18] Frederick C. McLewee,[19] Charles F. Wilbur,[20]

17. Charles W. Hackett (1854–1898) had a career based in the railroad business though he also moved into banking, insurance, and newspaper publishing. In 1896 he was chair of the Republican State Committee of New York. "Charles W. Hackett Dead," *NYTimes*, April 17, 1898, 1.

18. Rueben L. Fox (listed as R. S. Fox and sometimes known as Colonel Fox, circa 1850–1909) was chief clerk of the Republican State Committee. "Moving Now to Saratoga," *NYTimes*, 21 August 1896, 5.

19. Frederick C. McLewee (ca. 1855–1913) was inspector general of the State National Guard of New York, but was dismissed by the governor from that position on December 31, 1896, after releasing a critical report of the National Guard's performance.

20. Charles F. Wilbur was a good friend of Charles W. Hackett, chairman of the Republican State Committee, and a delegate to the Republican State Convention in 1896, representing the Nineteenth Assembly District. "Republican Conventions," *NYTimes*, 18 June 1896, 2. In 1900 he served as superintendent of the census for Manhattan and the Bronx. All this suggests that he was part of the political machine of Senator Thomas C. Platt. "M. Maurice Eckstein of Tropic Foods, Inc.," *NYTimes*, 8 September 1945, 15.

Thomas L. Hamilton,[21] Colonel Harry L. Swords,[22] Colonel John H. Black,[23] Francis H. Wilson,[24] Maurice Eckstein,[25] William Halpin,[26] and William R. Day of Canton.[27]]

21. Thomas L. Hamilton (1859–1908) was associated with the building firm of John L. Hamilton & Sons. He was first vice president of the New York County Republican Committee in 1895 and had been a member of that committee since 1888. Although a close personal friend of Fred S. Gibbs and associated with the Platt faction of the Republican Party, he was nonetheless appointed commissioner of electrical control in June 1895 by Mayor Strong. "Amos J. Cummings Removed," *NYTimes*, 28 June 1895, 8.

22. Harry L. Swords was sergeant at arms of the Republican National Committee. He later found a sinecure in the Custom House of New York. "Heard in the Corridors of Washington Hotels," *Washington Post*, 3 June 1918, 6.

23. John H. Black was in the book trade and in 1896 was president of both the Chicago Sound Money League and the Commercial Travelers' Sound Money League of the United States. Many of the salesmen in the Commercial Travelers' Association were normally Democrats who had supported Cleveland but were committed to McKinley because of his position on monetary policy. "Commercial Men for McKinley," *NYTimes*, 11 September 1896, 8; "Commercial Men in Line," *NYTimes*, 20 September 1896, 3; "Mr. Hanna Has Visitors," *NYTimes*, 4 August 1900, 3.

24. Francis Henry Wilson (1844–1910) was a lawyer and Republican congressman in the Third District of New York (Brooklyn, 1895–97). He was a close friend of McKinley and in September 1897 resigned his office to accept an appointment as postmaster of Brooklyn. Politics forced him out of that office in November 1901. "Congressman Wilson Resigns," *NYTimes*, 1 October 1897, 2; "Postmaster Wilson Has Resigned," *NYTimes*, 20 November 1901, 8.

25. Maurice Morris Eckstein (ca. 1869–1945) worked for a jewelry firm and became a member of the New York County and New York State Republican Committees. In 1897 he was appointed secretary to Senator Thomas C. Platt. He ran for county clerk in the 1896 election, losing to Democrat Henry D. Purroy.

26. William Halpin (1864–1937) was a Republican politician. When an assemblyman, he introduced the consolidation bill that united the five boroughs into greater New York City. "William Halpin, 72, Once Assemblyman," *NYTimes*, 23 August 1937, 19.

27. William R. Day (1849–1923) was a lawyer, longtime friend, and political adviser of William McKinley. They lived three doors away from each other in Canton. Day became first assistant secretary of state (1897–98) and then succeeded John Sherman as secretary of state (1898). He negotiated the peace with Spain and was an associate justice on the Supreme Court (1903–22).

DOCUMENT NO. 10

Bryan in a Peep Show

If You Can't See Him, See His Shadow
Make the Motions
When He's Elected SinJin Will Sell the Bonds for
Uncle Sam—Money Changers in the Temple—Amnon
Catches Candidate and Abe Gruber Sees a Vision.[28]

The one fear that has haunted Billy Bryan, the Boy Orator of the Platte, has been that he would not be able to talk to and shake hands with a majority of the voters of the country before election day. This same fear, it may be said, has haunted many of the people of the country. Thousands upon thousands who live in districts that Bryan has not approached have groaned under the misfortune that kept them where they could not see him. But it's all changed now. There needn't be any more haunting or any more fear. Billy Bryan is to spread over the country from the uppermost corner of Maine to the most southern corner of Florida and from the Atlantic to the Pacific. His speech is to fill the land, and every man, woman and child is to see and hear him. The vitascope man will manage it. Arrangements are said to be in progress now. The Boy Orator is to talk into a machine. His words are to be impressed on wax rolls and his motion on gelatin films. Every breath he breathes and every sound he utters is to be recorded. Every motion of his body, every gesture of his hands and arms, every wiggle of his eyebrow, the stock smile, the twinkling eye, and above all the wonderful mouth—every move of it—is to be caught and then on great canvases displayed to the waiting multitude. While the figure wriggles and the arms swing and the mouth wags open and shut, the wheels in the phonograph attachment are to go around, and speech is to issue. It is not decided yet, so the interested parties say, whether the crown of thorns and cross of gold speech is to be used or the Madison Square effort. Each is equally good in its way for stampeding purposes, and a stampede is what the Boy Orator wants. It may be that the small sum of 10 cents in silver will be charged to look at the show, and the proceeds may go to SinJin. (*New York Sun*, 28 September 1896, 2)

28. SinJin was apparently a regional accent for St. John. Perhaps referring to John the Baptist? Amnon was King David's oldest son, who raped his half-sister and was later killed by his half-brother in revenge. Abe Gruber was a local Republican who gave stump speeches and was an officer of a local Republican club. None of which fully explains this set of references.

DOCUMENT NO. 11

Thomas A. Edison's vitascope is in use both at Proctor's Pleasure Palace and at Proctor's Twenty-Third Street, and the proprietors of the device promised to have ready for showing this week a series of instantaneous photographs of William J. Bryan in the act of making a speech without a net from the platform of a railroad car. The apparatus wouldn't stand it; the draught from the speaker's mouth was too strong and the movement of his lips too rapid. The attempts make an interesting chapter in the record of scientific progress. The vitascope shows instantaneous pictures at the rate of forty a second, the photographs having been taken at the same speed. Imagine the number needed for a Bryan speech! They are inured to these matters at Menlo Park, and the twenty four and three-quarters miles of sensitive film required was prepared. A cable spool was borrowed from the Metropolitan Traction Company to wind it on and then the speed test began. At the first trial with a glib talker there was not the slightest difficulty in photographing the speaker. The machine followed every movement of the lips and seemed to be capable of thrice the speed. For further tests the apparatus was held before a steam blower and finally it was braced so that the draught on an exhaust fan ten feet in height did not interfere in the slightest degree with its delicate mechanism. Then the camera was set up at Orange, NJ and the Boy Orator's train was awaited.

As it hove in sight the Roarer of Platte was visible and from his gestures it was plain even to the nearsighted that he was speaking. The apparatus was set in motion, and just as it was started the fatal error in the careful calculation became apparent. The approaching spouter saw the machine, realized his picture was being taken, and put on more velocity. Immediately the ballast of the roadbed was laid bare, trees beside the tracks shed their foliage, and all this mass of sand, leaves and loose rails was lifted to go hurling ahead of the express train straight at the recording apparatus. In all but the one mentioned particular the plans were well laid. No part of the machine gave way and the photographer though grievously wounded by a flying fishplate, stuck to his post. As a result the first 4 ⅜ miles of the film now bear the best photographic reproduction of a wind storm ever seen. But for the leaves, limbs of trees, and wreckage of semaphores that dot the sand blast, it would be serviceable as a picture of an African monsoon, but the Boy, oh, where was he? He was right in it but invisible. The train collided with a freight car that had been blown from a siding, stopped just beyond the station, and was at once backed till the last car was opposite the vitascope. Then the speech was resumed, but the short range brought new troubles. The apparatus had been tested up to 4,926 records a second, and it had been planned to get the movement of the lips for each and every syllable, but the faithful operator soon became aware that the machine though working as well as ever was not going fast enough. The speaker's lips did not show at all, and the middle of his face looked like a gusty gash. Bleeding from his wounds and chilled in every pore, the heroic photographer surrendered so far as to strive only to take one picture per word. But his heart sank as mile after mile of the film sped by, showing nothing but an open countenance lugged with a blowpipe.

The worst came when the Nebraskan, unmindful of the fact that his cyclonic utterances were not directed toward a "dugout" of his own "perarrers," spoke in his fullest tones. Biff! went the car railing, and with a striking power of several thousand tons, landed on the photographer's neck. He dropped insensible, but, faithful to the end, shut off the machine in his fall. When he began to revive his first sensation was that he was in a close atmosphere. Staggering to his feet, he realized the dead truth: the wind's velocity was less than seventy miles an hour; the speech was ended, and this was but an echoing zephyr. But the orator was still there, hanging onto a remnant of the car platform and bowing to right and left. Before he fainted again, this Horatius[29] of photographers once more started his machine. The pictures then taken are well-nigh perfect. They show the wind raiser, bareheaded and unruffled, bowing and smiling to all sides as the train steams away. Edison's name stands as strongly as any one's can for persistency and stubbornness in overcoming obstacles, and money is no object when an end is to be attained, but the attempt will not be made again, and the present pictures at Proctor's are as near an approach as will be made to photographing the Bryan wind machine in operations. (*New York Sun*, 24 October 1896, 5)

DOCUMENT NO. 12

Mason Mitchell, an actor who was wounded in the gallant charge of Roosevelt's rough riders, put himself on public exhibition at Proctor's yesterday. He figures in what the programme styled an "illustrated recital of Actor Rough Rider Mason Mitchell." Before he showed himself, the white screen on which war views are usually displayed was lowered, and a small table set out. Mr. Mitchell, a stalwart man of middle age, wore the brown canvas uniform of the First Volunteer Cavalry. He began by telling of the rough riders' organization, their drilling at San Antonio, and their landing in Cuba. In all that preceded his reference to the order for the regiment to move inland in Cuba there was no other emphasis than those of easy narrative. In the description of the fights at El Caney and San Juan Hill, his speech was at times rapid, but there was no touch of theatric exaggeration, no suggestion of the melodramatic. It was a plain tale, not of personal experience, but of the doings of an army, more especially those of the brigade to which the rough riders belonged. Other regiments, especially the Seventy-first New York and the black troopers of the Tenth Regular Cavalry, came in for compliments, and

29. Horatius Cocles was a Roman officer who courageously and miraculously withstood a rain of missiles from the Etruscan enemy.

individuals upon whom the narrator dwelt with admiration were Capt. Capron, Hamilton Fish and Col. Roosevelt. Different treatment was accorded to the Spanish guerillas. The feature of the Cubans' make-up that stood out in the speaker's memory was what he styled their "grasping suavity." The eighteen-minute narrative's dramatic height was its praise of Roosevelt at the climax. The pictorial accompaniment was in the magic lantern way. During the narrative the footlights were burning bright, except when at intervals they were darkened in order that the picture thrown upon the screen might appear. A dozen pictures showed individual officers or soldiers grouped and fighting, the best of the subjects being of a sort already used by the war-graphs. (*New York Sun*, 6 September 1898, 7)

DOCUMENT NO. 13

Holmes Talks of Luzon

OPENS HIS SEVENTH SERIES OF LECTURES TO A CROWDED HOUSE.

Peaceful Manila and Its Background of War the Real
Topic—A Defense of United States Soldiers Against Charges
of Drunkenness—Prohibiting Cock-Fighting Is a Mistake,
the Lecturer Says—Motion and Stationary Pictures
of Admiral Dewey.

Burton Holmes inaugurated his seventh season as a public entertainer last night at Central Music Hall. The subject which speedily established sympathetic relations between Mr. Holmes and a "standing room only" audience—the sign at the front said so and the appearance of the house proved it—was "Manila." To call the outcome of Mr. Holmes' travels a lecture is to do it an injustice; it is in fact a dramatic entertainment of no mean order, and might properly be titled, "Peaceful Manila and Its Background of War." The idea of dramatic contrast prevailed from beginning to end.

In all the long lists of views, colored and motion pictures alike, there were none which showed the brutality of war and few that showed its suffering, yet there were not many which did not owe their effectiveness to military significance. The uniform of a soldier would thrust its way into the most peaceful scenes, and the ruins, which were picturesque, were of modern making.

The comments and explanations of the lecturer himself seemed framed to avoid any direct reference to the war and its progress without ever letting the fact of hostilities be forgotten. It was evident, also, that he desired covertly to convey the impression that he would have liked to tell more did he not think the frankness might be an injury to him as an entertainer. By repression he aimed to emphasize, and succeeded, through not committing himself, one fancies, more than he intended.

This is preliminary to saying that there is no manner of doubt that Mr. Holmes, the individual, was not pleased with what he saw in the Philippines. He did not refer, except with utmost indirectness, to any topic so pointed as expansion, but he took pains to tell the smallness of Luzon territory actually in American possession, and did not hesitate to say where he believed certain errors of administration had been committed. He took care, however, to praise the American soldiers in camp and out of it.

TALKS ON MATTERS OF NEWS.

Perhaps he would be better pleased if more attention were paid to the excellence of his views and the raciness of his descriptive utterances, but, inasmuch as he has insisted upon dragging matters of news into a place of amusement he must bear the penalty. His veiled allusions to an unpleasant state of affairs in the Philippines began with the minute he announced the safe arrival of his vessel in Manila Bay. Lying in quarantine, he said, he and his fellow passengers were startled at the breakfast table by sounds of heavy cannonading. Hastening to the deck they found that the entire American fleet was bombarding a Filipino position down the bay, twelve miles from Manila itself. Until then, he said, he had no idea what "insurgent boldness" meant or how closely they were pressing the Americans. Later on he told how narrow was the strip inland held by our army, saying it was bounded by not much more than the width of a railroad track, and in length a bare thirty miles. While he was at San Fernando, the post furthest outlying, it was attacked by Aguinaldo's army during the night. He did not lay claim to any particular bravery on the occasion.

The most outspoken criticism made by Mr. Holmes was upon the commanding General's action, or the government's in abolishing the universal inland sport of cock fighting.

COCK FIGHT ESTABLISHED SPORT.

"Cock fighting," he said, "was an established Filipino custom, had been so for two centuries or more. The Filipinos did not see anything harmful or brutal in it. When the sport was prohibited they felt as we would have done had an arbitrary decree been issued forbidding baseball or golf or football. They could see no reason for it. They thought it wantonly done. In time, when peace is a settled thing, when American rule—if it is to be—is established the cruel pastime might have been abolished. Coming when it did it roused a spirit of distrust, not to say hatred, which will be felt for a long while. The act is an example of the lack of tact, which has been displayed from the moment the United States army succeeded that of Spain on the islands. It is not more soldiers that are needed; it is a better understanding of Filipino nature, more common sense."

Mr. Holmes recurred again to current topics after showing a motion picture of a regiment passing through Manila.

DEFENDS THE AMERICAN SOLDIER.

"I want to say," he said, "that a story which has cast upon the American army the aspersion of being a body of drunkards is untrue; maliciously so, I believe. When our boys are on the firing line, sometimes for days at a time, they have no allowance of liquor of any kind, and generally there is little water to be had, sometimes not any. Their rations consist of damp hardtack; they eat while standing ankle deep likely in the water which the tropical downpours send coursing through the trenches. If they drank heavily when their regiments were brought into Manila for a little rest I for one would not blame them. But they do not. In proportion to number I saw extremely few intoxicated soldiers in Manila. The drink they get is beer, shipped from the United States. When I have seen a regiment come in I have felt like taking them out by companies and saying 'Boys, have one on me.' They are brave fellows and honorable; while they are fighting and dying they should at least be spared the slurring remarks."

TAKES A PICTURE OF ADMIRAL DEWEY.

While in Hongkong on his way to Manila Mr. Holmes met Admiral Dewey, and the consequence is an admirable view showing the Admiral in civilian dress, together with a motion picture showing all sides of the Olympia, taken from a launch which encircled the vessel. The motion pictures, of which Mr. Holmes presents a dozen or more, are, as a rule, exceptionally clear, though some of them were taken under unpropitious circumstances, weather and otherwise. One of the best in the lot is a view of a cock fight, secured despite police regulations. It has as a climax a raid by the provost marshal's guard and the arrest of all concerned, including the belligerent cocks. The views, motion and stationary, include a panorama of the Pasig River, a Filipino hotel room with its odd furniture, the Escolta, the Ninth Infantry crossing the bridge of Spain, a caravan of cars, a glimpse of Cavite, the defense of Baliung, and many examples of town and suburban architecture. One picture shows a regiment encamped in a church, though, it is explained, no sacrilege was offered, services being held every Sunday. Altogether the lecture seems designed to give an accurate account of present day life in the Philippines. (*Chicago Daily Tribune*, 27 October 1899, 5)

Abbreviations for Frequently Cited Newspapers

BaltSun	= *[Baltimore] Sun*
BrookEagle	= *Brooklyn Daily Eagle*
ChicTrib	= *Chicago Daily Tribune*
NYHerald	= *New York Herald*
NYJournal	= *New York Journal*
NYMail&Express	= *New York Mail and Express*
NYPress	= *New York Press*
NYSun	= *[New York] Sun*
NYTimes	= *New York Times*
NYTrib	= *New York Tribune*
NYWorld	= *New York World*

Notes

INTRODUCTION

1. "Barack Obama: Yes We Can," BarackObama.com, posted 9 January 2008, https://www.youtube.com/watch?v = Fe751kMBwms. As of July 2015 it had received more than 5,427,000 hits. This was one of numerous Internet postings in the election season; most have been taken down. "Obama's Most Famous Speech—Yes We Can," accessed 27 October 2015, http://www.seefeelchange .com/video/obamasspeech-yes-we-can/.

2. "Yes We Can Obama Song by will.i.am," YouTube will.i.am channel, posted 2 February 2008, https://www.youtube.com/watch?v = 2fZHou18Cdk.

3. "'O-B-A-M-A OBAMA!' song in Obama, Japan" YouTube, uploaded 8 March, 2008, https://www.youtube.com/watch?v = W4hX23r3Dpo. It had had more than one hundred thousand views when accessed 27 October 2015. The posting by the Swedish nanny has unfortunately disappeared. Music videos celebrating Obama's 2008 candidacy from Kenya, Italy, the United Kingdom, Mexico, and elsewhere are still on YouTube.

4. http://www.boxofficemojo.com/movies/?id = fahrenheit911.htm, accessed 24 July 2015.

5. Danny Schechter offered versions of this quotation in casual conversation with me and others on many occasions.

6. My first presentation on this subject was "From the Beginnings of Cinema to YouTube and Our Computers" at the Histories of Film Theories conference in Udine, Italy, March 25, 2009. Subsequent publications on the contemporary moment include Charles Musser, "Political Documentary, YouTube and the 2008 US Presidential Election: Focus on Robert Greenwald and David N. Bossie," *Studies in Documentary Film* 4, no. 1 (2010): 199–210; and Charles Musser, "Truth and Rhetoric in Michael Moore's *Fahrenheit 9/11*," in *Michael*

Moore: Filmmaker, Newsmaker, Cultural Icon, ed. Mathew Bernstein (Ann Arbor: University of Michigan Press, 2010), 167–201.

7. "Remarks by the President on Election Night," 7 November 2012, https://www.whitehouse.gov/the-press-office/2012/11/07/remarks-president-election-night. The phrase "the greatest nation on Earth" is, as Obama has pointed out in a different, postelection context, a cliché. "Obama Calls It 'a Cliche' to Say We're 'the Greatest Country on Earth,'" Cybercast News Service, 14 May 2013, accessed 9 August 2015, http://cnsnews.com/blog/craig-bannister/obama-calls-it-cliche-say-were-greatest-country-earth.

8. James W. Carey, *Communication as Culture: Essays on Media and Society* (Boston: Unwin, Hyman, 1989), 21.

9. John B. Thompson, *The Media and Modernity: A Social Theory of the Media* (Stanford, CA: Stanford University Press, 1995), 38.

10. Jeffrey C. Alexander, *The Performance of Politics: Obama's Victory and the Democratic Struggle for Power* (Oxford: Oxford University Press, 2010), 11.

11. Jeffrey C. Alexander and Bernadette N. Jaworsky, *Obama Power* (Malden, MA: Polity Press, 2014), 3.

12. Geoffrey Craig, *The Media, Politics and Public Life* (Crows Nest, Australia: Allen and Unwin, 2004), 6.

13. Lisa Gitelman, *Scripts, Grooves, and Writing Machines: Representing Technology in the Edison Era* (Stanford, CA: Stanford University Press, 1999), 125.

14. The term "mediascape" was coined and briefly characterized by Arjun Appadurai in "Disjuncture and Difference in the Global Cultural Economy," *Public Culture* 2 (1990) 2:9.

15. Christian Wolmar, *The Great Railroad Revolution: The History of Trains in America* (New York: Public Affairs, 2012).

16. Menahhem Blondheim, *News Over the Wires: The Telegraph and the Flow of Public Information in America, 1844–1897* (Cambridge, MA: Harvard University Press, 1994), 106, 190.

17. Gerald J. Baldasty, *E. W. Scripps and the Business of Newspapers* (Urbana: University of Illinois Press, 1999), 12–16.

18. John Brooks, *Telephone: The First Hundred Years* (New York: Harper and Row, 1976), 90–105; Robert V. Bruce, *Bell: Alexander Graham Bell and the Conquest of Solitude* (Ithaca, NY: Cornell University Press, 1990).

19. Warren Susman, *Culture as History: The Transformation of American Society in the Twentieth Century* (New York: Pantheon Books, 1984); John Higham, "The Reorientation of American Culture in the 1890s," in *The Origins of Modern Consciousness,* ed. John Weiss (Detroit: Wayne State University Press, 1965), 25–48.

20. H. Clark Johnson, "The Gold Deflation, France and the Coming of the Depression, 1919–1932" (PhD diss., Yale University, 1994).

21. Christina D. Romer, "Spurious Volatility in Historical Unemployment Data," *Political Economy* 94 (February 1986): 31. Lebergott's figures tend to be higher. See Stanley Lebergott, "Annual Estimates of Unemployment in the United States, 1900–1954," in *The Measurement and Behavior of Unemploy-*

ment Conference of the Universities-National Bureau Committee for Economic Research (Princeton, NJ: Princeton University Press [for NBER], 1957). See also J.R. Vernon, "Unemployment Rates in Post-Bellum America: 1869–1899," *Journal of Macroeconomics* 16 (1994): 701–14.

22. "Civil Rights Cases," in *West's Encyclopedia of American Law,* 2nd ed., accessed 29 December 2015, http://legal-dictionary.thefreedictionary.com /Civil+Rights+Cases.

23. The amendment to give women the right to vote in Idaho was on the November 1896 ballot, so women in Idaho could not vote for president until 1900.

24. Barbara Miller Solomon, *In the Company of Educated Women: A History of Women and Higher Education in America* (New Haven, CT: Yale University Press, 1985), 63.

25. Tom Gunning, "The Cinema of Attractions: Early Film, Its Spectator and the Avant-Garde," in *Early Cinema: Space, Frame, Narrative,* ed. Thomas Elsaesser (London: BFI, 1990), 58–59.

26. Robert Grau, *The Theater of Science* (New York: Broadway Publishing Company, 1914), 10.

27. Erkki Huhtamo and Jussi Parikka, eds., *Media Archaeology: Approaches, Applications, and Implications* (Berkeley: University of California Press, 2011); Jussi Parikka, *What Is Media Archaeology?* (Cambridge and Malden, MA: Polity Press, 2012); Simone Natale, "Understanding Media Archaeology," *Canadian Journal of Communication* 37 (2012): 523–27.

28. Paul Spehr, *The Man Who Made Movies: W.K.L. Dickson* (Hertfordshire, England: John Libbey, 2008), 444–53; Jonathan Auerbach, *Body Shots: Early Cinema's Incarnations* (Berkeley: University of California Press, 2007), 15–31; Charles Musser, *The Emergence of Cinema: The American Screen to 1907* (New York: Scribner, 1990), 150–55.

29. See the Oxford Dictionary, accessed 25 July 2015, https://www .oxforddictionaries.com/us/definition/american_english/media.

30. Thomas Elsaesser, "Between Knowing and Believing: The Cinematic Dispositive After Cinema," in *Cine-Dispositives: Essays in Epistemology Across Media,* ed. François Albera and Maria Tortajada (Amsterdam: University of Amsterdam Press, 2015), 32.

31. Carolyn Marvin, *When Old Technologies Were New: Thinking About Communication in the Late Nineteenth Century* (New York: Oxford University Press, 1988), 152.

32. Lisa Gitelman, *Always Already New: Media, History, and the Data of Culture* (Cambridge, MA: MIT Press, 2008), 7.

33. Walter Benjamin, "The Work of Art in the Age of Technological Reproducibility (Second Version)," in Walter Benjamin, *Selected Writings, Volume 3: 1935–1938,* ed. Howard Elland and Michael W. Jennings (Cambridge, MA: Harvard University Press, 2006), 103–33.

34. François Albera and Maria Tortajada, eds., *Cine-Dispositives.*

35. Both in conversations and through their scholarship, Brooks McNamara and Bernard Bate have been extremely helpful in thinking about oratory and pageantry as essential parts of the political process in the late nineteenth and

early twentieth centuries. See Brooks McNamara, *Day of Jubilee: The Great Age of Public Celebrations in New York, 1788–1909* (New Brunswick, NJ: Rutgers University Press; 1997); and Bernard Bate, *Tamil Oratory and the Dravidian Aesthetic* (New York: Columbia University Press, 2009).

36. Asa Briggs and Peter Burke, *A Social History of the Media: From Gutenberg to the Internet* (Cambridge and Malden, MA: Polity Press, 2009), 2.

37. Charles Musser, "Why Did Negroes Love Al Jolson and *The Jazz Singer*?: Melodrama, Blackface and Cosmopolitan Theatrical Culture," *Film History* 23, no. 2 (2011): 198–222; Charles Musser, "The Hidden and the Unspeakable: On Theatrical Culture, Oscar Wilde and Ernst Lubitsch's *Lady Windermere's Fan* (1925)," *Film Studies* 4 (Summer 2004): 12–47; Charles Musser, "Towards a History of Theatrical Culture: Imagining an Integrated History of Stage and Screen," in *Screen Culture: History and Textuality*, ed. John Fullerton (Eastleigh, England: John Libbey Publishing, 2004), 3–20.

38. Anthony R. Fellow, *American Media History*, 3rd ed. (Boston: Wadsworth, 2013); Paul Starr, *The Creation of the Media: Political Origins of Modern Communication* (New York: Basic Books, 2004); Carolyn Marvin, *When Old Technologies Were New*; Lisa Gitelman, *Always Already New*.

39. Jay David Bolter and Richard Grusin, *Remediation: Understanding New Media* (Cambridge, MA: MIT Press, 2000).

40. Brian Winston, *Media Technology and Society: A History: From the Telegraph to the Internet* (London: Routledge, 1998), 19–24.

41. Siegfried Zielinski, *Deep Time of the Media: Towards an Archaeology of Hearing and Seeing by Technical Means*, trans. Gloria Custance (Cambridge, MA: MIT Press, 2006), 101–57.

42. Important research on screen practice in the nineteenth century is being done by amateur historians (I use this term in a strong, positive sense) in the *Magic Lantern Gazette*, including Kentwood D. Wells on John Fallon's stereopticon and Terry and Deborah Borton on Joseph Boggs Beale. See Kentwood D. Wells, "What's in a Name? The Magic Lantern and the Stereopticon in American Periodicals 1860–1900," *Magic Lantern Gazette* 20, no. 3 (Fall 2008): 3–19; Kentwood D. Wells, "The Stereopticon Men: On the Road with John Fallon's Stereopticon, 1860–1870," *Magic Lantern Gazette* 23, no. 3 (Fall 2011): 3–34; Terry and Deborah Borton, *Before the Movies: American Magic-Lantern Entertainment and the Nation's First Great Screen Artist, Joseph Boggs Beale* (Herz, England: John Libbey, 2014). See also Terry Borton, "238 Eminent American 'Magic-Lantern' Showmen: The Chautauqua Lecturers," *Magic Lantern Gazette* 25, no. 1 (Spring 2013): 3–36. Likewise a few dissertations have been done on this topic, but X. Theodore Barber's was never published, and Artemis Willis is still in the process of completing hers. X. Theodore Barber, "Evenings of Wonder: A History of the Magic Lantern Show in America" (PhD diss., New York University, 1993); Artemis Willis, "The Magic Lantern Today: Archaeology, Apparatus and Aesthetics for a New Millennium" (PhD diss., University of Chicago, forthcoming).

43. André Gaudreault, *Film and Attraction: From Kinematography to Cinema*, trans. Timothy Barnard, foreword by Rick Altman (Urbana: University of Illinois Press, 2011). The term "cinema" is used in other ways that must con-

cern us. In many cases it is understood as an essential component of a larger media form that includes the peep-hole kinetoscope, nontheatrical motion picture exhibition, and so forth. The term is often used interchangeably with "movies" or "film." In this respect, projection is a dominant but nonessential element of this particular media form. "Cinema" as a term has been used synecdochically to refer to a wide range of modern motion picture practices—a form of shorthand, just as "film studies" and "cinema studies" are often used interchangeably even though we could argue that they don't mean quite the same thing. "Cinema" is also a term that can refer to film as art. Thus a bad movie or a how-to film would not be considered cinema.

44. Benedict Anderson, *Imagined Communities: Reflections on the Origin and Spread of Nationalism* (London: Verso, 1991).

45. Daniel J. Boorstin, *The Image: A Guide to Pseudo-Events in America* (New York: Atheneum, 1987). William D. Harpine also questions Boorstin's characterizations of pseudo-events in *From the Front Porch to the Front Page: McKinley and Bryan in the 1896 Presidential Campaign* (College Station: Texas A&M University Press, 2005), 38–39.

46. Terry Ramsaye, *A Million and One Nights: A History of the Motion Picture* (New York: Simon and Schuster, 1926), 326.

47. This effort to see how specific motion pictures disrupted a wide range of social and cultural practices is essential if we are to grasp the extent to which cinema was a wide-rangingly disruptive force from its outset. This applied to *The Passion Play of Oberammergau* (1898) as well as several different fight films. But it also applies to short one-shot films such as *The John C. Rice-May Irwin Kiss*, which had a widespread impact on the theatrical world. See Charles Musser, "The May Irwin Kiss: Performance and Early Cinema," in *Visual Delights Two: Exhibition and Reception*, ed. Vanessa Toulmin and Simon Popple (Eastleigh, England: John Libbey, 2005), 96–115.

48. Richard Abel, "The Pleasures and Perils of Big Data in Digitized Newspapers," *Film History* 25, nos. 1–2 (2013): 1–10; Richard Abel, *Menus for Movieland: Newspapers and the Emergence of American Film Culture, 1913–1916* (Berkeley: University of California Press, 2015), 1–19.

49. H. Wayne Morgan, *William McKinley and His America* (Kent, OH: Kent State University Press, 2003); William D. Harpine, *From the Front Porch to the Front Page*.

50. Patrick Joyce, "The Gift of the Past," in *Manifestos for History*, ed. Keith Jenkins, Sue Morgan, and Alum Munslow (London: Routledge, 2007), 89.

51. The president-elect consistently won New York State until 1916, when Woodrow Wilson was reelected while his opponent, former New York Governor Charles Hughes, won his home state.

CHAPTER ONE

1. James McGarth Morris, *Pulitzer: A Life in Politics, Print and Power* (New York: HarperCollins, 2010), 224–32.

2. Adlai Stevenson (1835–1914) was the grandfather of Adlai Stevenson II (1900–1965), the Democratic candidate for president in 1952 and 1956.

3. Women had voted in the territory of Wyoming since December 10, 1869.

4. "Is It Apathy?," *NYHerald*, 26 October 1892, 10; "Mr. Cleveland's Speech," *NYTimes*, 2 November 1892, 1; see also Harry W. Baehr Jr., *The New York Tribune Since the Civil War* (New York: Dodd, Mead and Co., 1936), 244.

5. George Harmon Knoles, *The Presidential Campaign and Election of 1892* (Stanford, CA: Stanford University Press, 1942), 9–48; Harry W. Baehr Jr., *The New York Tribune Since the Civil War*, 243–44.

6. Joanne Reitano, *The Tariff Question in the Gilded Age: The Great Debate of 1888* (University Park: Pennsylvania State University Press, 1994), xvi.

7. "The Two Candidates," *NYTimes*, 20 July 1892, 8. The figure of 20,000 comes from "Lost in Noise," *Boston Globe*, 21 July 1892, 1. Madison Square Garden could seat 8,000 but the *Baltimore Sun* estimated that between 25,000 and 30,000 were assembled there. "In Madison Square Garden," *BaltSun*, July 21, 1892, 1. On the other hand, the Republican *NYTrib* wrote of 6,000 to 8,000 in attendance. "Informing Their Leaders," *NYTrib*, 21 July 1892, 1.

8. "The Surprise Party Tonight," *Hartford Courant*, 20 July 1892, 4. In addition, the nomination of Adlai Stevenson was seen by some as saddling Cleveland with "an uncongenial and undesired associate." Ibid.

9. "Mr. Cleveland's Response," *NYTimes*, 21 July 1892, 2.

10. "The Clevelands at Greenwich Village," *NYTimes*, 9 October 1892, 9.

11. George Harmon Knoles, *The Presidential Campaign and Election of 1892*, 207; "A Great Cleveland Night," *NYTimes*, 2 November 1892, 1. Cleveland also participated in a campaign rally on November 5.

12. In response to the First Lady's illness and the constraints this put on the president, Cleveland cut back on his participation in public events. For this reason he declined to go to the dedication of the World's Columbian Exposition on October 21, 1892.

13. "Rising German Cheers," *NYTrib*, 4 November 1892, 1.

14. "Mr. Reid in Mamaroneck," *NYTrib*, 6 November 1892, 8. Saturday was the culmination of presidential campaigning. Candidates and their surrogates did not campaign on Sundays, and Monday was also relatively quiet since men worked and they needed to get up early the next day and vote.

15. "McKinley in Brooklyn," *NYHerald*, 1 November 1892, 5.

16. Paul Starr, *The Creation of the Media: Political Origins of Modern Communication* (New York: Basic Books, 2004), 150.

17. "New Tuesday Meeting," *NYPress*, 15 October 1892, 4.

18. "The Republican Calendar," *Brooklyn Standard Union*, 15 October 1892, 3.

19. "A Big Harlem Parade," *NYTrib*, 9 October 1892, 1.

20. Ibid.

21. "The Tariff Law," *Brooklyn Standard Union*, 15 October 1892, 3.

22. Henry Villard, *Memoirs of Henry Villard: Journalist and Financier* (New York: Houghton Mifflin, 1904), 361–62. New York financier William C. Whitney was another key Cleveland supporter.

23. *Puck*, the nation's first successful humor magazine, founded in 1871, was strongly Democratic. Some of its staff left in 1881 to establish a Republican counterpart, *Judge*.

24. Janet E. Steele, *The Sun Shines for All: Journalism and Ideology in the Life of Charles A. Dana* (Syracuse, NY: Syracuse University Press, 1993), 131–32, 148.

25. "Rising German Cheers," *NYTrib*, 4 November 1892, 1.

26. "No Apathy Exists Here," *NYTrib*, 18 October 1892, 1; "Make It a Great Parade," *NYTrib*, 23 October 1892, 1.

27. "The Big Parade Abandoned," *NYTrib*, 26 October 1892, 2.

28. "In Fourteenth Street, Opposite the Wigwam," *NYHerald*, 4 November 1892, 7.

29. "Never Such a Rally!" *NYSun*, 4 November 1892, 1.

30. "In Fourteenth Street, Opposite the Wigwam," *NYHerald*, 4 November 1892, 7.

31. "Business Men March and Cheer for Cleveland," *NYHerald*, 6 November 1892, 15.

32. "In the People's Theatre," *NYTimes*, 7 November 1892, 8.

33. "Ten to Nine on Cleveland," *NYSun*, 4 November 1892, 1.

34. Bill Nichols, *Representing Reality: Issues and Concepts in Documentary* (Bloomington: Indiana University Press, 1991).

35. Wheeler was a correspondent for a Red Bank Democratic Club during the 1880 election. See "The Contest," *BrookEagle*, 19 August 1880, 4.

36. "Death of John L. Wheeler," *NYTimes*, 1 December 1893, 9.

37. "Incidents of the Civil War," *BrookEagle*, 23 February 1886, 4, and 2 March 1886, 2; "Hours of Leisure," *NYSun*, 29 March 1886, 3.

38. "Hermon," *Ogdensburg Journal*, 8 December 1886, 4; "Ogdensburg" and "Hermon," *Gouverneur Free Press*, 15 December 1886, 3; "Amusements," *Watertown Daily Times* (New York), 15 October 1887; "Northfield, Mass.," *Vermont Phoenix*, 20 January 1888. See also the *Ogdensburg Advance and St. Lawrence Democrat*, 19 December 1889, 1.

39. "The Civil War," *BrookEagle*, 12 March 1886, 1. Wheeler gave another lecture at the Summerfield Methodist Episcopal Church in Brooklyn on December 6, 1886. The church was packed and his presentation applauded. "Incidents of the Civil War," *BrookEagle*, 7 December 1886, 2.

40. "Against Cleveland and Free Trade," *NYTrib*, 19 March 1888, 5.

41. "The Tariff Illustrated," *BrookEagle*, 6 August 1888, 2; "Notes on the Canvass," *NYTrib*, 10 August 1888, 3; and "Home News," *NYTrib*, 12 August 1888, 8.

42. "Our Main Objective," *American Economist*, 4 January 1889, 6.

43. "Annual Address of the President," *American Economist*, 18 January 1889, 34.

44. Ibid.

45. "New Harrison Recruits," *ChicTrib*, 1 September 1888, 4; "The Stereopticon Is Kept Busy," *NYTrib*, 23 August 1888, 3.

46. "The Tariff Question Illustrated," *Newark Union* (New York), 10 October 1888, 3.

47. *Bridgeport News*, quote in "The Tariff Illustrated," *Newark Arcadia Weekly Gazette* (New York), [13] October 1888.

48. "Very Sensitive Republicans," *NYTimes*, 18 September 1888, 1.

49. "Pictured Politics," *Buffalo Sunday Morning News*, 21 October 1888, 1.

50. *Syracuse Daily Journal*, 16 October 1888.

51. "Flashes from the Sun," *NYSun*, 12 February 1888, 10.

52. Jacob A. Riis, *How the Other Half Lives: Studies Among the Tenements of New York*, 2nd ed. (1890; New York: Young People's Missionary Movement, n.d.), 296.

53. "Flashed on Canvas," *Boston Globe*, 7 September 1888, 4.

54. "Shown on the Stereopticon," *Boston Globe*, 23 September 1888, 1.

55. "Digs by the Stereopticon," *NYSun*, 15 August 1888, 1.

56. "Daily Times of 1888 vs. Daily Times of '81, '3 and '4," *Watertown Re-Union*, 3 October 1888, 4.

57. "Politics on the Canal," *NYSun*, 4 November 1888, 10.

58. Charles Baudelaire, *The Painter of Modern Life and Other Essays*, ed. and trans. Jonathan Mayne (New York: Da Capo Press, 1964), 9.

59. "Digs by the Stereopticon," *NYSun*, 15 August 1888, 1.

60. Christina D. Romer, "Spurious Volatility in Historical Unemployment Data," *Political Economy* 94 (1986): 22.

61. H. Wayne Morgan, *From Hayes to McKinley: National Party Politics, 1877–1896* (Syracuse, NY: Syracuse University Press, 1969), 318.

62. *Jamestown Weekly Alert* (New York), 23 August 1888, 4.

63. "The Tin Plate Debate," *American Economist*, 29 August 1890, 129.

64. Joan Reitano, *The Tariff Question in the Gilded Age*, 129–30.

65. H. Wayne Morgan offers a more nuanced assessment of the tariff bill and McKinley's defeat, for instance noting that a Democratic Ohio legislature redistricted McKinley's seat in 1890 so his constituency leaned to the Democrats. Likewise, the Tariff Act of 1890, he argues, was sophisticated in the goods it targeted. H. Wayne Morgan, *From Hayes to McKinley*, 355.

66. "Short Tariff Sermons. The Tin-Plate Duty," *American Economist*, 23 September 1892, 163.

67. "Eighth Annual Meeting of the American Protective Tariff League," *American Economist*, 27 January 1893, 26; Judge John L. Wheeler, "Protection in the South," *American Economist*, 4 January 1889, 3–4.

68. "The Tariff Illustrated," *American Economist*, 24 June 1892, 335.

69. "Our Illustrated Lectures," *American Economist*, 9 September 1892, 148.

70. "The Tariff Illustrated," *American Economist*, 23 September 1892, 173.

71. "Good Work Through the State: Judge Wheeler Uses the Stereopticon Effectively at Middletown," *NYTrib*, 16 October 1892, 2; "Born and Bred a Democrat," *Port Jervis Union* quoted in the *Middletown Daily Press*, 17 October 1892, 1.

72. "The Tariff Illustrated," *Middletown Daily Press*, 17 October 1892, 1.

73. Ibid.

74. Ibid.

75. "The Tariff Illustrated," *American Economist*, 23 September 1892, 172.

76. "To Celebrate the Birth of the Republican Party," *NYTrib*, 2 August 1884, 7.

77. "Amsterdam," *Troy Daily Times*, 31 August 1892; "The Sheep Story Settled Him," *NYTimes*, 3 September 1891, 2.

78. D. G. Harriman, "Protection a Necessity," *American Economist*, 16 September 1892, 155–56.

79. "All Aflame: Republican Enthusiasm Throughout the City," *Brooklyn Standard Union*, 21 September 1892, 5. Harriman's illustrated tariff lectures were never mentioned in the *American Economist*.

80. "Pushing Campaign Work," *NYTrib*, 30 September 1892, 7. He presented at Montclair Hall, Montclair, New Jersey, on October 11; see "The Good Work Goes On," *NYPress*, 12 October 1892.

81. "Protection Discussed by Hon. D. G. Harriman at Criterion," *Brooklyn Standard Union*, 27 October 1892, 1. Conceivably the lack of flair was linked to the restraint required out of respect for Caroline Harrison's passing.

82. Advertisement, *Elkhart Daily Review* (Indiana), 16 August 1888, 2; "Patriotic Instructive Entertainment," *Pittsburg Dispatch*, 16 March 1889, 7; "Pleasant Entertainments," *Pittsburg Dispatch*, 26 November 1889, 4.

83. "Warwick," *Middletown Daily Press*, 27 March 1891, 2; "A Course of Sunday Evening Lectures in the New Casino," *Middletown Daily Press*, 6 January 1892, 3; "Evidence for Mayor Schieren," *NYTimes*, 16 August 1891, 20. Tully would eventually train members of the Law Enforcement Society in the uses of the Kodak Detective Camera to gather evidence of Sunday Dry Law violations. "Snap Shots at Tipplers," *NYSun*, 24 December 1894, 1.

84. "Fifth Ward Republicans," *BrookEagle*, 16 September 1892, 6.

85. "In and Around Flushing," *BrookEagle*, 3 August 1892, 3; "Political Odds and Ends," *NYTrib*, 14 September 1892, 3.

86. Reese was a resident of Westfield, New Jersey, and had offices in New York City. See "Union County Republicans Hopeful," *NYTrib*, 25 September 1892, 5; "Republican Meeting," *Warren Republican,* 28 October 1892, 3; "New Jersey Is Fighting," *NYTrib*, 31 October 1892, 3.

87. "Republican Rallies," *Hartford Courant*, 25 October 1892, 8.

88. "Rally at the Locks," *Hartford Courant*, 27 October 1892, 7.

89. "A New Brooklyn Park Commissioner," *NYTrib*, 31 January 1888, 1. Kennedy was a member of the insurance brokerage firm of Weed and Kennedy.

90. "Closing Meeting in the Thirteenth Ward," *BrookEagle*, 3 November 1888, 1; "About Brooklyn People," *BrookEagle*, 4 September 1892, 2.

91. "At Republican Headquarters," *NYWorld*, 2 October 1892, 7.

92. "E. R. Kennedy Speaks in East Orange," *NYTrib*, 7 October 1892, 2.

93. "Protection Illustrated," *NYTrib*, 25 October 1892, 3.

94. "For the Stereopticon," *NYTimes*, 28 October 1892, 4. The *New York Times* editorial was referring to a letter published as "Party Policy and the People," *NYTrib*, 9 August 1890, 7.

95. "Eighth Annual Meeting of the American Protective Tariff League," *American Economist*, 27 January 1893, 26.

96. "The Stereopticon in Politics," *Ogdensburg Journal*, 16 August 1892, 23.

97. John A. Logan (1826–1886) had been a Republican senator from Illinois and the Republican vice presidential candidate in 1884.

98. "Brodsky's Stereopticon Show," *NYSun*, 2 October 1892, A2; "Sam Engel's Light Is Out," *NYSun*, 12 October 1892, 9.

99. "Sausalito Republicans," *San Francisco Morning Call*, 24 October 1892, 1.

100. "Democratic Societies," *San Francisco Chronicle*, 3 November 1892, 10.

101. *NYTimes*, 5 August 1892, 4.

102. "Latest News," *Washington Evening Star*, 7 November 1892, 1.

103. "Amusements," *New Haven Morning News*, 8 November 1892, 2.

104. "Theater and Club House," *New Haven Morning News*, 9 November 1892, 2.

105. Few women ventured out to watch the returns. Sketches of the crowd in Washington, DC, that appeared in the *Washington Evening Star* depict only men, though men of all ages and all classes. "Flashing Out the News," *Washington Evening Star*, 9 November 1892, 9. The theater was seen as a more appropriate place for mixed-gender audiences.

106. "Night Scenes in the City," *NYSun*, 9 November 1892, 5.

107. "Theater and Club House," *New Haven Morning News*, 9 November 1892, 2; "News at the Theaters," *NYHerald*, 9 November 1892, 2.

108. "Taking pictures" were, one suspects, pictures that "took," or charmed, the public.

109. "Giving Out the News," *Hartford Courant*, 9 November 1892, 4.

110. "Hartford, Heavy Vote," *Hartford Courant*, 9 November 1892, 4. In addition, Proctor's Theatre in Hartford showed returns after its evening performance: "In Proctor's a big crowd saw 'Joseph' and most of them stayed to see the returns cast upon a screen by a stereopticon. But many went out and at midnight the audience was a slim one. Stereopticon pictures were shown between the bulletins." Ibid.

111. "About the Bulletins," *NYTimes*, 9 November 1892, 3.

112. There is considerable controversy around the World Building--its height, and its number of stories (varying from eighteen to twenty-six). Pulitzer sought to build the largest commercial building in the world, one that would dwarf his competitors. See Aurora Wallace, *Media Capital: Architecture and Communications in New York City* (Urbana: University of Illinois Press, 2012), 64–72.

113. "Up the 'World's' Ladder," *NYWorld*, 9 November 1892, 5.

114. "At the 'World's' Harlem Office," *NYWorld*, 9 November 1892, 5.

115. "Many Thousands Read the Signals," *NYHerald*, 9 November 1892, 7.

116. "By the Light of the Sun," *NYSun*, 9 November 1892, 5.

117. "At the Sun's Up-town Office," *NYSun*, 9 November 1892, 5.

118. Frank M. O'Brien, *The Story of "The Sun"* (New York: George H. Doran, 1918), 180.

CHAPTER TWO

1. A random word search of the *Guardian* and *Observer* in England shows that the term "optical lantern" first appeared in the 1880s but did not become common until the 1890s and virtually disappeared after World War I. Its deployment in Britain came later and ended sooner than did its counterpart ("stereopticon") in the United States.

2. For a brief history of the magic lantern from its invention by Christiaan Huygens through the early twentieth century, see Charles Musser, "Towards a History of Screen Practice," in *The Emergence of Cinema: The American Screen to 1907* (New York: Scribner, 1990), 15–54. This chapter corrects, elaborates on, and refines that history in the United States from the 1840s through the 1880s. Extensively researched articles on this topic now appear regularly in the *Magic Lantern Gazette: A Journal of Research.*

3. André Gaudreault and Philippe Marion briefly introduce the term "weak medium form" in "A Medium Is Always Born Twice," *Early Popular Visual Culture* 3, no. 1 (May 2005): 7.

4. For instance a search for the term "illustrated lecture" will generate fewer hits than a search in which the two words "illustrated" and "lecture" merely appear in the same item. In an earlier iteration of this undertaking I had tried to be more capacious, but this became methodologically problematic and impractical given changes and refinements in digitizing and search engines. For instance, recognition of a word in its plural form may have changed. So a search for "slide projector" may have recognized the phrase "slide projectors" at one point but does not at present.

5. "Amusements," *NYTimes*, 20 March 1881, 11. A search for the term "stereoptic" also generated some uses of the term "stereopticon" that suffered printing imperfections. Other exhibitors used the term "stereoscopic views."

6. Another explanation for the frequent appearance of "stereopticon" and "lecture" in the same *New York Times* news item has to do with the practice of grouping mentions and advertisements about such public events in a single file. As a result, a lecture at one location and the mention of a stereopticon at another will create a false co-relation.

7. "Religious Notices," *NYTimes*, 2 March 1879, 7, and 6 April 1879, 7.

8. Advertisement, *NYTimes*, 18 December 1858, 3. Combined uses of the words "magic lantern" and "lecture" might appear in reports from Europe where the idiom "stereopticon" was not employed. See "The Voltaire Centenary," *NYTimes*, 16 June 1878, 4.

9. One perhaps unique exception (which did not show up in a random word search) can be found in an advertisement by the optician J.B. Dancer, who offered a variety of lantern-related paraphernalia for sale, including stereopticons. His effort to introduce the American term did not catch on. Advertisement, *Manchester Guardian*, 5 January 1864, 2.

10. Advertisement, *Manchester Guardian*, 2 November 1864, 4.

11. Although the terms "lantern" and "lecture" appear in 374 items between 1850 and 1879, the number in which they have a meaningful intersection is small.

12. "Amusements," *NYTimes*, 19 January 1880, 7.

13. The term "documentary" or "documentary film" seems to have been imported to the United States from French-speaking parts of Europe. In "Vatican Repudiates Attack on Our Movies," *NYTimes*, 29 July 1927, 17, the Catholic Church applauds "instructive documentary films" being made in Belgium.

14. Advertisement, *NYTimes*, 2 May 1926, SM23.

15. "Educational Motion Pictures," *NYTimes*, 14 November 1926, X16.

16. "Our Parks as Teachers," *NYTimes*, 26 May 1935, X25. Classified ads for "lantern slide projectors" can be found in the *Chicago Tribune* and other newspapers by 1919. Photographic journals occasionally provide advertisements such as one for the Ingento Stereopticon, which is described as "the most perfect and complete lantern-slide projector on the market." Advertisement, *Photo Era*, 1 February 1913, 2.

17. Advertisement, *NYTimes*, 25 December 1940, 9.

18. "The Magic-Lantern," *The Manufacturer and Builder: A Practical Journal of Industrial Progress*, 1 July 1869, 199.

19. "Metropolitan Opera House," *NYTimes*, 6 March 1886, 5.

20. For information on early phantasmagoria performances in the United States see Charles Musser, *The Emergence of Cinema*, 24–29.

21. Patent no. 7,458, Improvement in Producing Photographic Pictures Upon Transparent Media, issued 25 June 1850.

22. Louis Walton Sipley, "The Magic Lantern," *Pennsylvania Arts and Sciences* 4 (December 1939): 39–43; Louis Walton Sipley, "W. and F. Langenheim-Photographers," *Pennsylvania Arts and Sciences* (1937): 25–31. The crucial work on the magic lantern in the United States remains Xenophon Theodore Barber, "Evening of Wonders: A History of the Magic Lantern Show in America" (PhD diss., New York University, 1993).

23. "W. & F. Langenheim's," *Philadelphia Inquirer*, 19 September 1849, 2.

24. "New Invention," *Philadelphia Inquirer*, 4 October 1849, 2.

25. Ibid.

26. "Langenheim's Talbotypes," *Dollar Newspaper*, 24 October 1849, 3.

27. "New Invention," *Boston Daily Argus*, 17 October 1849, 2.

28. "Novel Exhibition," *Boston Transcript*, 29 January 1850, 2; advertisement, *Boston Bee*, 1 February 1850, 3.

29. "Novel Exhibition," *Boston Transcript*, 29 January 1850, 2.

30. Advertisement, *Boston Bee*, 16 February 1850, 3.

31. Advertisement, *Boston Herald*, 13 March 1850, 3.

32. "Whipple's Dissolving Views," *Youth's Companion*, 14 March 1850, 23.

33. "John Adams Whipple," Wikipedia, accessed 21 September 2015, https://en.wikipedia.org/wiki/John_Adams_Whipple.

34. See "The Great Exhibition," *London Observer*, 4 May 1851, 5; "The Great Exhibition," *London Observer*, 7 May 1851, 2.

35. The Langenheims, quoted in the *Art-Journal* (London) (April 1851): 106.

36. "At the Polytechnic Lecture Rooms," *North American Gazette*, 3 May 1851, 2; "Langenheim's Physiorama," *Pennsylvania Freeman*, 8 May 1851, 3.

37. "Langenheim's Physiorama," *Pennsylvania Freeman*, 8 May 1851, 3.

38. Charles Musser, *The Emergence of Cinema*, 45–48; Laurent Mannoni, *The Great Art of Light and Shadow: Archaeology of the Cinema*, ed. and trans. Richard Crangle (Exeter, England: University of Exeter Press, 2000), 248–62. The book was originally published in French.

39. Advertisement, *Athenaeum*, 18 January 1851, 66.

40. This 1855 outfit apparently contained all the components of what would become known as the stereopticon. Their "large oxy-hydrogen lantern, with dis-

solving views" was "intended to itinerate through the two counties and give exhibitions in connection with the various societies. The apparatus will be placed in charge of a lecturer and exhibitor, who will travel with it. The dissolving views are sufficiently numerous to afford a series of six exhibitions arranged as follows: 1) The insect world (British insects and foreign). 2) The vegetable world. 3) Familiar objects in daily use (food and fluids). 4) Oriental scenery. 5. British scenery. 6. The capitals of Europe." "Institutional Association for Lancashire and Cheshire," *Manchester Guardian*, 17 November 1855, 5. For the British the light source was often foregrounded in this new configuration. The oxy-hydrogen microscope seems to have been in general use much earlier, by 1842. "The Royal Adelaide Gallery," *Manchester Guardian*, 25 December 1842, 2.

41. M. A. Root, "The Magic Lantern. Its History and Uses for Educational and Other Purposes," *Philadelphia Photographer*, 1 December 1874, 11 (italics in original). Laurent Mannoni gives valuable attention to Duboscq in *The Great Art of Light and Shadow*, 227–30, 236–41, but he overlooks the Langenheim connection.

42. Frederick Langenheim to H. H. Snelling, 19 September 1854, in "Personal and Fine Art Intelligence," *Photographic and Fine Arts Journal*, 1 October 1854, 319.

43. "Langenheim's New Series of Stereoscopic Views," *National Intelligencer* (Washington, DC), 24 March 1856, 4; "The Stereoscope," *NYTrib*, 9 November 1858, 3.

44. Francesco Casetti, "Elsewhere. The Relocation of Art," in *Valencia09/Confines* (Valencia: INVAM, 2009), 348–51.

45. "Another New Invention—The Stereomonoscope," *NYTimes*, 10 June 1858, 2; "Photographic Inventions," *Scientific American*, 25 May 1861, 326.

46. "An Optical Wonder," *Louisville Daily Journal*, 29 April 1863, 1. The same basic review was also reprinted in *The Merchants' Magazine and Commercial Review* 48 (May 1863): 430.

47. Kentwood D. Wells, "Fallon's Stereopticon," *Magic Lantern Gazette* 23, no. 3 (Fall 2011): 2–34. Wells's extensive article is a valuable achievement and underscores the incomplete (and so often inaccurate) sketch of stereopticons in the 1860s as presented in Charles Musser, *The Emergence of Cinema*, 29–42, and Charles Musser, "The Stereopticon and Cinema: Media Form or Platform?," in *Cine-Dispositives: Essays in Epistemology Across Media*, ed. François Albera and Maria Tortajada (Amsterdam: University of Amsterdam Press, 2104), 129–60.

48. "Amusements, Something New Under the Sun," *Philadelphia Inquirer*, 19 December 1860, 8.

49. "The Stereopticon," *Saturday Evening Post*, 5 January 1861, 2.

50. Kentwood D. Wells, "The Stereopticon Men: On the Road with John Fallon's Stereopticon, 1860–1870," *Magic Lantern Gazette* 23, no. 3 (Fall 2011): 3–34.

51. "Public Amusements," *Philadelphia Press*, 4 February 1861, 2; "Public Amusements," *Philadelphia Press*, 27 April 1861, 3.

52. "Amusements," *Philadelphia Inquirer*, 4 February 1861, 8.

53. "Amusements, Music, &c.," *Philadelphia Inquirer*, 4 April 1861, 5.

54. "Amusements, Music, &c.," *Philadelphia Inquirer*, 23 February 1861, 5; "Amusements," *Philadelphia Inquirer*, 29 March 1861, 1.

55. "Amusements," *Philadelphia Press*, 11 April 1861, 3.

56. "Amusements," *Philadelphia Press*, 22 April 1861, 3.

57. "The Stereopticon," *Arthur's Home Magazine* (April 1861): 254. Whether all these stereopticons can be attributed to Fallon is unclear. A stereopticon was shown at Temperance Temple in Baltimore on February 4, 1862, but it was quite possibly a renamed magic lantern and not Fallon's. "Temperance Temple," *BaltSun*, 4 February 1862, 2.

58. Advertisement, *Newark Daily Advertiser*, 1 May 1861, 3.

59. "Amusements," *Boston Evening Traveller*, 8 July 1861, 3; "Amusements," *Boston Evening Transcript*, 20 July 1861, 3.

60. Advertisement, *Philadelphia Press*, 1 April 1863, 3.

61. "Amusements," *Philadelphia Inquirer*, 25 May 1861, 8.

62. "Amusements," *NYTimes*, 4 August 1861, 5. In contrast, the first uses of the term "illustrated lecture" that appeared in the *New York Tribune* did not use lantern slides. They were for Dr. Robert A. Fisher's illustrated lecture "Gunpowder, Cannon and Projectiles," for which he used "diagrams, models, shells and chemical experiments." See "Lecture at Plymouth Church," *NYTrib*, 11 January 1862, 3.

63. "De Cordova's Lyceum," *Jewish Messenger*, 26 July 1861, 13.

64. "Fallon's Great Work of Art! The Stereopticon" [1862], American Broadsides and Ephemera, series 1, no. 22839. "Amusements," *Hartford Courant*, 18 December 1862, 2. Fallon's stereopticon then moved to Hartford's larger and more prestigious Allyn Hall for a week in mid-January. Advertisement, *Hartford Courant*, 12 January 1863, 3; "The Stereopticon," *Hartford Courant*, 14 January 1863, 2.

65. Mayor M. B. Kablefleisch et al. to John Fallon, 25 April 1863, reprinted in *BrookEagle*, 4 May 1863, 17.

66. "The Stereopticon at the Atheneum," *BrookEagle*, 15 April 1863, 3.

67. Francesco Casetti, "Elsewhere. The Relocation of Art," 348–51.

68. "Modern Miracles," *BrookEagle*, 15 April 1863, 3.

69. The *New York Journal of Commerce* as quoted in *Louisville Daily Journal*, 29 April 1863, 1.

70. *BrookEagle*, 29 April 1863, 1, and 15 May 1863, 1.

71. "The Stereopticon," *BrookEagle*, 7 May 1863, 3.

72. *NYTrib*, 4 May 1863, 7. The label "English stereopticon" was not without its ironies, since the term "stereopticon" was never employed in England, but the equipment was likely imported from London even if the name was American.

73. Advertisement, *NYTimes*, 22 May 1863, 7.

74. "Amusements," *NYTimes*, 16 July 1852, 3.

75. *NYTrib*, 17 May 1864, 3.

76. *NYTrib*, 30 May 1864, 3. The Worth Monument, the second oldest in New York, was built in 1857 and contains the reinterred remains of General William Worth (1794–1849), who fought in the War of 1812 and the Mexican-American War.

77. "Touro Hall," *Hartford Courant*, 24 December 1862, 2.

78. Tom Gunning, "Modernity and Cinema: A Culture of Shocks and Flows," in *Cinema and Modernity*, ed. Murray Pomerance (New Brunswick, NJ: Rutgers University Press, 2006), 297–315.

79. "Amusements," *NYTimes*, 4 July 1864, 4.

80. "Amusements," *NYTimes*, 30 September 1864, 4; "Amusements," *NYWorld*, 15 September 1864, 8.

81. "Amusements," *Philadelphia Inquirer*, 10 October 1864, 8; advertisement, *Philadelphia Press*, 15 October 1864, 3.

82. "Clinton Hall," broadside, 29 October 1864, collection of Terry and Deborah Borton.

83. "The Free Stereopticon," *ChicTrib*, 1 October 1871, 2.

84. "The Sign Boards of New York," *Scientific American*, 15 June 1872, 400.

85. "Scenes Around the Herald Square," *NYHerald*, 6 November 1872, 4.

86. *NYTimes*, 10 October 1872, 4.

87. "Ohio," *NYTrib*, 10 October 1872, 1; "Indiana," *NYTimes*, 10 October 1872, 1.

88. "Our Bulletin," *NYTimes*, 10 October 1872, 1.

89. "Receiving the News," *NYTimes*, 6 November 1872, 8.

90. "The Times' Stereopticon Bulletins," *NYTimes*, 14 January 1873, 5.

91. "Waiting for the Returns," *NYTimes*, 8 November 1876, 2; "The Election Excitement," *NYTimes*, 12 November 1876, 1.

92. "Great Republican Parade," *NYTrib*, 12 October 1880, 1.

93. "Good Use of a Stereopticon," *NYTrib*, 25 October 1880, 2.

94. "Cleveland Men in Line," *NYTimes*, 26 October 1884, 1.

95. "Reviewed by Mr. Blaine," *NYTimes*, 1 November 1884, 2.

CHAPTER THREE

1. "Depew's Hospitality," *NYTimes*, 30 May 1895, 1.

2. "To Fight Harrison," *NYHerald*, 1 June 1895, 3.

3. There is a significant body of excellent writing on various aspects of the 1896 presidential election. See Stanley L. Jones, *The Presidential Election of 1896* (Madison: University of Wisconsin Press, 1964); William D. Harpine, *From the Front Porch to the Front Page: McKinley and Bryan in the 1896 Presidential Campaign* (College Station: Texas A&M University Press, 2005); H. Wayne Morgan, *From Hayes to McKinley: National Party Politics, 1877–1896* (Syracuse, NY: Syracuse University Press, 1969). This chapter complements this body of work while exploring some significant areas that have been overlooked. Abner McKinley is overlooked; so has the role of the stereopticon and various new media forms.

4. "Topics Talked About," *NYPress*, 3 May 1891, 14.

5. Ibid.

6. "McKinley's Brother," *NYHerald*, 26 April 1896, 2F.

7. H. Wayne Morgan, *William McKinley and His America* (Kent, OH: Kent State University Press, 2003), 137.

8. For an account of McKinley's political maneuverings to win the nomination, see ibid., 140–59.

9. "Silver Rules the Day," *NYSun*, 9 July 1896, 1–2.

10. Ibid. Hill had sought the Democratic nomination for president in 1892 and had often opposed Cleveland's initiatives while in the Senate. So his vote to commend may not have been entirely sincere.

11. "Bryan Nominated," *NYSun*, 11 July 1896, 1. Bryan's "Cross of Gold" speech, the 1896 Democratic Convention, and the election more generally have been extensively covered in traditional scholarship as well as on Wikipedia.

12. "Revolt of the Press," *BrookEagle*, 10 July 1896, 1.

13. *NYSun*, 10 July 1896, 6.

14. "Bryan Nominated," *NYSun*, 11 July 1896, 1.

15. "The One Issue," *NYTimes*, 11 July 1896, 4.

16. Allen Churchill, *Park Row* (New York: Rinehart and Co., 1958), 94.

17. "Mr. Hannah in This City," *NYTimes*, 29 July 1896, 8.

18. "Long Distance Telephone Talks," *ChicTrib*, 19 August 1896, 12. See also "Political Machine in Motion," *Los Angeles Times*, 6 September 1896, 13.

19. "Chairman Jones in Town," *NYTimes*, 12 September 1896, 3. Long-distance telephone service had been installed in McKinley's home by the time of the Republican National Convention. H. Wayne Morgan, *William McKinley and His America*, 167.

20. William D. Harpine, *From the Front Porch to the Front Page*.

21. "Up at Daybreak," *Cleveland Plain Dealer*, 16 October 1896, 2, quoted in William D. Harpine, *From the Front Porch to the Front Page*, 18.

22. The oft-cited figure of $3.5 million comes from Charles G. Dawes, *A Journal of the McKinley Years* (Chicago: Lakeside Press, 1950), 106–7. Dawes's precise figure was $3,562,325.59, though it was only approximate for the New York headquarters.

23. Janice A. Petterchak, *Lone Scout: W. D. Boyce and American Boy Scouting* (Ann Arbor, MI: Legacy Press, 2003).

24. "Stereopticon in Politics," *Chicago Inter Ocean*, 16 September 1896, 3.

25. Ibid.; "Rousing Meeting at Lincoln Club," *ChicTrib*, 18 September 1896, 2; "Talks in the Tent," *ChicTrib*, 20 September 1896, 1; "Explains Popocracy with Views," *ChicTrib*, 29 September 1896, 2; "Novelty in a M'Kinley Meeting," *ChicTrib*, 5 October 1896, 5; "Pictures Illustrate Issues of the Campaign," *ChicTrib*, 25 October 1896, 42.

26. "In the Campaign Pilot Houses," *Washington Morning Times*, 17 September 1896, 4; "Political Gossip," *Washington Post*, 17 September 1896, 6. Mr. T.E. Shields may have been Theodore Edward Shields (1862–1921), a Catholic educator who was then based in the nation's capital.

27. "Belleville News," *St. Louis Post-Dispatch*, 30 September 1896, 6. The Brooklyn-based Max Forker was a presidential elector in New York State for Charles Matchett, who was running for president on the Socialist Labor Party ticket. Forker was an experienced political orator. See "Matchett on the Stump," *BrookEagle*, 16 July 1896, 4. In 1898 Forker would be the party's nominee for New York State comptroller.

28. See Charles Musser, "The May Irwin Kiss: Performance and Early Cinema," in *Visual Delights Two: Exhibition and Reception*, ed. V. Toulmin and S. Popple (Eastleigh, England: John Libbey, 2005), 96–115.

29. The actor Joseph Jefferson was widely known as a close friend of President Cleveland—just repudiated by the Bryan Democrats. Jefferson and his family were also early investors in the American Mutoscope Company.

30. "Other Callers of the Day," *NYTrib*, 16 September 1896, 2.

31. G. W. Bitzer, *Billy Bitzer: His Story* (New York: Farrar, Straus and Giroux, 1971), 11. For an excellent account of the Biograph company's filming of *McKinley at Home* and other scenes in Canton, Ohio, on September 18, 1896, see Paul Spehr, *The Man Who Made Movies: W. K. L. Dickson* (Herts, England: John Libby, 2008), 437–43.

32. G. W. Bitzer, *Billy Bitzer*, 12.

33. "A Big Success," *Somerset Herald*, 23 September 1896.

34. The *New York Herald* editorialized as the campaign came to an end, "The managers of New York have not been unmindful of the fact that once relieved of the political strain of the last three months men will find time after Tuesday to take their wives or sisters or other men's sisters to the theatre" (1 November 1896, 8).

35. Advertised under its own name, the biograph was described as "the '*dernier cri*' in the art of producing light and motion." Hammerstein's Olympia program, week of October 12, 1896, reprinted in Gordon Hendricks, *Beginnings of the Biograph: The Story of the Invention of the Mutoscope and the Biograph and Their Supplying Camera* (New York: Beginnings of the American Film, 1964), 48–49. Henderson was the first to trace the biograph's initial tour, which might be seen as an out-of-town tryout or preview before this official premiere—a chance to work out any problems before presenting the exhibition to the press.

36. Cross-promotion worked well not only for Edison and Sandow in March 1894, but also for Corbett and Edison in September 1894.

37. *NYHerald*, 12 October 1896, 4.

38. Hammerstein's Olympia program, 12 October 1896.

39. "The Biograph at the Olympia," *NYTimes*, 13 October 1896, 5.

40. Tom Gunning, "The Cinema of Attractions: Early Film, Its Spectator and the Avant-Garde," in *Early Cinema: Space, Frame, Narrative*, ed. Thomas Elsaesser (London: BFI, 1990), 58.

41. "Sergei Eisenstein," Russian Archives online, http://www.russianarchives .com/gallery/old/eisen.html.

42. Ibid.

43. "The Biograph at the Olympia," *NYTimes*, 13 October 1896, 5.

44. "Cheers at Olympia," *NYMail&Express*, 13 October 1896, 5. McKinley had no sons. He and his wife had two daughters, who died in infancy. If *McKinley at Home* was shown twice, as this review suggests, it was likely that the program showed two prints of the film, knowing that there would be demand for an encore.

45. "A Moving Picture of M'Kinley," *NYTrib*, 13 October 1896, 7.

46. "The Biograph at the Olympia," *NYTimes*, 13 October 1896, 5.

47. "Vaudeville," *NYMail&Express*, 17 October 1896, 13.

48. G. W. Bitzer, *Billy Bitzer*, 11.

49. "The Biograph at the Olympia," *NYTimes*, 13 October 1896, 5. General John McAuley Palmer (1817–1900) was a former governor and senator of Illinois. In 1896 he was the presidential candidate of the National Democratic Party, which supported the Gold Standard.

50. "The Olympia Music Hall," *NYTrib*, 15 September 1896, 3.

51. *The New York Mail and Express* failed to mention the Biograph in "Vaudeville: New Attractions at Hammerstein's Olympia and Other Music Halls" (10 October 1896, 14).

52. "Vaudeville Jottings," *New York Dramatic Mirror*, 17 October 1896, 18.

53. *NYMail&Express*, 12 October 1898, 2.

54. "Hammerstein's Olympia," *New York Dramatic Mirror*, 24 October 1896, 17.

55. "The Biograph at the Olympia," *NYTimes*, 13 October 1896, 5.

56. Charles G. Dawes, *A Journal of the McKinley Years*, 102; "Roosevelt Speaks Here Tonight," *ChicTrib*, 15 October 1896, 2.

57. "Last Week's Bills," *New York Dramatic Mirror*, 31 October 1896, 9.

58. "Hammerstein's Olympia," *NYMail&Express*, 20 October 1896, 4.

59. This offers a modest correction to *The Emergence of Cinema*, in which I mistakenly indicate that the biograph reopened at Koster & Bial's a week later, on November 2. Koster & Bial's advertisements and publicity notices running in the Sunday newspapers of October 25 failed to mention that the biograph would be on its bill in the coming week. It was obviously a last-minute addition.

60. "War of the Music Halls," *NYSun*, 11 October 1896, 4.

61. For a careful review of Williams and Walker's performance, see "Topics of Vaudeville," *NYSun*, 27 October 1896, 7. The Biograph company had quickly filmed a number of demeaning racialized images of the African Americans.

62. "Dramatic World," *NYMail&Express*, 26 October 1896, 5.

63. "At Other Theaters," *NYHerald*, 27 October 1896, 7. The *Herald* tended to add an "e" to the biograph's name and alternated between lower- and uppercase.

64. "Koster & Bial's," *NYMail&Express*, 3 November 1896, 4.

65. Ibid. "Popocrat" is an amalgam of Populist and Democrat, the two parties that had nominated Bryan. The same incident was described in less colorful terms by the *NYHerald*, 3 November 1896, 7.

66. Julius Cahn, *Julius Cahn's Official Theatrical Guide* (New York: Publication Office, Empire Theatre Building, 1897), 67, 69.

67. "Greatest of Parades," *NYTimes*, 1 November 1896, 1. The *New York Times* estimated that "100,000 Men March and Shout for Sound Money."

68. *The Phonoscope* (November 1896): 16.

69. Edison Manufacturing Company, *Edison Films* (March 1900): 36.

70. Stanley L. Jones, *The Presidential Election of 1896*, 345.

71. Abner McKinley and Biograph may have even thwarted an Edison company effort to film the Republican candidate (Edison personnel went to Ohio in May 1896 in what proved to be an unsuccessful filming trip).

72. William J. Bryan, *The First Battle: A Story of the Campaign of 1896* (Chicago: W. B. Conkey Co., 1896), 479.

73. Ibid.

74. *The Phonoscope* (April 1897): 14; "Bryan Traverses New Jersey," *NYTimes*, 24 September 1896, 2. Bryan would return to New Jersey later that month, speaking at Patterson and Newark.

75. "Proctor's Pleasure Palace," *NYMail&Express*, 20 October 1896, 4.

76. Ibid.

77. "Bryan in a Peep Show," *NYSun*, 28 September 1896, 2.

78. *NYSun*, 24 October 1896, 5.

79. Both Harrison and Cleveland made audio recordings, though neither was for campaign purposes. Gianni Bettini made a short recording of Harrison, though there is little consensus on dates (they vary from ca. 1889 to 1894–99). Uncertainty surrounds Cleveland's speech as well, though the National Archive dates it as 1893 (accessed 29 July 2015, https://research.archives.gov /id/121666).

80. "Phonograph in Politics," *San Francisco Call*, 6 August 1896, 1. See also "Phonographs in the Campaign," *NYTrib*, 16 August 1896, 24.

81. See for instance "Musical Supplement," *American Economist*, 23 October 1896, which featured sheet music for "McKinley Protection."

82. "Phonograph in Politics," *San Francisco Call*, 6 August 1896, 1.

83. Richard Bauman and Patrick Feaster, "'Fellow Townsmen and My Noble Constituents!': Representations of Oratory on Early Commercial Recordings," *Oral Tradition* 20, no. 1 (2005): 43, http://journal.oraltradition.org/issues/20i /bauman_feaster.

84. National Phonograph Company catalog, quoted in ibid., 42–43.

85. "Rejected the Bait," *Los Angeles Times*, 9 September 1896, 10.

86. "Bryan's Speech but Not His Voice," *NYTrib*, 31 August 1896, 3.

87. Ibid.

88. National Phonograph Company catalog quoted in Richard Bauman and Patrick Feaster, "Fellow Townsmen and My Noble Constituents!," 42.

89. "Gathered About Town," *NYTimes*, 6 October 1896, 8.

90. "How Presidential Candidates' Voices Look," *ChicTrib*, 20 September 1896, 41.

91. *Los Angeles Times*, 12 October 1896, 6.

92. "In a Gold League," *ChicTrib*, 9 September 1896, 1.

93. "Zeal for Chicago Day," *ChicTrib*, 16 September 1896, 4.

94. "To Ask M'Kinley Here," *ChicTrib*, 14 September 1896, 2.

95. "Parade to Be a Monster," *ChicTrib*, 1 October 1896, 7.

96. "Chicago Day on Wires," *ChicTrib*, 2 October 1896, 2.

97. "Chicago Day," *ChicTrib*, 10 October 1896, 1.

98. "Chicago's Marching Host," *NYSun*, 10 October 1896, 1.

99. "The Cheers Echoed in Canton," *NYTrib*, 10 October 1896, 2.

100. "Sent to Distant Ears," *ChicTrib*, 10 October 1896, 9.

101. "Heard at Canton," *Detroit Free Press*, 10 October 1896, 10.

102. "The Noise of It Heard Here," *NYTrib*, 10 October 1896, 2. John Peter Altgeld (1847–1902) was the Democratic governor of Illinois from 1893 to

1897. A progressive, he introduced child labor laws and pardoned the three surviving men convicted in the Haymarket Riots.

103. "Sent to Distant Ears," *ChicTrib*, 10 October 1896, 9.

104. "Long Distance Telephone Concerts," *Scientific American*, 28 February 1891, 130.

105. "Among the Electricians," *NYTimes*, 17 February 1889, 14.

106. "Entertained by Telephone," *NYTimes*, 21 January 1893, 1.

107. H. Wayne Morgan, *William McKinley and His America*, 167.

108. "Parades Elsewhere," *BaltSun*, 2 November 1896, 6.

109. "Foraker Sees His Chief," *ChicTrib*, 1 November 1896, 6. See also, "McKinley to Talk with Buffalo," *NYTimes*, 31 October 1896, 2.

110. Charles G. Dawes, *A Journal of the McKinley Years*, 95; "In Gold War on Wheels," *ChicTrib*, 20 September 1896, 11.

111. "First Gun in Cook," *ChicTrib*, 3 September 1896, 1.

112. "McKinley Men on Bikes," *ChicTrib*, 2 October 1896, 7.

113. "His Record Is Broken," *ChicTrib*, 4 October 1896, 5.

114. Ibid.

115. "October 17 Wheelmen's Day," *Washington Post*, 7 October 1896, 3.

116. "Wheelmen Will Parade Anyway," *ChicTrib*, 24 October 1896, 2.

117. "Wheelmen in Line Also," *ChicTrib*, 25 October 1896, 3.

118. "The Republican Clubs," *NYMail&Express*, 6 October 1896, 6.

119. "Wheelmen Parade: A Picturesque Sound-Money Demonstration by Bicyclists," *NYTimes*, 31 October 1896, 2.

120. In the Baltimore area and elsewhere, the wheelmen were supposed to deliver campaign literature to those outside the city. "Bicycles in the Campaign," *NYTrib*, 14 September 1896, 2.

121. See for instance "The Republican Clubs," *NYMail&Express*, 19 October 1896, 4.

122. "River Ablaze and for Gold," *NYHerald*, 25 October 1896, 5A.

123. "Pageant of Patriotism," *NYHerald*, 1 November 1896, 5A.

124. "Greatest of Parades," *NYTimes*, 1 November 1896, 1.

125. "They Marched 150,000 Strong," *BrookEagle*, 1 November 1896, 1.

126. "As Seen in Wall Street," *NYTimes*, 1 November 1896, 3.

127. "Will Review by Telephone," *NYTimes*, 31 October 1896, 6.

128. Ibid.

129. It was announced that "the audiences will be able to distinguish faces in the ranks" of the big McKinley parade. "Koster & Bial's," *NYMail&Express*, 7 November 1896, 13.

130. "Manhattan for M'Kinley," *NYHerald*, 4 November 1896, 4.

131. "Crowds at the Bulletins," *NYTimes*, 4 November 1896, 5.

132. Ibid.

133. Ibid.

134. Ibid.

135. Ibid.

136. "Herald's News of Victory," *NYHerald*, 4 November 1896, 8. The first film mentioned was *In the Dentist Chair* (Edison, January 1895), initially made for the peep-hole kinetoscope.

137. "Election Night in New York City," *NYWorld*, 8 November 1896.

138. "All the News for All," *NYWorld*, 1 November 1896, 11.

139. *New York Evening Journal*, 3 November 1896, 3.

140. Advertisement, *New York Clipper*, 14 November 1896, 595.

141. *New York Evening Journal*, 3 November 1896, 3.

142. Ibid. The Cinographoscope was made by A. & J. Pipon (French Patent no. 254 394, 2 March 1896). See "A. J. Pipon," accessed 26 August 2015, http://cinematographes.free.fr/pipon.html. Thanks to Laurent Mannoni for bringing this reference to my attention.

143. Laurent Mannoni to Charles Musser, email, 19 August 2015.

144. "Scenes and Incidents in Brooklyn," *BrookEagle*, 4 November 1896, 14.

145. Ibid.

146. "New York's Wild Joy," *NYSun*, 4 November 1896, 3.

147. "Before the Globe's Bulletins," *Boston Globe*, 4 November 1896, 2.

148. "How Returns Are Gathered and Given," *San Francisco Chronicle*, 8 November 1896, 25.

149. "The Story of the Making of a President," *ChicTrib*, 1 November 1896, 29.

150. Ibid.

151. "Returns on the Fly," *ChicTrib*, 4 November 1896, 10.

152. Ibid. Mary Ellen Lease was a controversial feminist from Kansas who had backed the Populists and then broken with them.

153. Jenny Bourne Taylor, "Structure of Feeling," in *Dictionary of Cultural and Critical Theory*, ed. Michael Payne, Blackwell Reference Online, 9 February 2010, http://www.blackwellreference.com/subscriber/tocnode?id = g9780631207535_chunk_g978063120753522_ss1-37.

154. "McKinley Preaches Hope," *NYSun*, 25 October 1896, 7. If one is looking for acknowledgment of citizens who were marginalized along the lines of identity politics, two women's marching clubs visited Canton, Ohio, on October 1 and "paraded the muddy streets with a total disregard for bedraggled skirts and subsequent sore throats." "Women Parade to See M'Kinley," *NYHerald*, 2 October 1896, 5. Likewise there were various efforts to include African Americans, including a "colored glee club" that sang campaign songs at various events. "What They Want Is Work," *NYTrib*, 13 October 1896, 1; "Bicyclists Raise a Banner," *NYTrib*, 9 October 1896, 2. W. T. Crump visited Canton and spoke to McKinley on behalf of African American voters of West Virginia. "An Army Invades Canton," *NYTrib*, 18 October 1896, 3.

155. Republican Congressional Committee, *The Republican Textbook for the Campaign of 1902* (Philadelphia: Republican National Committee, 1902), 23.

CHAPTER FOUR

1. This does not mean that important surprises don't pop up, as Vanessa Toulmin recently demonstrated with her work on the British film producers and showmen Mitchell and Kenyon. See Vanessa Toulmin, *Electric Edwardians: The Films of Mitchell and Kenyon* (London: BFI, 2007), and Vanessa Toulmin

and Simon Popple, eds., *The Lost World of Mitchell and Kenyon: Edwardian Britain on Film* (London: BFI, 2004).

2. André Gaudreault, *Film and Attraction: From Kinematography to Cinema*, trans. Timothy Barnard, foreword by Rick Altman (Urbana: University of Illinois Press, 2011); André Gaudreault and Philippe Marion, "A Medium Is Always Born Twice," *Early Popular Visual Culture* 3, no. 1 (May 2005): 3–15.

3. André Gaudreault, *Film and Attraction*, 34.

4. Dudley Andrew, *What Cinema Is!: Bazin's Quest and Its Charge* (Chichester, England: Wiley-Blackwell, 2010), xiii.

5. Ibid., xiv.

6. Edgar Morin, *The Cinema, or the Imaginary Man*, trans. Lorraine Mortimer (Minneapolis: University of Minnesota Press, 2005), 48.

7. Virginia Woolf, *Mr. Bennett and Mrs. Brown* (London: Hogarth Press, 1923), 4–5.

8. Jacques Deslandes and Jacques Richard, *Historie Comparée du Cinema*, vol. 2, *Du Cinematographe au Cinema, 1896–1906* (Paris: Casterman, 1968).

9. Gaudreault offers two periods before institutionalization, which occurs around 1915. The first—the system of monstrative attractions—goes to 1908. The second, "the system of narrative integration" (53) or the proto-institutional period, goes from 1908 to 1914 (90).

10. David Bordwell, Janet Staiger, and Kristin Thompson, *The Classical Hollywood Cinema: Film Style and Mode of Production to 1960* (New York: Columbia University Press, 1985).

11. If we consider cinema in the context of the long history of screen practice, we might want to call the initial formation of cinema in 1895–96 something like Screen 4.0 (to take a somewhat arbitrary number). Or if sync-sound films circa 1927 is seen as 2.0, then Gaudreault's birth of cinema might be Cinema 1.4 or 1.5.

12. My first article on early cinema denounced the common use of the birth metaphor by film scholars. Charles Musser, "The Early Cinema of Edwin S. Porter," *Cinema Journal* 19, no. 1 (Fall 1979): 1–38, reprinted with a historiographic introduction in *The Wiley-Blackwell History of American Film*, vol. 1, ed. Cynthia Lucia, Roy Grundmann, and Art Simon (Malden, MA: Wiley-Blackwell, 2012), 39–86. I have been surprised and somewhat dismayed to see it reemerge in this context. Gaudreault and Marion suggest that "it is quite difficult to avoid biological metaphors here." André Gaudreault and Philippe Marion, "A Medium Is Always Born Twice," 6. With this I respectfully disagree.

13. André Gaudreault and Philippe Marion, "A Medium Is Always Born Twice," 5–7. This brief if provocative essay sees the "second birth of cinema" primarily as a question of the changing nature of its intermediality but avoids identifying a particular moment or period of its occurrence. Again, their ideas of self-consciousness (by which the authors mean a sense of film as an art?), autonomy, and institutionalization are in tension with one another.

14. This definition of mass media is using Melvin L. Defleur and Everette E. Dennis, *Understanding Mass Communication* (New York: Houghton Mifflin Co., 1985), 5–11. See Charles Musser, *Before the Nickelodeon: Edwin S. Porter*

and the Edison Manufacturing Company (Berkeley: University of California Press, 1991), 372. It is worth noting that with the rise of the Internet, Defleur and Dennis felt compelled to modify substantially what they were defining ("mass communication" rather than "mass media") and how they defined it. See Melvin L. Defleur and Everette E. Dennis, *Understanding Mass Communication: A Liberal Arts Perspective*, 7th ed. (Boston: Houghton Mifflin Co., 2002), 16–19.

15. Charles Musser, "Pre-Classical American Cinema: Its Changing Modes of Film Production," in *Silent Film*, ed. Richard Abel (New Brunswick, NJ: Rutgers University Press, 1996), 85–108.

16. Charles Musser, "The Early Cinema of Edwin S. Porter," *Cinema Journal* 19, no. 1 (Fall 1979): 1–38. Tom Gunning, *D. W. Griffith and the Origins of American Narrative Film* (Urbana: University of Illinois Press, 1991).

17. Charles Musser, *The Emergence of Cinema: The American Screen to 1907* (New York: Scribner, 1990), 417.

18. François Albera, Maria Tortajada, and Franck Le Gac, "Questioning the Word 'Dispositif': Note on the Translation," trans. Franck Le Gac, in *Cine-Dispositives: Essays in Epistemology Across Media*, ed. François Albera and Maria Tortajada (Amsterdam: Amsterdam University Press, 2015), 11–14.

19. "A Moving Picture of M'Kinley," *NYTrib*, 13 October 1896, 7.

20. "Life, Color, and Motion," *BrookEagle*, 28 November 1896, 9.

21. Charles Musser, *The Emergence of Cinema*, 338.

22. André Gaudreault and Philippe Marion, "Measuring the 'Double Birth' Model Against the Digital Age," *Early Popular Visual Culture* 11, no. 2 (2013): 158–77.

23. Charles Musser, *The Emergence of Cinema*, 15.

24. The illustrated lecture combining slides and film continued after 1903, perhaps becoming even more common as the cost of films and film production went down. Burton Holmes among others continued such practices into the 1920s and beyond. However, the rise of the nickelodeons in 1906 and cinema presence as mass entertainment made this residual practice relatively peripheral in comparative terms.

25. In *Film and Attraction*, Gaudreault argues "that 'cinema' was not invented in 1890 by Thomas Edison and W. K. L. Dickson with the Kineto-graph, nor by Auguste and Louis Lumière in 1895 with their Cinématographe, nor by any other supposed inventor of cinema. The only things invented by those who are generally recognized as having invented cinema were the devices to make cinema. It is a subtle distinction, but the device used to make cinema is not the same as cinema itself." André Gaudreault, *Film and Attraction*, 5. Would this suggest that Gaudreault and I are thinking along similar lines? I am not so sure, though we are both trying to understand similar phenomena. Also, as one of the presumed "partisans of Edison" (p. 33, though they go unmentioned by name), I would like to reiterate and so clarify my position. There is no question in my mind: *Edison neither invented the cinema nor the device to make cinema.* Cinema is, to my mind, *projected* motion pictures in a commercial, theatrical setting. This is what the Lumières did with their cinématographe (and what Armat and Jenkins did with their phantoscope). Edison and Dickson

invented a motion picture system that relied on the peep-hole kinetoscope to exhibit films, which was *a pre-cinematic device*. But the system itself inevitably had a set of discrete but interrelated practices associated with it. Of course the kinetoscope turned out to be a fad or novelty; by the winter of 1895–96 it was passé and a money-losing proposition. Its contribution to the history of motion pictures is fundamental because so many of its protocols were incorporated into the rejuvenated motion picture field, spurred by the addition of projection.

26. In other writings I have distinguished between two somewhat different cinema formations in the period from 1897 to 1903. To simplify: the innovation of a reframing device circa 1898 avoided film screenings that could be marred by split-frame images on the screen. It was one factor that enabled motion pictures to become a permanent attraction in New York vaudeville houses in 1898–99, which in turn provided a significant element of commercial stability.

27. "Le Prince, Louis Aimé Augustin," in *Encyclopedia of Early Cinema*, ed. Richard Abel (London and New York: Routledge, 2005), 378.

28. Charles Musser, "1896–1897: Movies and the Beginnings of Cinema," in *American Cinema 1890–1909: Themes and Variations*, ed. André Gaudreault (New Brunswick, NJ: Rutgers University Press, 2009), 45–65. See also Yuri Tsivian, "The Rorschach Test of Cultures: On Some Parallels Between Early Film Reception in Russia and the United States," *Yale Journal of Criticism* 7, no. 2 (1994): 177–88. One might see both *The Corbett-Fitzsimmons Fight* (March 1897) and *The Horitz Passion Play* (November 1897) as functioning within the post-novelty period.

29. Yuri Tsivian, "'What Is Cinema?' An Agnostic Answer," *Critical Inquiry* 34, no. 4 (Summer 2008): 755.

30. "President Goes to Canton," *NYTimes*, 22 September 1900, 3.

31. "Let Well Enough Alone," *BrookEagle*, 4 November 1900, 18.

32. "Roosevelt Ends His Tour," *NYTimes*, 3 November 1900, 2.

33. "110,000 in Line for Sound Money," *BrookEagle*, 4 November 1900, 1; "Men in the Big Column," *NYTimes*, 4 November 1900, 4.

34. Joanne Morreale, *The Presidential Campaign Film: A Critical History* (Westport, CT: Praeger, 1996), 32–33. The claim of Vitagraph owners J. Stuart Blackton and Albert E. Smith to have been in Cuba during the Spanish-American War was fanciful showmanship—something they asserted when presenting their own Spanish-American War programs—and so they figured, why not just keep saying it? It was also part of an unsuccessful effort to conceal their duplication of Edison films taken by William Paley, who did get to Cuba. In any case, given Abner McKinley's active involvement with the American Mutoscope Company and the 1896 McKinley program, it seems hard not to conclude that McKinley was the first US president to understand film's propagandistic appeal.

35. When the California Entertainment Company advertised its moving picture offerings in San Diego, it cited "Flying Trains, Battle of San Juan Hill, Charging Cavalry, Naval Battles of Spanish War, etc. etc." Advertisement, *San Diego Evening Tribune*, 17 September 1900, 4.

36. The 1896 campaign had been an exception for all kinds of reasons: McKinley had received more votes than Bryan in New York City and won the state by a 19 percent margin.

37. "30,000 Men to Be in Line," *NYTimes*, 9 September 1900, 2.

38. "Pictures for Voters," *Prosperity*, 25 August 1900, 1.

39. "Populists Use Passes Generously," *Topeka Capital*, 7 September 1900, 1; "New Campaign Idea," *Topeka Capital*, 7 September 1900, 6.

40. "Moving Pictures of Bryan," *NYSun,* as reprinted in the *Boston Globe*, 1 July 1900, 16.

41. Stephen Bottomore, "1900," *Film History* 24, no. 4 (2012): 394–95.

42. "A Moving Picture," *Lincoln Nebraska State Journal*, 3 July 1900, 4.

43. Josh Wink, "Farmer Bryan's Photographs," *Boston Globe*, 9 July 1900, reprinted in its entirety in Stephen Bottomore, "1900," 394–95.

44. *Washington Post*, 16 August 1900, 6.

45. Edison's Kinetograph Department focused much of its energies on filming scenes of the 1900 Paris Exposition and meeting demand for Galveston flood pictures. Although Edison's principal commercial strategy was to shut down all rival American producers for patent violations, the inventor also came close to selling his business to Biograph in the summer of 1900. When that fell through, efforts to revive his business included the hiring of Edwin S. Porter in November 1900 and the building of a motion picture studio in Manhattan. See Charles Musser, *Before the Nickelodeon*, 156.

46. "He Is on the Film," *Grand Rapid Press*, 19 July 1900, 1.

47. Advertisement, *ChicTrib*, 14 August 1900, 5.

48. "Attractions for the Week," *ChicTrib*, 26 August 1900, 4.

49. "Vaudeville's Best," *Detroit Free Press*, 9 September 1900, A6.

50. Advertisement, *NYTimes*, 28 October 1900, 23. Huber's generally used Percival Waters Kinetograph service, which was closely aligned with the Edison Manufacturing Company, so perhaps its staff filmed the candidates after all. If so, the Edison company did not bother to copyright the pictures, nor to advertise them.

51. "Foyer and Greenroom Gossip," *Boston Globe*, 21 October 1900, 23.

52. Advertisement, *Moving Picture World*, 25 July 1908, 67.

53. "Shakespeare in Motion Pictures," *Moving Picture World*, 1 August 1908, 80.

54. "Mr. Bryan's Speech of Acceptance," *NYTimes*, 9 August 1900, 8.

55. "Bryan Talks to Phonograph," *NYTimes*, 14 August 1900, 3.

56. "Irish Societies to Hear Bryan," *Birmingham Age*, 14 August 1900, 1.

57. "Sue for Democratic Oratory," *Washington Post*, 8 September 1900, 10. The graphophone was the name and trademark of an improved version of the phonograph.

58. "Refused Bryan's Speeches," *Washington Post*, 14 September 1900, 10.

59. "Campaign Records," *New Haven Register*, 22 October 1900, 12.

60. "Prosperity Host in a Pageant," *ChicTrib*, 27 October 1900, 1.

61. "President's Letter Sent by Bicycle," *NYTrib*, 14 October 1900, 5.

62. "In the Automobile World," *NYTimes*, 9 September 1900, 10.

63. "Democratic Leaders Confer," *NYTimes*, 22 July 1900, 4.

64. "Ideas for the Campaign," *NYTimes*, 16 September 1900, 14.

65. "Votes Made by Pictures," *ChicTrib*, 4 November 1900, 32.

66. "Ideas for the Campaign," *NYTimes*, 16 September 1900, 14.

67. "Roosevelt for Governor," *NYTimes*, 13 July 1898, 4; "Roosevelt for Governor," *NYTimes*, 16 July 1898, 4.

68. "Theatrical Notes," *Washington Post,* 31 July 1898, 18.

69. Advertisement, *NYSun*, 4 September 1898, 12.

70. "Pleasure Palace," *New York Clipper*, 17 September 1898, 482.

71. "Theater: Seen on the Stage," *Vogue*, 8 September 1898, iii; "Four Theaters Reopened," *NYSun*, 6 September 1898, 7.

72. Theodore Roosevelt to Mason Mitchell, 29 September 1898, accessed 4 August 2015, http://www.shapell.org/manuscript/theodore-roosevelt-promotes-the-rough-riders.

73. "Roosevelt in Gloversville," *NYTimes*, 23 October 1898, 2.

74. "Lecture on the Battle of Santiago," *San Francisco Call*, 23 September 1898, 2.

75. "Elmendorf Is Out," *NYTimes*, 20 April 1896, 2.

76. "Meetings and Entertainments," *NYTrib*, 2 April 1897, 7.

77. "Professor Bickmore's Travels," *NYTimes*, 19 September 1897, 17. Elmendorf also gave his own lectures on photographic work for the Camera Club. "Choice of Subject and Exposure," *Camera Notes,* 1 April 1898, 1, 4.

78. "War Views at University Club," *NYTrib*, 19 October 1898, 9.

79. "New York," *New York Observer and Chronicle*, 24 November 1898, 671. See also "Lecture of Santiago Campaign," *NYTimes*, 25 November 1898, 2; "Military Social Function," *NYTimes*, 13 January 1899, 4.

80. "War Through a Camera," *NYTimes*, 18 January 1899, 7.

81. "City History Club," *NYTrib*, 24 February 1899, 7; "A Tour of the West Indies," *BrookEagle*, 11 April 1899, 3.

82. Dwight L. Elmendorf Spanish-American War lantern slides, Roosevelt R560.3.EL64, Theodore Roosevelt Collection, Harvard College Library.

83. Advertisement, *Philadelphia Inquirer*, 26 April 1898, 9.

84. "Town Topics," *Worcester Spy*, 14 January 1897, 7.

85. "Rev. W. G. Cassard's Lecture," *Washington Post*, 2 February 1899, 1.

86. "Social Side," *Boston Journal*, 1 May 1898, 13.

87. "Views of Naval Battles," *St. Louis Post-Dispatch*, 20 November 1899, 2. "The Man Behind the Gun" was the title of a new march by John Philip Sousa.

88. "City News in Brief," *Oregonian*, 11 December 1898, 5.

89. Clifford Putney, *Muscular Christianity: Manhood and Sports in Protestant America, 1880–1920* (Cambridge, MA: Harvard University, 2001); Donald E. Hall, ed., *Muscular Christianity: Embodying the Victorian Age* (New York: Cambridge University Press, 1994). See for instance Rev A. C. Smither's New Year's sermon on "Expansion": "At the Churches Yesterday," *Los Angeles Times*, 2 January 1899, 8.

90. "News from Our Churches," *The Advance*, 19 May 1898, 35.

91. Ibid.

92. David Francis email to Charles Musser, 1 October 2015. Francis reports that the set of slides, lecture booklet, and other materials come from a small-time showman who presented his program in the back room of a bar at the beginning of the twentieth century.

93. "South Hadley," *Springfield Republican*, 30 June 1898, 8.

94. "Berkshire County," *Springfield Republican*, 20 May 1898, 9.

95. Advertisement, *Springfield Republican*, 2 December 1898, 1; "In and About Springfield," *Springfield Republican*, 30 November 1898, 4.

96. "Lively Days at Behoboth," *BaltSun*, 6 August 1898, 8.

97. "Sunday Services," *Cleveland Plain Dealer*, 2 April 1898, 6.

98. "Ranks It with Treason," *NYTrib*, 3 February 1899, 9.

99. "Yonkers," *NYTrib*, 28 March 1898, 16.

100. *Philadelphia Inquirer*, 21 April 1895, 5.

101. "They Cheered Flag Loudly," *Pawtucket Times*, 16 April 1898, 6; "A Patriotic Lecture," *Pawtucket Times*, 28 May 1898, 9; "Will Be Big Benefit," *Pawtucket Times*, 10 May 1898, 6.

102. "Illustrated Lecture on Cuba," *Cleveland Plain Dealer*, 22 May 1898, 2.

103. "A Lecture on Cuba," *NYTrib*, 28 June 1898, 9.

104. Advertisement, *Plattsmouth Semi-Weekly News*, 23 April 1898, 1.

105. Advertisement, *BaltSun*, 7 April 1898, 1; "Lecture on the Cuban War," *BaltSun*, 9 April 1898, 12.

106. "Cuba and Maine by Stereopticon," *Duluth News Tribune*, 31 March 1898, 5.

107. "Cuba and Its People," *NYTimes*, 24 October 1898, 10.

108. "On Cuba and Spain," *Boston Herald*, 2 April 1898, 6.

109. "American Soldiers Praised in Berlin," *NYHerald*, 9 December 1989, 9.

110. "Lecture on Cuba," *Harrisburg Patriot*, 29 June 1898, 4.

111. "Should Keep Them," *Grand Rapids Herald*, 9 May 1898, 3.

112. "Causes of the Revolt," *Boston Herald*, 27 May 1898, 6.

113. "The Day's Gossip" *NYTrib*, 10 November 1898, 5.

114. "The Association Course," *Philadelphia Inquirer*, 15 October 1893, 3; "A Lecture on Manila," *NYTrib*, 17 March 1899, 6.

115. "Manila and the Philippines," *Fort Worth Morning Register*, 6 December 1899, 7.

116. "Lectured on the Philippines," *Argus and Patriot* (Montpelier), 28 December 1899, 4.

117. "Entertainment Last Night," *Omaha Daily Bee*, 3 December 1898, 2.

118. "To Tell About the Fighting," *San Jose Evening News*, 21 March 1899, 8.

119. Advertisement, *Duluth News-Tribune*, 25 March 1899, 2.

120. "What Is Going on To-day," *NYTrib*, 20 May 1899, 12.

121. "Lecture on Philippine War," *Rockford Morning Star* (Illinois), 21 February 1900, 2.

122. "Illustrated Lecture," *Oregonian*, 10 September 1899, 12; "Compliments Montana Boys," *Helena Independent*, 28 November 1899, 2; "War in the Philippines," *Anaconda Standard* (Montana), 3 December 1899, 6.

123. "In Society's Realm," *Anaconda Standard* (Montana), 21 January 1900, 18.

124. *Butte Weekly Miner* (Montana), 12 April 1900, 6; *Anaconda Standard* (Montana), 8 April 1900, 16.

125. "Lecture on Philippines," *Wilkes-Barre Times*, 20 November 1899, 8.

126. "Priest on the Philippines," *NYTimes*, 30 October 1899, 3; "Affairs at Manila," *San Jose Evening News*, 16 November 1899, 8.

127. "Free Lectures," *NYTimes*, 6 January 1900, BR11; "Free Lectures for the People," *NYTrib*, 15 November 1899, 7.

128. Ira M. Price, "Our New Island Possessions," *The Dial*, 16 June 1899, 394.

129. "Columbia Lectures," *NYTimes*, 30 December 1900, 7.

130. "Institute Programmes," *BrookEagle*, 17 December 1899, 37.

131. "Hospitality and Hawaii," *BaltSun*, 25 January 1899, 10.

132. "Institute Programmes," *BrookEagle*, 17 December 1899, 37.

133. "Holmes Talks of Luzon," *ChicTrib*, 27 October 1899, 5.

134. Ibid.

135. "The Lectures of One Day," *NYTrib*, 9 March 1900, 8.

136. Ibid.

137. Burton Holmes, "Manila," in *The Burton Holmes Lectures*, vol. 5 (Battle Creek, MI: Little-Preston, 1901), 336.

138. E. Berkeley Tompkins, *Anti-Imperialism in the United States: The Great Debate, 1890–1920* (Philadelphia: University of Pennsylvania Press, 1970), 122–33; Michael Patrick Cullinane, *Liberty and American Anti-Imperialism, 1898–1909* (New York: Palgrave Macmillan, 2012), 51–114.

139. "Anti-Imperialists Meet," *NYTimes*, 25 September 1900, 3.

140. "Anti-Imperialists in Mass Meeting," *NYTimes*, 25 May 1900, 1.

141. "Peace Speech Not Peaceful," *BrookEagle*, 2 October 1899, 1.

142. Ibid.

143. Ibid. Halstead was later given a plum position by the Republican National Committee as it prepared for its national convention. "Design for the Republican National Convention Tickets and Badges Agreed Upon," *BrookEagle*, 30 March 1900, 3.

144. Louis W. Koenig, *Bryan: A Political Biography of William Jennings Bryan* (New York: G.P. Putnam's Sons, 1971), 331.

145. Ibid.

CODA

1. David Nasaw has argued that the Hearst family had large interests in gold as well as silver mines, and so his pro-Bryan position was not in the publisher's strict economic self-interest. See *The Chief: The Life of William Randolph Hearst* (Boston: Houghton Mifflin Co., 2006), 118. This raises a number of issues, including the question: How radical would the Free Silver platform have been if it had been instituted? Economists suggest that its impact would likely have been quite small.

2. James McGarth Morris, *Pulitzer: A Life in Politics, Print and Power* (New York: HarperCollins, 2010), 221–32.

3. N.S. Balke and R.J. Gordon, "The Estimation of Prewar Gross National Product: Methodology and New Evidence," *Journal of Political Economy* 97, no. 1 (1989): 84.

4. Bill Nichols discusses documentary's expository mode in *Representing Reality: Issues and Concepts in Documentary* (Bloomington: Indiana University Press, 1991), 32–38.

5. Lisa Gitelman, *Scripts, Grooves, and Writing Machines: Representing Technology in the Edison Era* (Stanford, CA: Stanford University Press, 1999), 125.

6. Terry Ramsaye, *A Million and One Nights: A History of the Motion Picture* (New York: Simon and Schuster, 1926), 326.

7. At one point Michael Moore was planning to make a follow-up documentary entitled *Fahrenheit 9/11 and ½* but wisely shelved those plans, aware that the resulting effort would have been counterproductive.

8. Douglas G. Craig, *Fireside Politics: Radio and Political Culture in the United States, 1920–1940* (Baltimore: Johns Hopkins University Press, 2000), 143.

9. Jack Redding, *Inside the Democratic Party* (Indianapolis: Bobbs-Merrill, 1958), 254; Joanne Morreale, *The Presidential Campaign Film: A Critical History* (Westport, CT: Praeger, 1996), 36–37.

10. Richard Dyer MacCann, *The People's Films* (New York: Hastings House, 1973), 56–86.

11. Douglas Kellner and Dan Streible, "Emile de Antonio: Documenting the Life of a Radical Filmmaker," in *Emile de Antonio*, ed. Douglas Kellner and Dan Streible (Minneapolis: University of Minnesota Press, 2000), 46–47.

12. In New York City, *Millhouse* played at the Olympia Theater on Broadway and 101st Street for three days during 1972: on March 2, November 6, and Election Day, November 7. Movie advertisements, *NYTimes*, 2 March 1972, 3; and 6 November 1972, 52.

13. Emile de Antonio, "Mr. Hoover and I (1989)," in *Emile de Antonio*, 330. Home VCRs, DVD players, and the Internet would make such containment much more difficult.

14. Soon after President McKinley's assassination in September 1901, Abner became ill with Bright's disease, dying less than three years after his sibling.

15. But again the media was foregrounding white women and white men. The *New York Times* devoted three lines to Plessy v. Ferguson, the Supreme Court decision that legalized state laws requiring racial segregation, simply noting, "Judgment affirmed, with costs." See "Federal Courts," *NYTimes*, 19 May 1896, 3.

16. Warren Susman, *Culture as History: The Transformation of American Society in the Twentieth Century* (New York: Pantheon Books, 1984); John Higham, "The Reorientation of American Culture in the 1890s," in *The Origins of Modern Consciousness*, ed. John Weiss (Detroit: Wayne State University Press, 1965).

17. The field's principal academic society, the Society for Cinema Studies, changed its name in 2002 to the Society for Cinema and Media Studies. Yale University finally followed suit in 2014 when its Film Studies Program became the Film and Media Studies Program.

18. Charles Musser, "The Early Cinema of Edwin S. Porter," *Cinema Journal* 19, no. 1 (Fall 1979): 1–38, reprinted in *The Wiley-Blackwell History of*

American Film, vol. 1, ed. Cynthia Lucia, Roy Grundmann, and Art Simon (Malden, MA: Wiley-Blackwell, 2012), 39–86; André Gaudreault, "Detours in Film Narrative: The Development of Cross-Cutting," *Cinema Journal* 19, no. 1 (Fall 1979): 39–59, reprinted in *Early Cinema: Space, Frame, Narrative*, ed. Thomas Elsaesser (London: BFI, 1990), 133–50; Noël Burch, "Porter or Ambivalence," *Screen* 19, no. 4 (Winter 1978–79): 91–105.

19. Gerald Mast, *A Short History of the Movies* (Indianapolis: Bobbs-Merrill, 1976), 42–43.

20. In *D. W. Griffith and the Origins of American Narrative Film: The Early Years at Biograph* (Urbana: University of Illinois Press, 1991), Tom Gunning argues that Griffith was a key innovator in terms of film style in his development of "the narrator system." Jay Leyda, who regularly taught a continuing course on the Griffith Biograph films, was a major influence on the study of early cinema. He was both my and Tom Gunning's dissertation adviser.

21. André Bazin, "The Evolution of Film Language," in *What Is Cinema?*, ed. and trans. Hugh Gray (Berkeley: University of California Press, 1967), 23–40.

22. Tom Gunning, "The Non-Continuous Style of Early Film (1900–1906)," in *Cinema 1900–1906: An Analytical Study*, compiled by Roger Homan (Brussels: FIAF, 1982), 219–30.

23. Tom Gunning, "The Cinema of Attractions," in Thomas Elsaesser, ed., *Early Cinema*, 56–62. My own reservations regarding some of the formulations of the "cinema of attractions" paradigm can be found in Charles Musser, "Rethinking Early Cinema: Cinema of Attractions and Narrativity," *Yale Journal of Criticism* 7, no. 2 (1994): 203–32, reprinted in *Cinema of Attractions Reloaded*, ed. Wanda Stauven (Amsterdam: Amsterdam University Press, 2006), 389–416.

24. Noël Burch, *Theory of Film Practice* (New York: Praeger, 1973).

25. Besides those mentioned above, the Brighton group also included David Francis (then director of the National Film Archive in London), Eileen Bowser and Jon Gartenberg (then curator and assistant curator, respectively, at the Museum of Modern Art, New York), John and Williams Barnes (Barnes Museum, Philadelphia), John Fell (San Francisco State University), Paul Spehr (Library of Congress), Michael Chanan, Barry Salt, David Levy, Tjitte de Vries, Martin Sopocy, and John Hagen. Others such as Thomas Elsaesser soon joined this scholarly interest group. Given our shared interests, the concerns of the Brighton Group did not always mesh easily with the work of other scholars interested in early cinema such as Robert C. Allen or Anthony Slide.

26. C. W. Ceram, *Archaeology of the Cinema* (New York: Harcourt, Brace and World, 1965). Noël Burch, in fact, embraced the term "primitive cinema" when talking about cinema before Griffith.

27. Laurent Mannoni, *The Great Art of Light and Shadow: Archaeology of the Cinema*, ed. and trans. Richard Crangle (Exeter, England: University of Exeter Press, 2000).

28. Who invented cinema had been a technical question for lawyers involved in patent disputes, and was taken up by film historians such as Georges Sadoul in *Histoire générale du cinéma. Tome 1. L'invention du cinéma* (1946; reprint,

Paris: Denoël, 1975). Whether film scholars should take this approach seems dubious.

29. David Bordwell, Janet Staiger, and Kristin Thompson, *The Classical Hollywood Cinema: Film Style and Mode of Production to 1960* (New York: Columbia University Press, 1985).

30. Anthony Slide, *Early American Cinema* (New York: A. S. Barnes, 1970), 7. Slide also emphasized the importance of Porter's *Life of an American Fireman* while valorizing the Library of Congress copyrighted version with its temporal repetitions—associating it with Alain Resnais's *Last Year at Marienbad* (1961). Ibid., 13.

31. We were separated by geography. On the East Coast the better-known books on the silent era were Gordon Hendricks, *The Edison Motion Picture Myth* (Berkeley: University of California Press, 1961), Kevin Brownlow, *The Parade's Gone By* (New York: Ballantine Books, 1968), George Pratt, *Spellbound in Darkness: A History of the Silent Film* (Greenwich, CT: New York Graphic Society, 1966), and Terry Ramsaye, *A Million and One Nights*, as well as several volumes by Georges Sadoul and Jacques Deslandes.

32. Thomas Elsaesser, ed., *Early Cinema*.

33. Jennifer M. Bean and Diane Negra, eds., *A Feminist Reader in Early Cinema* (Durham, NC: Duke University Press, 2002).

34. John Fell, ed., *Film Before Griffith* (Berkeley: University of California Press, 1983).

35. John L. Fell, *Film and the Narrative Tradition* (Norman: University of Oklahoma Press, 1974); Marion Froger et al., "Le Centre de recherché sur l'intermédialité, *Visio* 6, nos. 2–3 (Spring–Summer 2001): 317–26. André Gaudreault's many presentations on intermediality from this period include "Rapports d'intermédialité entre les séries culturelles dans le cinéma des premiers temps," Séminaire Fotogenia, Università degli Studi di Bologna, 1997. See also André Gaudreault, "The Diversity of Cinematographic Connections in the Intermedial Context of the Turn of the Century," in *Visual Delights: Essays on the Popular and Projected Image in the 19th Century*, ed. Simon Popple and Vanessa Toulmin (Trowbridge, England: Flicks Books, 2000), 8–15.

36. Erkki Huhtamo and Jussi Parikka, "Introduction," in *Media Archaeology: Approaches, Applications, and Implications*, ed. Erkki Huhtamo and Jussi Parikka (Berkeley: University of California Press, 2011), 12.

37. Thomas Elsaesser, ed., *Early Cinema*, 1, 3. In fact, Elsaesser was regularly using the term "the new film history" as early as 1986 in his review essay "The New Film History," *Sight and Sound* 55, no. 4 (Fall 1986): 246–51.

38. Thomas Elsaesser, "The New Film History as Media Archaeology," *Cinémas: Journal of Film Studies* 14 (2004): 75. By the year 2000 he was regularly teaching a required course at the University of Amsterdam entitled "Media Archaeology."

39. Ibid., 99.

40. "Michel Foucault," Stanford Encyclopedia of Philosophy, accessed 22 October 2015, http://plato.stanford.edu/entries/foucault/#3.2. The differences between the connotations of certain terms in the American and European contexts are striking. This was true not only for the term "archaeology" but for

"primitive" as well. Noël Burch, who was based in Paris, had used "primitive" to characterize pre-1908 cinema while those of us in New York rejected it because we wanted to separate ourselves from Ramsaye's terminology (and his historiographical approach) as well as reject a more general tendency to dismiss (or condescend to) pre-Griffith cinema as quaint and ultimately uninteresting. Interestingly, Elsaesser saw Burch as taking a Foucauldian position in his work on early cinema, while most of us in the United States read *Theory of Film Practice* as an inspiring mix of Russian formalism and Marxism. Thomas Elsaesser, "Film History as Media Archaeology," in Elsaesser, *Film History as Media Archaeology: Tracking Digital Cinema* (Amsterdam: University of Amsterdam Press, 2016), 9.

41. Thomas Elsaesser, "The New Film History as Media Archaeology," 75.

42. Simone Natale, "Review Essay," *Canadian Journal of Communication* 37 (2012): 524.

43. Jussi Parikka, *What Is Media Archaeology?* (Cambridge and Malden, MA: Polity Press, 2012), 6.

44. See Erkki Huhtamo and Jussi Parikka, "Introduction," in *Media Archaeology*, 2.

45. Jussi Parikka, *What Is Media Archaeology?*.

46. Angelica Das, "Sundance: Is It Documentary or Journalism?," *IndieWire*, 4 February 2015, accessed 22 October 2015, http://www.indiewire.com/article/sundance-is-it-documentary-or-journalism-20150204.

Bibliography

Abel, Richard, ed. *Encyclopedia of Early Cinema*. New York: Routledge, 2005.

———. *Menus for Movieland: Newspapers and the Emergence of American Film Culture, 1913–1916*. Berkeley: University of California Press, 2015.

———. "The Pleasures and Perils of Big Data in Digitized Newspapers." *Film History* 25, nos. 1–2 (2013): 1–10.

Albera, François, and Maria Tortajada, eds. *Cine-Dispositives: Essays in Epistemology Across Media*. Amsterdam: University of Amsterdam Press, 2015.

Alexander, Jeffrey C. *The Performance of Politics: Obama's Victory and the Democratic Struggle for Power*. Oxford: Oxford University Press, 2010.

Alexander, Jeffrey C., and Bernadette N. Jaworsky. *Obama Power*. Malden, MA: Polity Press, 2014.

Allen, Robert C. *Vaudeville and Film, 1895–1915: A Study in Media Interaction*. PhD diss., University of Iowa, 1977. New York: Arno Press, 1980.

Allen, Robert C., and Douglas Gomery. *Film History Theory and Practice*. New York: Alfred A. Knopf, 1985.

Altick, Richard D. *The Shows of London*. Cambridge, MA: Harvard University Press, 1978.

Anderson, Benedict. *Imagined Communities: Reflections on the Origin and Spread of Nationalism*. London: Verso, 1991.

Andrew, Dudley. *What Cinema Is!: Bazin's Quest and Its Charge*. Chichester, England: Wiley-Blackwell, 2010.

Appadurai, Arjun. "Disjuncture and Difference in the Global Cultural Economy." *Public Culture* 2, no. 2 (1990): 1–24.

Auerbach, Jonathan. *Body Shots: Early Cinema's Incarnations*. Berkeley: University of California Press, 2007.

Baehr Jr., Harry W. *The New York Tribune Since the Civil War*. New York: Dodd, Mead and Co., 1936.

Baldasty, Gerald J. *E. W. Scripps and the Business of Newspapers*. Urbana: University of Illinois Press, 1999.

Balke, Nathan S., and Robert J. Gordon. "The Estimation of Prewar Gross National Product: Methodology and New Evidence." *Journal of Political Economy* 97, no. 1 (1989): 38–92.

Barber, X. Theodore. "Evenings of Wonder: A History of the Magic Lantern Show in America." PhD diss., New York University, 1993.

Barnes, John. *The Beginnings of the Cinema in England*. New York: Barnes and Noble, 1976.

———. *The Rise of the Cinema in Great Britain*. London: Bishopgate Press, Ltd., 1983.

Barnouw, Erik. *Documentary: A History of the Non-Fiction Film*. New York: Oxford University Press, 1974.

———. *The Magician and the Cinema*. New York: Oxford University Press, 1981.

Bate, Bernard. *Tamil Oratory and the Dravidian Aesthetic*. New York: Columbia University Press, 2009.

Baudelaire, Charles. *The Painter of Modern Life and Other Essays*. Edited and translated by Jonathan Mayne. New York: Da Capo Press, 1964.

Bauman, Richard, and Patrick Feaster. "'Fellow Townsmen and My Noble Constituents!': Representations of Oratory on Early Commercial Recordings." *Oral Tradition* 20, no. 1 (2005), http://journal.oraltradition.org/issues/20i/bauman_feaster.

Bazin, André. *What Is Cinema?* Edited and translated by Hugh Gray. Berkeley: University of California Press, 1967.

Bean, Jennifer M., and Diane Negra, eds. *A Feminist Reader in Early Cinema*. Durham, NC: Duke University Press, 2002.

Benjamin, Walter. "The Work of Art in the Age of Technological Reproducibility (Second Version)." In *Walter Benjamin: Selected Writings, Volume 3: 1935–1938*, 103–33. Edited by Howard Elland and Michael W. Jennings. Cambridge, MA: Harvard University Press, 2006.

Bensel, Richard Franklin. *Passion and Preferences: William Jennings Bryan and the 1896 Democratic National Convention*. New York: Cambridge University Press, 2008.

Bitzer, G. W. *Billy Bitzer: His Story*. New York: Farrar, Straus and Giroux, 1973.

Black, Alexander. *Miss Jerry*. New York: Scribner's, 1897.

———. *Photography Indoors and Out: A Book for Amateurs*. New York: Houghton, Mifflin and Co., 1893.

Blondheim, Menahhem. *News Over the Wires: The Telegraph and the Flow of Public Information in America, 1844–1897*. Cambridge, MA: Harvard University Press, 1994.

Bolter, Jay David, and Richard Grusin. *Remediation: Understanding New Media*. Cambridge, MA: MIT Press, 2000.

Boorstin, Daniel J. *The Image: A Guide to Pseudo-Events in America*. New York: Atheneum, 1987. First published 1961.

Bordwell, David, Janet Staiger, and Kristin Thompson. *The Classical Hollywood Cinema: Film Style and Mode of Production to 1960*. New York: Columbia University Press, 1985.

Borton, Terry. "238 Eminent American 'Magic-Lantern' Showmen: The Chautauqua Lecturers." *Magic Lantern Gazette* 25, no. 1 (Spring 2013): 3–36.

Borton, Terry and Deborah Borton. *Before the Movies: American Magic-Lantern Entertainment and the Nation's First Great Screen Artist, Joseph Boggs Beale.* Herz, England: John Libbey, 2014.

Bottomore, Stephen. "Filming, Faking and Propaganda: The Origins of the War Film, 1897–1902." PhD diss., Utrecht University, 2007.

———. "1900." *Film History* 24, no. 4 (2012): 394–95.

Braverman, Harry. *Labor and Monopoly Capital: The Degradation of Work in the Twentieth Century.* New York: Monthly Review Press, 1974.

Briggs, Asa, and Peter Burke. *A Social History of the Media: From Gutenberg to the Internet.* Cambridge and Malden, MA: Polity, 2009.

Brownlow, Kevin. *Hollywood: The Pioneers.* New York: Alfred A. Knopf, 1979.

———. *The Parade's Gone By.* New York: Ballantine Books, 1968.

Bryan, William J. *The First Battle: A Story of the Campaign of 1896.* Chicago: W.B. Conkey Co., 1896.

Burch, Noël. *Correction Please: A Study Guide.* London: Arts Council of Great Britain, 1980.

———. *Life to Those Shadows.* Edited and translated by Ben Brewster. London: BFI Publishing, 1990.

———. "Porter or Ambivalence." *Screen* 19, no. 4 (Winter 1978–79): 91–105.

———. *Theory of Film Practice.* New York: Praeger, 1973.

Caldwell, Genoa. *The Man Who Photographed the World.* New York: Harry N. Abrams, 1977.

Carey, James W. *Communication as Culture: Essays on Media and Society.* Boston: Unwin, Hyman, 1989.

Casetti, Francesco. "Elsewhere. The Relocation of Art." In *Valencia09/Confines,* 348–51. Valencia: INVAM, 2009.

Ceram, C.W. [Kurt Wilhelm Marek]. *Archaeology of the Cinema.* New York: Harcourt, Brace, 1965.

Chanan, Michael. *The Dream That Kicks.* London: Routledge and Kegan Paul, 1980.

Churchill, Allen. *Park Row.* New York: Rinehart and Co., 1958.

Craig, Douglas G. *Fireside Politics: Radio and Political Culture in the United States, 1920–1940.* Baltimore, MD: Johns Hopkins University Press, 2000.

Craig, Geoffrey. *The Media, Politics and Public Life.* Crows Nest, Australia: Allen and Unwin, 2004.

Crary, Jonathan. *Techniques of the Observer: On Vision and Modernity in the Nineteenth Century.* Cambridge, MA: MIT Press, 1990.

Cullinane, Michael Patrick. *Liberty and American Anti-Imperialism, 1898–1909.* New York: Palgrave Macmillan, 2012.

Dawes, Charles G. *A Journal of the McKinley Years.* Chicago: Lakeside Press, 1950.

Defleur, Melvin L., and Everette Dennis. *Understanding Mass Communication.* 2nd ed. New York: Houghton Mifflin Co., 1985.

———. *Understanding Mass Communication: A Liberal Arts Perspective.* 7th ed. Boston: Houghton Mifflin Co., 2002.

Deslandes, Jacques. *Histoire comparée du cinema*, vol. 1: *De la cinématique au cinématographe, 1826–1896*. Tournai, Belgium: Casterman, 1966.

Deslandes, Jacques, and Jacques Richard. *Historie comparée du cinema*, vol. 2: *Du cinématographe au cinéma, 1896–1906*. Paris: Casterman: 1968.

Ellison, Robert H., ed. *A New History of the Sermon: The Nineteenth Century*. Leiden, the Netherlands: Brill, 2010.

Elsaesser, Thomas. *Film History as Media Archaeology: Tracking Digital Cinema*. Amsterdam: University of Amsterdam Press, 2016.

———. "The New Film History." *Sight and Sound* 55, no. 4 (Fall 1986): 246–51.

———. "The New Film History as Media Archaeology." *Cinémas: Journal of Film Studies* 14 (2004): 75–117.

Elsaesser, Thomas, ed. *Early Cinema: Space, Frame, Narrative*. London: BFI, 1990.

Fell, John. *Film and the Narrative Tradition*. Norman: University of Oklahoma Press, 1974.

Fell, John, ed. *Film Before Griffith*. Berkeley: University of California Press, 1983.

Fellow, Anthony R. *American Media History*. 3rd ed. Boston: Wadsworth, 2013.

Fielding, Ray, ed. *A Technological History of Motion Pictures and Television*. Berkeley: University of California Press, 1967.

Fullerton, John, ed. *Screen Culture: History and Textuality*. Eastleigh, England: John Libbey Publishing, 2004.

Gaudreault, André. "Detours in Film Narrative: The Development of Cross-Cutting." *Cinema Journal* 19, no. 1 (Fall 1979): 39–59. Reprinted in *Early Cinema: Space, Frame, Narrative*, 133–50. Edited by Thomas Elsaesser. London: BFI, 1990.

———. "The Diversity of Cinematographic Connections in the Intermedial Context of the Turn of the Century." In *Visual Delights: Essays on the Popular and Projected Image in the 19th Century*, 8–15. Edited by Simon Popple et Vanessa Toulmin. Trowbridge, England: Flicks Books, 2000.

———. *Film and Attraction: From Kinematography to Cinema*. Translated by Timothy Barnard, foreword by Rick Altman. Urbana: University of Illinois Press, 2011.

———. *From Plato to Lumière: Narration and Monstration in Literature and Cinema*. Translated by Timothy Barnard, preface by Paul Ricoeur, preface to the English-language edition by Tom Gunning. Toronto: University of Toronto Press, 2009.

Gaudreault, André, ed. *American Cinema 1890–1909: Themes and Variations*. New Brunswick, NJ: Rutgers University Press, 2009.

Gaudreault, André, and Philippe Marion. "A Medium Is Always Born Twice." *Early Popular Visual Culture* 3, no. 1 (May 2005): 7.

Gelatt, Roland. *The Fabulous Phonograph 1877–1977*. 2nd ed. New York: Collier Books, 1977.

Gitelman, Lisa. *Always Already New: Media, History, and the Data of Culture*. Cambridge, MA: MIT Press, 2008.

———. *Scripts, Grooves, and Writing Machines: Representing Technology in the Edison Era*. Stanford, CA: Stanford University Press, 1999.

Gitelman, Lisa, and Geoffrey B. Pingree, eds. *New Media, 1740–1915*. Cambridge, MA: MIT Press, 2003.

Goffman, Erving. *The Presentation of Self in Everyday Life*. New York: Anchor Books, 1959.

Grau, Robert. *The Business Man in the Amusement World*. New York: Broadway, 1910.

———. *Theater of Science*. New York: Broadway, 1914.

Gunning, Tom. "The Cinema of Attractions: Early Film, Its Spectators and the Avant-Garde." In *Early Cinema: Space, Frame, Narrative*, 56–62. Edited by Thomas Elsaesser. London: BFI, 1990.

———. *D. W. Griffith and the Origins of American Narrative Film*. Urbana: University of Illinois Press, 1991.

———. "Modernity and Cinema: A Culture of Shocks and Flows." In *Cinema and Modernity*, 297–315. Edited by Murray Pomerance. New Brunswick, NJ: Rutgers University Press, 2006.

———. "The Non-Continuous Style of Early Film (1900–1906)." In *Cinema 1900–1906: An Analytical Study*, 219–30. Compiled by Roger Homan. Brussels: FIAF, 1982.

Gutman, Herbert G. *Work, Culture and Society in Industrializing America*. New York: Vintage Books, 1977.

Hall, Donald E., ed. *Muscular Christianity: Embodying the Victorian Age*. New York: Cambridge University Press, 1994.

Harpine, William D. *From the Front Porch to the Front Page: McKinley and Bryan in the 1896 Presidential Campaign*. College Station: Texas A&M University Press, 2005.

Harris, Neil. *Humbug: The Art of P. T. Barnum*. Boston: Little Brown and Co., 1973.

Hendricks, Gordon. *Beginnings of the Biograph: The Story of the Invention of the Mutoscope and the Biograph and Their Supplying Camera*. New York: Beginnings of the American Film, 1964.

———. *Eadweard Muybridge: The Father of the Motion Picture*. London: Secker and Warberg, 1975.

———. *The Edison Motion Picture Myth*. Berkeley: University of California Press. New York: Arno, 1972. First published in 1961.

———. *The Kinetoscope: America's First Commercially Successful Motion Picture Exhibitor*. New York: Beginnings of the American Film, 1966.

Higham, John. *Hanging Together: Unity and Diversity in American Culture*. New Haven, CT: Yale University Press, 2001.

Hobsbawm, Eric. *The Age of Empire (1875–1914)*. New York: Vintage Books, 1989.

Hofstader, Richard. *The Age of Reform: From Bryan to F. D. R*. New York: Knopf, 1955.

Holman, Roger, comp. *Cinema 1900/1906: An Analytical Study by the National Film Archive (London) and the International Federation of Film Archives*. 2 vols. Brussels, Belgium: Federation Internationale des Archives du Film,

1982. Vol. 1: *Brighton Symposium, 1978*. Vol. 2: *Analytical Filmography (Fiction Films), 1900–1906*.

Holmes, Burton. "Manila." In *The Burton Holmes Lectures*, vol. 5. Battle Creek, MI: Little-Preston Co., 1901.

Hopwood, Henry V. *Living Pictures*. New York: Arno, 1970. First published 1899.

Huhtamo, Erkki, and Jussi Parikka, eds. *Media Archaeology: Approaches, Applications, and Implications*. Berkeley: University of California Press, 2011.

Jenkins, C. Francis. *Animated Pictures; An Exposition of the Historical Development of Chronophotography, Its Present Scientific Applications and Future Possibilities*. Washington, DC: H. L. McQueen, 1898.

———. *Picture Ribbons*. Washington, DC: H. L. McQueen, 1897.

Jenkins, C. Francis, and Oscar B. Depue. *Handbook for Motion Picture and Stereopticon Operators*. Washington, DC: Knega, 1908.

Jenkins, Keith, Sue Morgan, and Alum Munslow, eds. *Manifestos for History*. London: Routledge, 2007.

Jenkins, Reese V. *Images and Enterprise: Technology and the American Photographic Industry, 1839–1925*. Baltimore: Johns Hopkins University Press, 1975.

Johnson, H. Clark. "The Gold Deflation, France and the Coming of the Depression, 1919–1932." PhD diss., Yale University, 1994.

Jones, Stanley L. *The Presidential Election of 1896*. Madison: University of Wisconsin Press, 1964.

Klinghard, Daniel. *The Nationalization of American Political Parties, 1880–1896*. New York: Cambridge University Press, 2010.

Knoles, George Harmon. *The Presidential Campaign and Election of 1892*. Stanford, CA: Stanford University Press, 1942.

Koenig, Louis W. *Bryan: A Political Biography of William Jennings Bryan*. New York: G. P. Putnam's Sons, 1971.

Lempert, Michael, and Michael Silverstein. *Creatures of Politics: Media, Message and the American Presidency*. Bloomington: Indiana University Press, 2012.

Lyons, James, and John Plunkett. *Multimedia Histories: From the Magic Lantern to the Internet*. Exeter, England: University of Exeter Press, 2007.

Mannoni, Laurent. *The Great Art of Light and Shadow: Archaeology of the Cinema*. Edited and translated by Richard Crangle. Exeter, England: University of Exeter Press, 2000.

Marcy, L. J. *Marcy's Sciopticon: Priced Catalogue of Sciopticon Apparatus and Magic Lantern Slides*. 6th ed. Philadelphia: L. J. Marcy, ca. 1878.

———. *The Sciopticon Manual. Explaining Marcy's New Magic Lantern and Light, Including Lantern Optics, Experiments, Photographing and Coloring Slides, Etc.* 5th ed. Philadelphia: Sherman and Co., 1874.

Marvin, Carolyn. *When Old Technologies Were New: Thinking About Communication in the Late Nineteenth Century*. New York: Oxford University Press, 1988.

Marx, Karl. *Capital: A Critique of Political Economy*, vol. 1. Moscow: Progress Publishers, 1978. First published 1867.

Mast, Gerald. *A Short History of the Movies*. Indianapolis: Bobbs-Merrill, 1976.

McAllister, T. H. *Catalogue and Price List Stereopticons*. New York: The Company, 1885.

McNamara, Brooks. *Day of Jubilee: The Great Age of Public Celebrations in New York, 1788–1909*. New Brunswick, NJ: Rutgers University Press, 1997.

Morgan, H. Wayne. *From Hayes to McKinley: National Party Politics, 1877–1896*. Syracuse, NY: Syracuse University Press, 1969.

———. *William McKinley and His America*. Kent, Ohio: Kent State University Press, 2003.

Morin, Edgar. *The Cinema, or the Imaginary Man*. Translated by Lorraine Mortimer. Minneapolis: University of Minnesota Press, 2005. First published 1956.

Morreale, Joanne. *The Presidential Campaign Film: A Critical History*. Westport, CT: Praeger, 1996.

Morris, James McGarth. *Pulitzer: A Life in Politics, Print and Power*. New York: HarperCollins, 2010.

Musser, Charles. *Before the Nickelodeon: Edwin S. Porter and the Edison Manufacturing Company*. Berkeley: University of California Press, 1991.

———. "The Early Cinema of Edwin S. Porter." *Cinema Journal* 19, no. 1 (Fall 1979): 1–38. Reprinted with a historiographic introduction in *The Wiley-Blackwell History of American Film*, vol. 1, 39–86. Edited by in Cynthia Lucia, Roy Grundmann, and Art Simon. Malden, MA: Wiley-Blackwell, 2012.

———. *Edison Motion Pictures, 1890–1900: An Annotated Filmography*. Friuli, Italy: Giorante del Cinema Muto, 1997.

———. *The Emergence of Cinema: The American Screen to 1907*. New York: Scribner's, 1990.

———. *High-Class Moving Pictures: Lyman H. Howe and the Forgotten Era of Traveling Exhibition, 1880–1920*. Princeton, NJ: Princeton University Press, 1991.

———. "Historiographic Method and the Study of Early Cinema." *Cinema Journal* 44, no. 1 (Fall 2004): 101–7.

———. "Political Documentary, YouTube and the 2008 US Presidential Election: Focus on Robert Greenwald and David N. Bossie." *Studies in Documentary Film* 4, no. 1 (2010): 199–210.

———. "Toward a History of Screen Practice." *Quarterly Review of Cinema Studies* 9, no. 1 (Winter 1984): 59–69.

———. "Truth and Rhetoric in Michael Moore's *Fahrenheit 9/11*." In *Michael Moore: Filmmaker, Newsmaker, Cultural Icon*, 167–201. Edited by Mathew Bernstein. Ann Arbor: University of Michigan Press, 2010.

Musser, Charles, et al. *Motion Picture Catalogs by American Producers and Distributors, 1894–1908: A Microfilm Edition*. Frederick, MD: University Publications of America, 1985.

Nasaw, David. *The Chief: The Life of William Randolph Hearst*. Boston: Houghton Mifflin Co., 2006.

Natale, Simone. "Understanding Media Archaeology." *Canadian Journal of Communication* 37 (2012): 523–27.

Nichols, Bill. *Representing Reality: Issues and Concepts in Documentary.* Bloomington: Indiana University Press, 1991.

Niver, Kemp R., ed. *Biograph Bulletins, 1896–1908.* Los Angeles: Locare Research Group, 1971.

O'Brien, Frank M. *The Story of "The Sun."* New York: George H. Doran, 1918.

Parikka, Jussi. *What Is Media Archaeology?* Cambridge and Malden, MA: Polity Press, 2012.

Petterchak, Janice A. *Lone Scout: W. D. Boyce and American Boy Scouting.* Ann Arbor, MI: Legacy Press, 2003.

Pratt, George C. *Spellbound in Darkness: A History of the Silent Film.* Greenwich, CT: New York Graphic Society, 1966.

Proceedings of the 1890 Convention of Local Phonograph Companies of the United States Held at Chicago, May 28 and 29, 1890. Milwaukee: Phonograph Printing Co., 1890.

Proceedings of the Second Annual Convention of Local Phonograph Companies of the United States, 16, 17, 18 June 1891. New York: Printed by Linotype Reporting and Printing, 1891.

Putney, Clifford. *Muscular Christianity: Manhood and Sports in Protestant America, 1880–1920.* Cambridge, MA: Harvard University, 2001.

Ramsaye, Terry. *A Million and One Nights: A History of the Motion Picture.* New York: Simon and Schuster, 1926.

Redding, Jack. *Inside the Democratic Party.* Indianapolis: Bobbs-Merrill, 1958.

Reitano, Joan. *The Tariff Question in the Gilded Age: The Great Debate of 1888.* University Park: Pennsylvania State University Press, 1994.

Riis, Jacob A. *How the Other Half Lives: Studies Among the Tenements of New York.* 2nd ed. New York: Young People's Missionary Movement, n.d. First published 1890.

Robinson, David, Stephen Herbert, and Richard Crangle, eds. *Encyclopedia of the Magic Lantern.* London: Magic Lantern Society, 2001.

Romer, Christina D. "Spurious Volatility in Historical Unemployment Data." *Political Economy* 94 (February 1986): 1–37.

Sadoul, Georges. *Histoire generale du cinema.* Vol. 1: *L'Invention du cinema.* Vol. 2: *Les Pionniers du cinema: De Melies a Pathe, 1897–1909.* Paris: Les Editions Denoel, 1947–48.

Schechter, Danny. *The Death of Media and the Fight to Save Democracy.* Hoboken, NJ: Melville House, 2005.

———. *Embedded: Weapons of Mass Deception: How Media Failed to Cover the War on Iraq.* Amherst, NY: Prometheus Books, 2003.

———. *News Dissector: Passions, Pieces, and Polemics, 1960–2000.* New York: Akashic, 2001.

———. *When News Lies: Media Complicity and the Iraq War.* New York: SelectBooks, 2006.

Schechter, Danny, and Roland Schatz, eds. *Mediaocracy, Hail to the Thief: How the Media "Stole" the U.S. Presidential Election 2000.* New York: InnoVatio, 2001.

Schiller, Herbert I. *Culture, Inc.: The Corporate Takeover of Public Expression.* New York: Oxford University Press, 1989.

Sipley, Louis Walton. "The Magic Lantern." *Pennsylvania Arts and Sciences* 4 (December 1939): 39–43.

————. "W. and F. Langenheim-Photographers." *Pennsylvania Arts and Sciences* (1937): 25–31.

Sklar, Robert. *Movie-Made America.* New York: Random House, 1975.

Slide, Anthony. *The Big V: A History of the Vitagraph Company.* 2nd ed. Metuchen, NJ: Scarecrow Press, 1987.

————. *Early American Cinema.* New York: A. S. Barnes, 1970.

Smith, Albert C., with Phil A. Koury. *Two Reels and a Crank.* Garden City, NY: Doubleday, 1952.

Solomon, Barbara Miller. *In the Company of Educated Women: A History of Women and Higher Education in America.* New Haven, CT: Yale University Press, 1985.

Spehr, Paul. *The Man Who Made Movies: W. K. L. Dickson.* Hertfordshire, England: John Libbey, 2008.

————. *The Movies Begin: Making Movies in New Jersey, 1887–1920.* Newark, NJ: Newark Museum and Morgan and Morgan, 1977.

Starr, Paul. *The Creation of the Media: Political Origins of Modern Communication.* New York: Basic Books, 2004.

Stauven, Wanda, ed. *Cinema of Attractions Reloaded.* Amsterdam: Amsterdam University Press, 2006.

Steele, Janet E. *The Sun Shines for All: Journalism and Ideology in the Life of Charles A. Dana.* Syracuse, NY: Syracuse University Press, 1993.

Stoddard, John L. *John L. Stoddard's Lectures.* 10 vols. Boston: Balch Brothers, 1897–98.

Susman, Warren. *Culture as History: The Transformation of American Society in the Twentieth Century.* New York: Pantheon Books, 1984.

Taylor, Jenny Bourne. "Structure of Feeling." *Dictionary of Cultural and Critical Theory.* Edited by Michael Payne. Oxford: Blackwell Publishing, 1997. Blackwell Reference Online, 9 February 2010, http://www.blackwellreference.com/subscriber/tocnode?id=g9780631207535_chunk_g978063120753522_ss1–37.

Thompson, John B. *The Media and Modernity: A Social Theory of the Media.* Stanford, CA: Stanford University Press, 1995.

Toulmin, Vanessa. *Electric Edwardians: The Films of Mitchell and Kenyon.* London: BFI, 2007.

Toulmin, Vanessa, and Simon Popple, eds. *The Lost World of Mitchell and Kenyon: Edwardian Britain on Film.* London: BFI, 2004.

————. *Visual Delights Two: Exhibition and Reception.* Eastleigh, England: John Libbey, 2005.

Trachtenberg, Alan. *The Incorporation of America: Culture and Society in the Gilded Age.* New York: Hill and Wang, 1982.

Tsivian, Yuri. "The Rorschach Test of Cultures: On Some Parallels Between Early Film Reception in Russia and the United States." *Yale Journal of Criticism* 7, no. 2 (1994): 177–88.

———. "'What Is Cinema?' An Agnostic Answer." *Critical Inquiry* 34 (Summer 2008): 754–76.

Vernon, J.R. "Unemployment Rates in Post-Bellum America: 1869–1899." *Journal of Macroeconomics* 16 (1994): 701–14.

Villard, Henry. *Memoirs of Henry Villard: Journalist and Financier.* New York: Houghton Mifflin, 1904.

Virilio, Paul. *War and Cinema: The Logistics of Perception.* London: Verso, 1989.

Wallace, Aurora. *Media Capital: Architecture and Communications in New York City.* Urbana: University of Illinois Press, 2012.

Walls, Howard Lamarr. *Motion Pictures, 1894–1912.* Washington, DC: Library of Congress, 1953.

Washbourne, Neil. *Mediating Politics: Newspapers, Radio, Television and the Internet.* New York: Open University Press, 2010.

Wells, Kentwood D. "The Stereopticon Men: On the Road with John Fallon's Stereopticon, 1860–1870." *Magic Lantern Gazette* 23, no. 3 (Fall 2011): 3–34.

———. "What's in a Name? The Magic Lantern and the Stereopticon in American Periodicals 1860–1900." *Magic Lantern Gazette* 20, no. 3 (Fall 2008): 3–19.

Williams, Raymond. *Marxism and Literature.* Oxford: Oxford University Press, 1977.

———. *Problems in Materialism and Culture: Selected Essays.* New York, Schocken, 1981.

Willis, Artemis. "Between Nonfiction Screen Practice and Nonfiction Peep Practice: The Keystone '600 Set' and the Geographical Mode of Representation." *Early Popular Visual Culture* 13, no. 4 (December 2015): 293–312.

———. "The Magic Lantern Today: Archaeology, Apparatus and Aesthetics for a New Millennium." PhD diss., University of Chicago, forthcoming.

Wilson, Edward. *Wilson's Lantern Journeys.* 3 vols. Philadelphia: published by the author, 1874–86.

Winston, Brian. *Media Technology and Society: A History: From the Telegraph to the Internet.* London: Routledge, 1998.

Wolmar, Christian. *The Great Railroad Revolution: The History of Trains in America.* New York: Public Affairs, 2012.

Woolf, Virginia. *Mr. Bennett and Mrs. Brown.* London: Hogarth Press, 1923.

Zielinski, Siegfried. *After the Media.* Translated by Gloria Custance. Minneapolis: Univocal, 2013.

———. *Deep Time of the Media: Towards an Archeology of Hearing and Seeing by Technical Means.* Translated by Gloria Custance. Cambridge, MA: MIT Press, 2006.

Index